50

The German Shepherd Dog

Ernest H. Hart

Acknowledgments

My most heartfelt thanks to Allan H. Hart, B.V.Sc. and his wife Julie Hart, B.V.Sc. for help with the chapter on veterinary medicine; to Mary E. Schuetzler for the lists of Grand Victors and Victrixes and other valuable information; to Paul and Ingeborg Theissen for the new rules and scoring in Schutzhund; to the breeders and handlers who supplied me with needed pictures; and to the many other photographers, professional and amateur, who helped lend pictorial substance to this book.

Front cover: Photo by Isabelle Francais. Courtesy of Elli Matlin of Highland Hills German Shepherds and John McDonnell.
Back cover: Family portrait of Pela Preussenblut, CD, Issac Preussenblut, CD, OFA, and Lahngold's Charm with children, Elizabeth and Richard. Pela and Issac are by VA Baer v. Klosterbogen, SchH III "a" ex Carla v. Haus Rena, SchH I "a." Photo courtesy of Bob and Ute Santella of the vom Linderhof Kennel, New York.

Black and white illustrations by the author, except as noted.

ISBN 0-86622-031-3

Distributed in the UNITED STATES by T.F.H. Publications, Inc., 211 West Sylvania Avenue, Neptune City, NJ 07753; in CANADA by H & L Pet Supplies Inc., 27 Kingston Crescent, Kitchener, Ontario N2B 2T6; Rolf C. Hagen Ltd., 3225 Sartelon Street, Montreal 382 Quebec; in ENGLAND by T.F.H. Publications Limited, 4 Kier Park, Ascot, Berkshire SL5 7DS; in AUSTRALIA AND THE SOUTH PACIFIC by T.F.H. (Australia) Pty. Ltd., Box 149, Brookvale 2100 N.S.W., Australia; in NEW ZEALAND by Ross Haines & Son, Ltd., 18 Monmouth Street, Grey Lynn, Auckland 2 New Zealand; in SINGAPORE AND MALAYSIA by MPH Distributors (S) Pte., Ltd., 601 Sims Drive, # 03/07/21, Singapore 1438; in the PHILIPPINES by Bio-Research, 5 Lippay Street, San Lorenzo Village, Makati Rizal; in SOUTH AFRICA by Multipet Pty. Ltd., 30 Turners Avenue, Durban 4001. Published by T.F.H. Publications Inc., Ltd. the British Crown Colony of Hong Kong.

"In life the firmest friend,
the first to welcome,
foremost to defend."

 Lord Byron

*To my wife Kay,
and to all the German Shepherds
we have shared over the years.*

Contents

Foreword

In 1955 I wrote, with no little trepidation and some collaboration from William Goldbecker, my first book, *This Is The German Shepherd,* and in 1966 I wrote a revised edition of the same book. The years between then and now have seen a host of canine generations pass and have worn away most all of what was written then. What was foresight has become hindsight and can be critically re-examined only in that capacity.

In the light of fresh knowledge and new experience it was decided that an entirely new book must be written, with pristine approaches to breeding, bloodlines, canine medicine, care and feeding, genetics and all the other more esthetic and philosophical paths followed by the more intense Shepherdists; the book that must be molded to an understanding of what motivates the various component elements of what we term the Shepherd "fancy." The data collected—recent, pertinent and informative—must now be sorted, scrutinized, and transcribed for your edification and discernment.

Since the time of that initial writing I have written seventeen books and a multitude of short stories, painted numerous paintings, illustrated a number of books, owned a quantity of German Shepherds and traveled to most of the cities, towns and jungles in the world. I have lived in Spain and South America and, I presume, in the process have become a citizen of the globe, with a greatly broadened concept of mankind's role on this planet. I have judged dog shows in many diverse areas of the world, and wherever civilization was to be found I have also found, with few exceptions, the German Shepherd Dog.

"First Lessons," a watercolor painting by the author.

The breed is almost universal in its appeal, its sterling attributes lending it distinction and importance wherever man needs a helper, a companion, a guard for self, household goods or livestock, or where there is a specialized job to be accomplished. The German Shepherd Dog is so staunch in its simple and honest affection and willingness to please—and so unlike some of the people who own Shepherds and reach desperately for transitory elements of prestige through their dogs—that sometimes it seems that the dogs and the "dog game" are two disparate entities that have no common denominator. Perhaps with this book I can help to bring the two closer together, to serve a more useful purpose and reach a closer union.

Over the years I have seen much change take place in the breed and many false gods abandoned for the worship of new deities and collusive philosophies. All of it is here in these pages, all that there is of the German Shepherd: the history, the foibles, the theories and the unbiased truth as we know it today, gleaned from experience and the study of all the new and relevant factors involved.

I hope you enjoy and find helpful that which is printed here. It is written for you much in the nature of a report, but with some entirely personal observations. If it serves its purpose, to entertain and instruct, then my labors will be well rewarded.

Ernest H. Hart
Florida, U.S.A.

Chapter 1

Dog and Man . . .
From the Beginning

We don't know whether this universe of ours achieved genesis with a "big bang" or a whimper; there are scientific theories that support both assumptions. We do know that it evolved some billions of years ago, found its orbit and began a dramatic time of forming.

The seething fires in its inner core caused great upheavals, cracking the outer earlier-formed surface and pushing up boiling areas of shifting land, great bubbling seas and steaming virginal mountains. Volcanoes thrust upwards and exploded in primordial fury, vomiting forth the contents of the writhing earth's inner bowels. All the planet surged and roared in the awesome grip of a world's nativity.

Eventually, as billions of years faded into obscurity, there came a time of relative calmness and then, about three hundred to four hundred million years ago, an unprecedented, wholly unique and miraculous event occurred. In the murky seas, close to shore, a strange anomaly took place, a combining of chemicals, atmosphere and nutrients in the soupy water mixed with other elements in a witch's brew, and there was a yeasty stirring, a movement—and life, very tiny, very primitive and one-celled, was formed; with life came its shadow-twin, death.

Over the milleniums that tiny spark of almost invisible life survived the prodigious vagaries of that ancient world and slowly but surely prospered as though it had partaken of Amrita, the Hindu beverage of immortality. Environmental change and evolution molded the organisms into varied channels, and the participants in this dangerous game grew larger and stronger and took diverse shapes, in the seas establishing at last a host of fish creatures that assured the continuance of life on the planet. First the invertebrates, then the fishes and then the amphibians, strange monsters half fish and half reptile that crawled out of the sea onto the land. In time some returned to the womb of the waters, but others remained on the land, developing physical properties that made their decision suitable. In the *Paleozoic* era, of 370 million years duration, these primitive reptiles in the mud and swamps of that damp and humid time began a pilgrimage toward a fantastic variety of forms and sizes and, roughly 160 million years ago, the Age of the Dinosaurs began.

The dinosaurs established dominance over the land and ruled the earth over a period of 100 million years. The largest of these creatures were the plant-eating brachiosaurids and the monstrous flesh-eaters such as *Tyrannosaurus rex*. The dinosaurs prospered and evolved into specialized species of great variety and size; they finally fell prey to overspecialization, racial senescence and genetic resistance to the physical and mental modifications necessary for survival. It is rather shocking to give so little space to so many millions of years of bygone time, but we must progress rapidly for there is so much to say about more pertinent matters.

During the latter part of the era of the dinosaurs some of the smaller of the saurians had begun to mutate and so avoided the racial decline of the larger dinosaurs. And as these giants vanished the *Cenozoic* era was ushered in—the age of the mammals.

The mammalian family Miacidae, true, early carnivores, rather ferret-like in appearance, were the earliest known ancestors of the dog. From them issued a plastic genetic tide that also included the ancestors of the weasels (Mustelidae); raccoons (Procyonidae); hyenas (Hyaenidae); bears (Ursidae); civets (Viverrinae); and cats (Felidae); as well as the dogs (Canidae). Since man and dog are both mammals we have reached a focus in time from which both the canine and primate races will emerge.

Approximately 40 million years ago the grazing animals moved across the earth, and the first ape-like creatures became visible in the heights of the giant trees. The emerging canines like *Dapheonodons* ran in packs and hunted the grazing herbivorous animals. Then, about 15 to 20 million years ago, a great leap forward was made in the evolution of the canine species. Four prototype canine races appeared, evolving from the loins of the predatory *Tomarctus*. A contemporary pro-canine type *Cynodesmus* was also present at the time, but the four prototype canines were the fountainhead of all the dog breeds known to man. Both *Tomarctus* and *Cynodesmus* left enough fossil remains for paleontologists to tell us that both species were quite common in North America at that time.

Not long later, using our million year yardstick as a marker, during the *Pleiocene* era, the genus *Canis* (including the now recognizable wolves, jackals, foxes, coyotes, and wild dogs) migrated from North America to Asia. At this same time the first hominid, *Ramapithacus*, put in a less than prepossessing

Miacis, the long-tailed, slender-bodied carnivore from which such creatures as bears, raccoons, weasels, cats, and dogs evolved.

Tomarctus was the prototype dog.

appearance in Africa, the womb of the universe that labored to give birth to man. An ape with some human aspects, it was probably the ancestor of both the modern apes and man.

Between the time of *Ramapithacus* and *Australopithecus afarensis*, from 5 to 8 million years ago, ape and man split into two divergent races. The incipient man, *Australopithecus*, was about four feet tall, walked upright, had forsaken the trees for the pampas and was indeed a true, but quite apelike, human being. From the time of his advent on the stage of prehistory, man progressed steadily away from the primeval primate, from *A. afarensis* to *Paranthropus*, then advanced *Australopithecus, Homo erectus*, early *Homo sapiens*, Neanderthal Man, Cro-Magnon Man, and finally Modern Man, *Homo sapiens*. He walked erect, freeing his hands for other tasks; his brain enlarged and taught those clever hands to make tools and weapons, and with those weapons man became a hunter, and it was in this capacity that he first made social contact with the dog—and a new scenario was fashioned for the canine and human species.

The earliest known dog was discovered in the Pleistocene region of Palegawra cave in Iraq and has a radiocarbon date of 12,000 years before the present time. It is entirely possible that the domestic dog, *Canis familiaris*, and the Asian (Chinese) and African wolf possessed a close and common ancestor. Canine fossils are fragile and not too frequently found, but some were discovered in close association with Peking Man, dated approximately 500,000 years ago. Dogs were initially camp followers finding easy sustenance in the meat and bones man cleaned out of his living quarters. They were also the first alien creatures adopted and domesticated by man. But did this find of canine bones deposited at the same approximate time as those of Peking Man indicate that the dog had lived with man or been eaten by him? We don't know, but we lean toward the belief that the dog was a part of the household of that early man. The move from scavenger outside to household companion inside man's dwelling would not have been an inconceivable step at that time.

Man was no longer a stupid ape, and it would certainly not have taken him long to recognize the dog's superior attributes as a hunting partner; the dog had greater speed, greater strength of the jaws and a keener olfactory and hearing ability, and he soon formed a pact with man as a hunting companion and a protector of the hearth. Man also found a loyal friend and companion.

We do know that the canine species was well established as a part of the human household of *Homo sapiens neanderthalensis* 70 thousand years ago. Late Paleolithic cave paintings depict dogs with Mouflon sheep, the canine types always the same: a curled heavily haired tail, erect ears about the size of those of a Siberian Husky, a coat like that of a German Shepherd, and always as the hunting companion of man. These canines (and the use of fire) aided man to find and kill game that supplied him with both food and protective skins for clothing during the dreaded ages when the world was covered with

Thüringer Shepherd Dog *(above)* and Württemberger Shepherd Dog *(below)*. From these two German herding breeds came many of the genetic factors that fashioned the German Shepherd Dog breed.

ice and penetrating cold. The dog also became a pack animal hauling man's goods.

The human animal evolved with greater rapidity than all other creatures on earth, and soon man gathered and held the herbivorous creatures captive in flocks and herds to control his supply of meat and milk, rather than having to follow a nomadic existence pursuing the herds. He had only to periodically move them to new forage.

Soon he planted seeds and watched the products of his labor grow, and finally he completely controlled his environment; thus the agricultural age came into being. For his friend the dog he found new employment, guarding and moving the flocks to new pastures and watching over his planted fields; and in what later became Germany, as in many other parts of the world, a specific type of dog was selected for, one that could hold and herd the livestock man had domesticated. Thus, in several diverse sections of the middle of the European continent, dogs with varied physical attributes were bred as herding animals.

On the northern flatlands of Germany, a lithe trotting dog was selected for; in the mountain regions a heavier, sturdier dog evolved; and in central Germany a long-coated shepherd dog was found best suited to the job. All of these canines mirrored the feral type, for dog and wolf had evolved along parallel lines.

Selection differed with the environment, and type, color and coat texture varied. Many of these variables are still carried as recessives down through uncounted generations to occasionally appear in litters even today. White shepherds, blues, livers and even brindles, long-coated and sometimes wire-coated, these are the crosses breeders must bear for the long and arduous milleniums of the breed's evolution.

Man developed his towns and cities and new means of transportation and communication, and he found a common bond of interest with other men in discussion of herds, crops, weather and shepherd dogs. Soon, through type breeding to the best sheepherding dogs, a crude kind of genetic selection developed in primitive Germany, and a general utilitarian type began to emerge that best suited the overall terrain—and the German Shepherd Dog was crudely fashioned.

Chapter 2

A Breed is Born

The European heartland that later became Germany nurtured a vast number of sheep and a lesser, but still large, number of canines to tend them. By 1883 the greater number of German Shepherd Dogs in the fatherland were rugged, intelligent and generally sound in structure, but they had not yet acquired complete conformational standardization. Then a new and extremely important element became part of the breed's eventual destiny. The ingredient that was to affect the breed to such an enormous extent was a man, a military man, Rittmeister (cavalry captain) Max Emil Frederich von Stephanitz.

While attending one of the first all-breed dog shows ever held in Germany (in Karlsruhe, 1899) von Stephanitz and his friend and companion Artur Meyer came upon a gray dog of wolfish appearance but great dignity, a German Shepherd dog that stood quietly at the side of his handler. Both von Stephanitz and his friend had been keenly interested in dogs of this native breed, having seen them work sheep in Wurttemberg, Thuringia and Saxony and having marveled at their intelligence and innate ability. But never had they seen a specimen of the breed that was, to them, the epitome of the German Shepherd Dog . . . until now.

They examined the big gray dog with mounting excitement. This was the dog von Stephanitz had dreamed of, a perfect example of the true German Shepherd. A conversation with the dog's handler elicited the fact that the animal was essentially a herding dog and spent his life in that capacity; they also learned that the dog had been born with certain instinctive herding attributes that had needed but slight training to bring to the fore and make him proficient at his job. This dog perfectly fit the motto von Stephanitz had coined for the breed: "Utility and intelligence."

The dog's name was Hector Linksrhein; von Stephanitz bought him immediately and rechristened him on the spot as Horand von Grafrath and took him home to his Grafrath Kennels. In the same year, on April 3, the Rittmeister founded the Club For The German Shepherd Dog *(Verein für Deutsche Schäferhunde, S.V.),* became its first president and, with Teutonic thoroughness, wrote the first standard for the breed.

Eight years earlier, in 1891, another group had formed to advance the cause of the German Shepherd. Called the Phylax Society, it soon succumbed to lack of interest and its own inertia. But it had awakened fanciers to the possibilities of the breed, and when von Stephanitz formed his own club he used those fanciers as a nucleus membership and based the preliminary format of the club on the one that had been formulated by the Phylax Society. He was an energetic man and totally dedicated to the breed, and within a short period of time he fashioned the German Shepherd Dog to fit his own standard of excellence. He completely dominated the Shepherd fancy, and the owners and breeders of Shepherds followed his ideas without question.

He was the iron hand in the velvet glove, and his word was law. He was the leader, the man in the military uniform, an obvious badge of authority. His domination was predicated upon the facts that Chancellor von Bismarck had brought the country to the height of its military might and that martial power was the guiding force behind Germany's political policies throughout the world. Linked with the Hohenzollern monarchy wielding the weapon of Prussian imperialism, von Stephanitz in his military uniform was an obvious symbol of autocracy. Dictatorily he became the voice of authority of the *Verein für Deutsche Schäferhunde* and became breeding master, judge, breed inspector and arbiter of all things pertaining to German Shepherds in the fatherland. Only at that specific time, under those circumstances, and under the auspices of such a man as Rittmeister Max von Stephanitz could such an organization as the *Verein* be nurtured into the largest dog club dedicated to a specific breed in all the world, with 31,000 members and hundreds of small allied clubs scattered throughout the land.

It was a notable achievement for the man whose life's work was to be dedicated to the breed and the club he had fathered. Von Stephanitz became known as "The father of the breed," a title he cherished—one that drove him to write and distribute numerous pamphlets about the breed, culminating in his writing of the prestigious tome *The German Shepherd Dog In Word And Picture,* a book that was for many years the bible of fanciers of the German Shepherd.

Under the Rittmeister's guidance, Horand von Grafrath was destined to shape the German Shepherd breed for posterity. The Captain searched throughout Germany for bitches of the same type as Horand. They were hard to find, for von Stephanitz was a purist, and few females could be found that approached his ideal. When the wanted bitches were found they were cher-

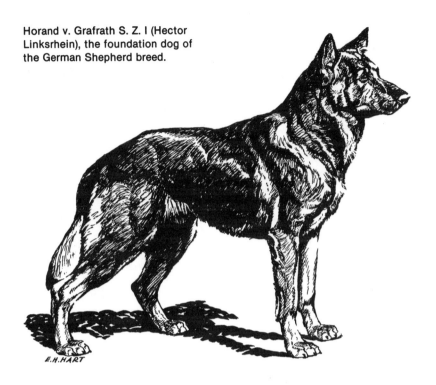

Horand v. Grafrath S. Z. I (Hector Linksrhein), the foundation dog of the German Shepherd breed.

ished and bred to Horand and their get judiciously inbred. Freya von Grafrath, registered number 7, was bred to Horand four times.

The Captain, even in his day, evidently possessed a vast knowledge of breeding and what was needed to produce the foundation animals of a strain. He knew that to coalesce and concentrate wanted genetic values it would be necessary to closely inbreed, and that was indeed what he did. He austerely culled each litter and kept the best of the lot until they were old enough to be critically analyzed, then he would select again. Only the very best were kept for future breeding; soon, with Horand as the alpha stud, the Grafrath Kennels was producing a family of Shepherd dogs that mirrored Horand's many qualities—his conformation and desired temperament, his beauty and utilitarian type.

The most important of Horand's many sons was Hektor von Schwaben, who was out of the good bitch Mores Plieningen. Hektor, in turn, sired Beowulf and his brother, Pilot III. They were both out of Thekla I von der Krone, a bitch sired by Horand. Heinz von Starkenburg, another important son of Hektor's, had as his dam Lucie v. Starkenburg. One can immediately envision the extreme inbreeding indulged in by the Rittmeister to set type and the reason for the intense culling in which he necessarily had to indulge.

The three sons of Horand mentioned in the preceding paragraph were the trio of studs that transferred their sire's prepotency to later generations. Pilot III, through his grandson Graf Eberhard von Hohen Esp, lent his genetic qualities to the von Boll and Kriminalpolizei strains, very important in their day, and to branches of Eichenpark, Reidekenburg, Harras von der Juch and Mohr Secretainerie. Beowulf sired great bitches that produced the bloodlines to Geri von Oberklamm and from Geri to Attilos Argos and Cito Bergerslust.

Heinz von Starkenburg was, of the three, the most important of Hektor's sons. On November 1, 1903 Heinz produced a litter out of Bella von Starkenburg in which there appeared an all-black male puppy. Von Stephanitz watched this puppy with immense concentration, for it was evident, almost from birth, that this youngster was special. As he matured there was no doubt in the minds of the Rittmeister and his colleagues that this puppy was a mutant embodying all that was dominant and estimable in the bloodlines.

The name of this important youngster was Roland von Starkenburg. He matured into a model for the breed and the one stud of his time who prepotently and constantly produced the type that the Rittmeister wished to perpetuate, though he was not quite sure in temperament. All German Shepherd Dogs living today can trace their lineage back to the redoubtable Roland. His great-grandsire and great-great-grandsire were Horand von Grafrath, both through Hektor von Schwaben; his sire and dam were Heinz von Starkenburg and Bella von Starkenburg, both out of the bitch Lucie von Starkenburg. Since Lucie was Roland's double grandmother, Pollux and Prima appear twice in the third generation. This pedigree is a classic example of the art of inbreeding, and that it was utilized at that time is quite

Roland v. Starkenburg, 1906-1907 Sieger. He was the black mutant whose genetic qualities did so much to shape the breed. Intense inbreeding gave Roland his marked prepotency.

Horst v. Boll by Munko v. Boll ex Hella v. Boll. Big, powerful, square, Horst was used more frequently than any other stud dog of his era.

Tell v. Kriminalpolizei by Luchs v. Kalsmunt-Wetzlar ex Herta v.d. Kriminalpolizei. He was considered the best German Shepherd of his day.

remarkable. It produced, in Roland, a giant step forward, for it granted him the best in his genetic line and blessed him, because of his close breeding, with enormous prepotency.

Hettel Uckermark, Roland's finest son, became Sieger in 1909, and through Bella von der Leine, Hettel sired Alex von Westfalheim who, through Hettel-Roland-Dewett-Krone breeding, begat the famous 1920 Sieger and International Grand Champion Erich von Grafenwerth. The same basic stock produced other strains of importance, the most memorable being Reidekenburg, Kriminalpolizei and von Boll.

Erich von Grafenwerth was a handsome specimen of the breed with a roomy, easy gait. Though he was sired by Alex, his beauty of conformation

Ch. Erich v. Grafenwerth by Alex v. Westfalenheim ex Bianka v. Riedekenburg. The 1920 Sieger and an International Grand Champion "destined to influence generations to come...".

Flora Berkemeyer by Harras v. Lippestrand ex Cilla Distelbruch. Mother of the Riedekenburg strain. Through the "A," "B," and "D" litters Riedekenburg she established her vital worth.

can be attributed to Hettel Uckermark, who stops both male lines in the second generation. Also of major importance genetically is Flora Berkemeyer in the lower female line; she was a pillar of the Reidekenburg bloodline and a superb bitch whose beauty and balance were passed on to Erich.

Hettel Uckermark was a dog of excellent temperament, but Erich was not blessed with his double grandsire's character, inheriting instead a social unsureness from his sire Alex, his grandsire Roland and the lovely Flora Berkemeyer. This slight character fault possessed by Erich led to employment by the *Verein* (SV) of more rigid temperament testing and a warning not to breed to Alex von Westfalheim because of the temperament taint. Since the warning also extended to Erich, he was reluctantly offered for sale and was purchased by an American and brought to the United States. Erich carried a slightly wavy coat, and to this day when we see a German Shepherd displaying this coat texture we refer to it as an "Erich" coat. Erich, despite his temperament defect, was one of the greatest sires of his time; he influenced many of the generations that came after him.

The 1920's saw a surge forward of many fine dogs in Germany, and quite a few of them found new homes in America and England and as far away as Japan and China. The major strains that flourished then were Uckermark (large, with strong structure and good bone, especially through Hettel); Kriminalpolizei (weak pigmentation, some imperfect dentition and uneven temperament, but still large, handsome and flashy animals). A rather typical example of what was known as the "young" Kriminalpolizei line was Nores von Kriminalpolizei. He was oversized but handsome, and he sported a short tail inherited from his dam, Lori von Brenztal. The von Bolls were heavy and square and possessed excellent temperament and intelligence. Dogs of the Riedekenburg strain were generally rather refined; they had excellent conformation and uneven temperament, ranging from unsureness to staunchness. Their genetic background was through Roland von Starkenburg and Lucie von Starkenburg.

During the early 1920's American fanciers purchased some of the finest show stock that Germany was willing to part with. Unfortunately, though the Americans paid large sums for the stock they purchased, the *Verein für Deutsche Schäferhunde* had issued warnings against many of these animals because of transmittable faults. The Americans had not done their homework and, because of the language barrier, had not learned all they needed to know about the dogs they had bought, dogs the Germans wanted to get rid of, and did ... at high prices.

Importing of Shepherds from Germany had begun as early as 1904, but not in any great numbers. Some time later, in 1913, Anne Tracy of New York and Benjamin H. Throop of Pennsylvania organized the German Shepherd Dog Club of America, the initial step toward true recognition of the breed in the United States. In 1914 a dog of some importance who had been a top show winner on the Continent but had been criticized by German judges for transmitting light pigmentation and a lack of secondary sex characteristics to his progeny, Apollo von Hunenstein, was exported to America. He had, in Germany, sired the excellent "D" litter Riedekenburg when bred to Flora Berkemeyer, and he proved to be a worthy stud in the United States. He was but one of several elite imports.

In those early days of the breed's struggle for a foothold in the United States, some of the Americans who embraced the breed and deserve mention here were: Mr. and Mrs. Halstead Yates; Mrs. Alvin Untermeyer; Mrs. Elliot Dexter, prominent on the west coast; Thomas F. Ryan; A.B. Widener of Joselle Kennels; and John Gans, whose Hoheluft Kennels were destined for greatness.

During World War I anything German became anathema to the American public, and in England the name of the breed was changed to the "Alsatian." During the war the Germans utilized their German Shepherds to their full utilitarian capacities as messengers, scouts and guard dogs, and the dogs gained fame as peerless war dogs. Tales of their exploits were brought back by Allied fighting men, and when the war ended many returning American soldiers brought German Shepherds home to the States with them.

Rin-Tin-Tin and Strongheart (Etzel von Oeringen) filled the screens of movie theaters throughout the country with their daring rescues and cliff-hanging escapes from danger. So great was the effect of these two dogs on the hearts and minds of the movie-going public, so celebrated did they become, that the popularity of the breed shot skyward. Everyone wanted a German Shepherd, a Rin-Tin-Tin or a Strongheart, and soon backyard breeders and puppy factories were spawned and flourished, selling sickly, undernourished, carelessly bred puppies with often falsified pedigrees and every imaginable physical and psychological defect. Most of these hucksters knew nothing about the breed and cared less. All they wanted was the money they could demand from an unsuspecting public for their "German Police" puppies. We can be thankful that no trace of those poor canine monstrosities lingers in our modern-day dogs.

Meanwhile earnest and knowledgeable breeders were selecting from excellent genetic material to elevate the general quality of the German Shepherd throughout the world. It was during this time that Mrs. Harrison Eustis founded her famous Fortunate Fields Kennels in Switzerland. She approached the kennel concept from a purely scientific viewpoint, and an immense amount of time and money was expended. The end result was the production of working German Shepherd dogs that could perform well any task within the design of their genetic structure. The usefulness of some of this stock was taken full advantage of by the Seeing Eye Kennels in Morristown, New Jersey, where the animals were employed as guide dogs for the blind.

Germany's economy had been devastated by the war. During the early 1920's inflation gripped and impoverished the nation, food was scarce and high in price, as were many other items of normal living, and the Germans put down a great many dogs whose breeding value was not impeccable. They fed and cared for the remaining animals as well as they could and from this nucleus continued to produce fine, generally superior German Shepherd Dogs. American dollars were exceedingly popular with German breeders, as they and Italian lire and Japanese yen are today, and many fine dogs of that era found their way to America's shores.

In 1922 the *Verein für Deutsche Schäferhunde* introduced breed surveys. German judges reviewed breed representatives in various areas of the country, graded them as to conformation, temperament and pedigree, issued an unbiased and thorough critique of each animal and recommended, in general terms, the breeding partner best suited to the specific dog.

American fanciers thought this a splendid idea and made surveys of their own, importing German judges for this purpose. But the surveys in America were not successful. German breeders followed the recommendations of the survey judges; American breeders didn't.

Some of the fine animals imported into the United States by 1925 included the best Germany had to offer: Cito Bergerslust, Gerri von Oberklamm, Alf von Tollensettel, Iso von Doernerhof, Harras von der Juch, Roland von Riedekenburg, Apollo von Hunenstein, Anni von Humboltspark, Dolf Dusternbrook and many more top dogs of great potential. Many of the imported dogs, rich in the desired genetic material, were overlooked while the breedings went to better-advertised and thus more popular animals. It is a shame that this happened, for some of the Shepherd dogs I refer to could have given much to the breed in the United States. Gerri von Oberklamm comes to mind in this category, as does Alf von Webbelmanslust, Caspar von Hain, Armin von Pasewalk, Cito Bergerslust, Alrich von Jena-Paradies and a host of other fine specimens. A parallel can be drawn in later years by the disregard breeders showed for such dogs as Attila Argos, Dewet von der Starrenberg and other Shepherds of great genetic worth who deserved more patronage than they received.

In the United States by the middle of the 1920's, many new and vital people had become fanciers of the breed. Names in the *Shepherd Dog Review* and in show catalogues of the day are familiar even today to the fancy. The New England Shepherd Dog Club and the German Shepherd Dog Club of America were engaged in torrid contention. Specialty shows were becoming larger and more frequent, and many novices were entering the ranks of ardent Shepherd fanciers. Such well known and celebrated seers of the breed as Rex Cleveland, a true gentleman, and Elliot S. Humphrey wrote articles about the German Shepherd that imparted jewels of wisdom for the edification of the interested. Humphrey, associated with the Fortunate Fields experiment in Switzerland with the collaboration of Lucien Warner, wrote the absorbing book *Working Dogs,* a detailed account of their activities during that valuable investigation.

There was a good deal of activity in the ranks of the German Shepherd fancy as the 1920's wore on. More knowledge of the breed and of genetics and the backgrounds of the important dogs was being absorbed and examined by serious breeders, and it was definitely a time of general growth and expansion. But no one, in Germany or in America, was completely aware of the fact that before 1925 was out a new era would dawn for the German Shepherd Dog.

Chapter 3

A New Era Dawns

The world was bigger in 1925. International travel was not as much a part of the social pattern as it is today, and the age of air travel had not yet shrunk the world. Of the tiny section of the world's populace dedicated to the owning and breeding of German Shepherds, few were aware of the outcome of the Sieger Show in Czechoslovakia in 1923. But that show was to have vast significance for the future of the German Shepherd Dog throughout the world.

Max von Stephanitz was aware of what had happened in Czechoslovakia and had given the results serious study. It bothered him that the dogs of Germany were becoming too high and short in body and, because of this anatomical failure, were losing the fluidity of movement necessary for a herding dog. Something had to be done immediately to check this tendency.

Before the 1925 Sieger Show was to be held, an unprecedented meeting of German Breeding Masters was called and chaired by von Stephanitz in his capacity as President of the *Verein für Deutsche Schäferhunde*. Not a whisper by any of those present as to the reason for the assembly was revealed. But Shepherd people throughout Germany were aware that something of moment was about to happen.

The Sieger Show that year was held in Frankfort Am Main. An air of expectancy pervaded the crowd, for they were aware that an event of definite import was about to occur there, at the Mecca for enthusiasts of the German Shepherd Dog. To the annual Sieger Show would come all the greats of the breed, from foreign countries and, of course, from all sections of Germany, and a new Sieger and Siegerin would be crowned who would influence the breed throughout the world for the next several years.

Judging began in the several rings, the young dog classes being the first to be judged, the Youth Class *(Jugendklasse* 12 to 18 months); then the Young Dog Class *(Junghundklasse* 18 to 24 months), then while these classes continued, von Stephanitz began judging the Utility Class *(Gebrauchshundklasse Ruden* 24 months and older) from which would come the 1925 World Sieger. The *Gebrauchshundklasse Hündinen* (Females) is, of course, also important, for the Siegerin would emerge from this class. But the female class does not have the significance of the male class—for a very obvious mathematical reason. A bitch, at most, can produce two litters a year, or about 12 to 14 puppies each year. But a top winning male, a Sieger, is used an average of sixty times a year, producing approximately three hundred and sixty progeny, so he influences the breed to a much greater extent than a female.

In the Utility Dog ring the handlers and their dogs were called into the spacious ring in catalogue order. There were many famous champions of Germany and many other countries. And then began the long and tedious examinations of both conformation and temperament, the latter very severely tested. Then the moving, the gaiting, the seemingly interminable trotting around the ring. Then the culling, this dog and that leaving the ring to be given a lesser rating or excused for some basic fault. At last the day came to an end. The best of all the dogs, the cream of the crop so to speak, were still in competition and on the morrow would reach their final placements.

The next day the judging began early, and the dogs began their perpetual gaiting around the ring as the Rittmeister intensely watched them, closely scrutinizing their every move; the functioning of the muscles and the skeletal framework beneath them; the firmness of joints and ligaments; the rhythm of their movement and the strength and thrust that propelled them forward. The handlers were periodically requested to walk their dogs and they did so, at approximately 120 steps a minute. Certain animals were asked to pick up the pace for a round of the ring as the Captain searched for faults that might be seen only under greater physical pressure. Handlers were changed often, as they tired; the dogs, however, continued their steady gaiting.

Finally the moment so long awaited had arrived. Von Stephanitz brought a dog from the middle of the line into third place. A few more rounds of the arena and, with a sweep of his arm, the Captain signalled the dog into second place. Then he pointed at the dog and dramatically motioned him to the lead as the watching crowd went wild. The judge had made his decision. The 1925 World Sieger was . . . Klodo vom Boxberg, the gray dog that in 1923 had been crowned Czechoslovakian Sieger. He was the symbol of the shape of things to come, the new era German Shepherd Dog.

What was he like, this dog that was to mold the breed to a new standard? He was primarily different from former Siegers in his balance and outline. He was not tall or square, as they had been. Von Stephanitz had decided, and had conveyed his wishes with his customary authority in the closed door meeting

Sieger and Ch. Klodo v. Boxberg by Erich v. Grafenwerth ex Elfe v. Boxberg . . . a new era was born!

Utz v. Haus Schutting, ZPr by Klodo v. Boxberg ex Donna z. Reuer. The famous German Sieger who started a controversy that exists to this day.

at Ossig, that a new type, a drastic change in the dog selected for World Sieger, must be made to bring the breed back to the wanted earlier-envisioned conformation standard, and Klodo was that type. He was longer than high in body yet short in back and loin, stationed lower and deeper, perfectly balanced and proportioned, and with a flowing, reaching gait of great power and fluidity. He was a son of the redoubtable Erich von Grafenwerth, and out of the good bitch Elfie von Boxberg. Linebred on Hettel Uckermark and combining the best of the Uckermark and Kriminalpolizei breeding, Klodo was a model of all that was best in his genetic background. His character and temperament were impeccable, and his selection for the Sieger title was quite

Odin v. Stolzenfels, ZPr by Curt v. Herzog-Hedan ex Bella v. Jagdschloss Platte. The 1933 Sieger, Odin was a basic and prepotent stud who sired a host of valuable Shepherds.

Vicki v. Bern, ZPr by Utz v. Haus Schutting ex Olle v. Bern. Dam of Gockel and Dachs v. Bern. "The dog Germany refused to part with...".

dramatic, as von Stephanitz wanted it to be, to make his point denoting change. The 1925 Sieger Show became known as the stepping stone from the "old blood" to the "new blood." (Klodo's win overshadowed the triumph of the breeding acumen of Tobias Ott, whose Sultan v. Blasienberg became Reserve Sieger, while his sister Seffe became Siegerin. Sultan became one of the basic studs in the Fortunate Fields experiment and, though gunshy, was otherwise invaluable in producing excellent working quality stock.)

Klodo was undoubtedly the best progeny of his sire, Erich. He produced many fine animals, his best sons being Utz von Haus Schutting, Odin von Stolzenfels and Curt von Herzog Hedan. Klodo carried a long-coat recessive,

Dachs v. Bern by Alex v. Ebersnacken ex Vicki v. Bern. Sire of the great Pfeffer and Odin. His genetic heritage molded early type in America.

Ingo v. Piastendamm, SchH II by Gockel v. Bern ex IIIa v. Oppeln-Ost. A superb individual and great sire.

and when Curt and Odin were inbred to Klodo bitches, a percentage of long-coated progeny appeared in the litters. Klodo's son Utz von Haus Schutting was successful in Germany in shows and at stud; he was then exported to the United States. He was not a prepossessing animal, being rather small and quiet. But once in the show ring he became a different dog; his structure, beautiful balance and grace in motion were appreciated by dedicated German Shepherdists.

Of great importance because of his breeding potential was the excellent Alex von Ebersnacken. He was the sire of Viki von Bern, who was the dam of Dachs von Bern, and Dachs sired both Odin von Busecker Schloss and Pfeffer von Bern, who were so important in basic American breeding. Alex was also the grandsire of Ingo vom Piastendamm, who is linebred on Utz von Haus Schutting.

Through the critiques, written material and word of mouth we are aware that perhaps the best sire line came through Rolf von Osnabruckerland. The upper bracket of this line featured Weigand v. Blasienburg, Gockel v. Bern, Ingo v. Piastendamm, Trutz aus der Schwanenstadt and Lex Preussenblut. Another line well liked in Germany for its excellent quality was that of Ingo von Piastendamm and his sire, Gockel von Piastendamm. Both were individually fine animals as well as excellent producers.

The dogs from Rolf von Osnabruckerland were noted for their excellent fronts and shoulder angulation, strong heads, good movement and the wanted secondary sex characteristics. They also generally produced a bit too much length in body and a lack of rear angulation. Sigbert Heidegrund was the fountainhead of another excellent German line. He was by Odin von Stolzenfels, and his dam was an Utz daughter. Sigbert gave Germany the top "Q" litter Durmersheim and the excellent Baldur von Befreiungsplatz. Baldur, in turn, sired Arry von der Gassenquelle and Pirol von der Buchenhohe. Quelle von Fredeholz, imported to the United States by Ernie Loeb, was a Pirol son.

In Germany the Piastendamm line was considered of great importance. It stems basically from Gockel von Bern. Both Ingo von Piastendamm and his son Harras were considered models of the breed. Their intrinsic value can be measured by the superiority of the stock that they produced. Another stud to be reckoned with was Brando von Heidelbeerberg, though he carried a recessive for long coats and sometimes passed on to his progeny a lack of staunchness in temperament. Curt von Herzog Hedan, Bodo von der Brahmenau and his son Onyx von Forrellenbach, all occasionally found in American pedigrees as well as German papers, were bearers of the long-coat recessive. There were many other strong sires in Germany including Immo vom Hasenfang, Vali von Wiegerfelsen, Siggo Corneliushof and the excellent Axel von Deninghauserheide, the sire of Sieger Alf vom Nordfelsen. Axel sometimes transmitted a tendency for weak ears, but we must mark his name well because he greatly influenced the quality and prepotency of the spectacular Americanbred, Lance of Fran-Jo, through Axel's son, Troll von Richterbach.

The fine show dog and sire Atlas von Dinas-Eck was sired by Vali v. Wiegerfelsen. Other procreators of merit were Siggo von Corneliushof, his son Arno von der Pfaffenau and Arras vom Nibelungengold.

At this point in time, built upon these established and thoughtfully conceived bloodlines dedicated to the improvement of the breed, a new phase of breeding legerdemain came into being in Germany. The important kennels cannily began to weave the genetic material at their disposal into new and

Rolf v. Osnabruckerland, SchH III by Lex Preussenblut ex Maja v. Osnabruckerland. One of Germany's early leading sires. Product of a genetically dominant line.

Bodo v. Brahmenau, HGH, ZPr by Donar v. Zuchtgut ex Fanny v. Neuerburg. A prominent German sire. 1938 Sieger (Japan). "A tendency to produce long coats . . .".

more pliable forms. Condor von Hohenstamm became a much sought-after stud and sired the 1962 Sieger, Mutz aus der Kuckstrasse, who was sold to Pakistan, but not before he had become the direct progenitor of many fine animals, particularly good bitches. The 1964 Siegerin, Blanka von Kisscamp, was a Mutz daughter. Condor von Hohenstamm is a grandson of the ubiquitous Axel von Deininghauserheide and Rolf von Osnabruckerland, a highly potent breeding cross.

The breeding of Arras von Adam-Riesezswinger to Halla aus der Eremitenklause is a classic example of a true "nick." It was repeated several times and, though an "open" breeding, proved to be entirely efficacious. The

Axel v. d. Deininghauserheide, SchH III, DPH, FH by Immo v. Hasenfang, SchH III ex Helma v. Hildegardsheim, SchH III. A famous show dog and sire of a host of great German dogs.

Alf v. Nordfelsen, SchH III by Axel v. d. Deininghauserheide, SchH III, DPH, FH ex Carin v. Bombergachen Park, SchH II. 1955 German Sieger and famous progenitor of fine show and working-type Shepherds.

"K" litter that produced Klodo a.d. Eremitenklause, Youth Sieger and a worthy sire, was the best of the several breedings. Klodo came to America and stamped his type on his get. He produced good type and backs, excellent balance, a slightly long body, occasionally weak ears and sometimes not quite the wanted 90 degree angulation in shoulders.

Hein von Richterbach, Gero von Katherinentor and Casar von der Malmannsheide all gave rich pigmentation to their get. Hein was an important pillar of the breed and appears in German as well as American pedigrees, notably in the breeding of Lance of Fran-Jo, in the lower bracket, as sire of the imported Grand Victor Bill von Kleistweg. Gero was a medium-size dog of harmonious build, good bone and a floating gait. Casar and his brother Dick

Hein v. Richterbach, SchH III, FH by Billo v. Oberviehland ex Rosel v. Osnabruckerland. A powerful, muscular, impressive dog, richly pigmented and of excellent temperament. Hein is a foundation dog in many German and American lines.

Bill v. Kleistweg by Hein v. Richterbach ex Adda v. Reiffeck. 1956 Grand Victor. A fine German import who finished his championship at the Specialty. Great-grandsire of Lance of Fran-Jo.

(from another litter) and Grief von Elfenhain (imported to the United States) were all sired by Hein, who was a son of Rosel von Osnabruckerland, sister to the famous Rolf. From film that Charles Kaman and I took in Germany at the Sieger Show, I would postulate (though I do not possess X-ray vision) that Casar von der Malmannsheide had hip dysplasia.

A son of Rolf von Osnabruckerland, Alf vom Waldorf-Emst, was a strong, heavy-boned animal who was progenitor of the excellent producer Marko vom Boxhochburg (who is behind Fred v.d. Bechtaler Burg, another good producer). The line carries long coats as a recessive. The "D" and "C" litters von Elfenhain were quite successful. The procreator was Arno von Haus Gersie, who was sired by Axel von der Deninghauserheide, also the father of

Perle v. Zollgrenzschutz-Haus, SchH II *(above)* by Igor v. Tempelblick, SchH III ex Krafta v. Zollgrenzschutz-Haus, SchH III. This strong, "Vörzuglich" bitch was the dam of the famous "V" litter v. Zollgrenzschutz-Haus. Harry v. Donaukai, SchH III *(below)* by Falk v. Emsschleuse, SchH II ex Freia v. Donaukai, SchH II. A top dog in Germany, Harry was sire of the great "V" litter Zollgrenzschutz-Haus. Imported, he became Canadian Grand Victor and Champion, as well as American Champion. Owned by Arbor Kennels.

Troll von Richterbach, found in the pedigree of Lance of Fran-Jo as previously mentioned. Arno von Haus Gersie produced sound working-type dogs. Good examples of his worth as a progenitor was the "V" litter Busecker Schloss (Valet, Veit, etc.) who, in their turn, produced remarkably good stock. Yet another top VA dog, Erko von Dinkelland, sired by the well liked Kay von Hexenkolk and himself the sire of the lovely bitch Quelle vom Bergischen Tal, was later imported to the United States by Jane Lightner and quickly made his championship. Erko also sired VA Pascha von der Bayernwaldperle and the many times top "V" dog Imbis aus Wattenscheid.

Josef Wasserman bred a superior litter at his Zollgrenzschutz-Haus Kennels when he bred Perle von Zollgrenzschutz-Haus to Harry von Donaukai (later imported to the United States). The best of the litter, Volker, was a model of what a Shepherd should be. Youth Sieger, then twice World Sieger, he was unsurpassed in his time. His breeding was not from the mainstream of Germany's breeding stock, so he was considered a valuable outcross. The author owned Volker's best son, Austrian Sieger Condor von Sixtberg, and a daughter who lived with us in Spain, "V" Della von Devrienthof, twice German Sheep Herding Siegerin and first in Service Dog Competition in Berlin. She was truly an extraordinary animal. Carmen von Sixtberg, litter sister to Condor von Sixtberg, was the dam of the four times "VA" dog and Reserve Sieger, Condor von Zollgrenzschutz-Haus, and Condor sired Quanto von Weinerau, one of the greatest dogs of the breed. Volker was brought to the United States for a limited time and was at stud in the kennels of my good friend Dr. Al Mehlman in Connecticut, but few American breeders took advantage of his heredity, a rather surprising commentary on the discernment of American breeders.

Gero and Ingo von Haus Elkemann, excellent animals themselves, proved to be valuable studs, giving to their offspring their own rich coloration and general balance. Zibo and Witz von Haus Schutting were very highly rated, Zibu achieving the title of Sieger in 1964. I was still living in Spain at that time but flew to Germany and saw Zibu made Sieger, a not very popular win since he was bred in the kennels of the judge, Dr. Funk. Greatly applauded was the Siegerin, Blanka von Kisskamp, a daughter of former Sieger Mutz aus der Kuckstrasse. Witz sired, among other fine dogs, 1965 Sieger Hanko von Hetschmule, Claus von Obergrombacher-Schloss, Nice von Heckhauser Weg and the "H" and "D" litters von Sixtberg. Witz was eventually shipped to Japan. Among the best of Zibu's get were Quido von Haus Schutting and Jacko von Bimohlen. The gray dog Brix von Grafenkrone was brought to America. He had sired nice stock in Germany, as did also Bar von der Starenheimet; both Brix and Bar were sons of Bar von Weissen Pforte.

The value of the "R" litter von Osnabruckerland line became so apparent that it was heavily bred upon and, as a result of this massing of genetic material, recessive faults combined and surfaced. Outcross lines were soon

Double Sieger Volker v. Zollgrenzschutz-Haus, SchH III, CACIB by Harry v. Donaukai, SchH III ex Perle v. Zollgrenzschutz-Haus, SchH II. "...Finally, what made the decision in his favor is that he comes from a good 'family,' and that he has already proven his qualities in breeding." (Dr. W. Funk, after awarding the Sieger title to Volker for the second time.) Volker was bred and owned by Josef Wassermann.

needed; luckily, they were available. German breeders had been aware that there would be a need for outcross material because of the confluence of breeding lines. They immediately, but cautiously, utilized this fresh genetic pool as a countermeasure to the intense "R" litter lines, and new strength, rejuvenated vigor and a correction of unwanted recessives occurred.

German breeders are aware that the greater the gene-pool the broader the breed basis and the easier it is to correct lines that have produced faults through excessive linebreeding or inbreeding. German Shepherd Dog type has changed drastically since 1925 and the Klodo von Boxberg era. Progress can be made in animal breeding only when the pattern of genetic traits, the faults and the virtues, are understood and objectively evaluated. Those who decide the fate of the breed in Germany periodically do this, and in so doing bring the breed back to a stabilized breeding base. But by outcrossing they cover, rather than eliminate, faults.

Condor v. Zollgrenzschutz-Haus, SchH III, AD by Condor v. Schnapp, SchH II ex Carmen v. Sixtberg, SchH II. Landesgruppen Youth Sieger, Bundessieger, four times VA at Sieger shows. A fine show and working dog, this handsome Shepherd, whose dam was a "V" litter sister to Condor v. Sixtberg, is the product of a great producing line and was sire of the great Quanto v.d. Wienerau. Bred and owned by Josef Wassermann of Germany.

GERMAN IMPORTS IN THE UNITED STATES

Klodo von Boxberg did not stay long in Germany. He was imported to America and stood at stud in the Maraldene Kennels of A.C. Gilbert (of Erector Set fame) in Hamden, Connecticut. I remember well a dark-haired boy in knickers and high socks, a boy of fifteen who hitch-hiked to the Gilbert estate to see the great Sieger Klodo. He walked hesitantly through the great iron gates and strode toward the big kennels, full of a bursting eagerness and anticipation. A big, richly-hued black and tan Shepherd with slightly soft ears greeted him and loped along beside him with lolling red tongue. This was Alf vom Tollensetal, a fine import in his own right. The boy spoke softly to the big dog and petted him and then, in an outside run, he saw a gray dog floating effortlessly back and forth. There was no doubt who this was in the boy's mind; this was the great Klodo. It had to be—no other dog in the world could move with such grace and power. His heart pounding with excitement, the

Ch. Pfeffer v. Bern, ZPr, MH by Dachs v. Bern ex Clara v. Bern. A German Sieger and Double U.S. Grand Victor.

boy half ran to the wire enclosure then stood there speechless, captured by the beauty of the animal before him.

It happened in 1925, and the author was the 15-year-old boy who watched the gray dog with such complete rapture. It was a long time ago, longer than I like to remember, but the memory of that moment is still alive and young in my mind.

In the United States, the German Shepherd gained steadily in popularity during 1925 and 1926 until, registered with the American Kennel Club, there were 21,596 German Shepherds listed out of an all-breed total of 59,496. Then the bandwagon began to roll and, due to the activities of the backyard breeders, puppy factories, bad publicity and stupid breeding practices by fanciers who should have had more integrity, the bottom fell out of the breed's popularity. By 1934 only 792 Shepherds were registered with the A.K.C. throughout the country.

The breed, during those years, may have declined in America, but fine animals were still being produced by a nucleus of earnest breeders in this country—Marie Leary of Giralda Farms fame, Jim and Eleanor Cole and their Dornwald Kennels, good friends that are gone now. There were the Llano Estacado Kennels, San Miguel on the coast, Celler Schloss,

Robinsway, Bee Jay, Liebestraum, Longworth, Grafmar, Waldesruh, Sarego, Lahngold, Hessian and so many more.

Then, in 1936, John Gans bought a young male from Franz Schorlin in Hanover and brought him to his Hoheluft Kennels in the United States. The dog's name was Pfeffer von Bern and, when Pfeffer had matured, Gans returned him to Germany to enter him in the Sieger Show at Munich in 1937. What happened then is history . . . Pfeffer von Bern won the World Sieger title. His show career in this country was also brilliant, and his sister Perchta von Bern, a lovely bitch, was also purchased for the Hoheluft Kennels. She had an exceptional show career even though she was missing four teeth. It is impossible to imagine a German Shepherd of today having any kind of a show career with that many missing teeth.

Before I continue the story of Pfeffer and his genetic background, I feel it necessary to mention here that on April 22, 1936, Max Emil Friedrich von Stephanitz passed away after a lingering illness. He had the good fortune to have seen his life's work fully accomplished and the German Shepherd Dogs he loved accepted around the globe as a breed without peer in the canine world. Von Stephanitz's lifetime dedication in the service of a breed of dogs is, without doubt, unparalleled in the history of dogdom.

Returning to Pfeffer von Bern, we find that he was sired by Dachs von Bern and his dam was Clara von Bern, a daughter of Ado von Pagensgrub, who was a son of Utz von Haus Schutting. Dach von Bern's sire was Alex von Ebersnaken, and Dach's dam was the lovely Vicki von Bern, whose owner refused to sell her at any price. Vicki was a daughter of Utz.

Pfeffer was possessed of great nobility. He was richly colored black and red-tan and had outstanding secondary sex characteristics; he had a beautifully laid-back shoulder, an excellent forequarter assembly, particularly fine hindquarter angulation for his day, good depth and a nice croup. One would have liked to have seen a trifle shorter loin, a bit firmer back, a somewhat shorter hock and a little more drive in the hindquarters during movement—but this is nit-picking. I merely mention that he could have used a bit of improvement in these areas. The fact is that he was World Sieger in Germany and had a great show career in the United States.

He was linebred on Utz von Haus Schutting and was a prepotent sire, giving lavishly of his dominant gifts to most of his offspring. The best of these was the Grand Victor Nox of Ruthland, his brother Noble and sister Nora, Grand Victrix Lady of Ruthland, Ch. Vetter of Dornwald, Ajax and Amigo von Hoheluft and many, many more great and near-great animals. But to his offspring, we must not forget, he passed on also the hidden recessive faults of his heritage.

Pfeffer's illustrious son, Double Grand Victor Nox of Ruthland (who carried a recessive for long coats), begat a multitude of fine dogs. His dam, Carol of Ruthland, produced many excellent offspring when bred to Pfeffer, a

Grand Victor and Ch. Nox of Ruthland by Ch. Pfeffer v. Bern ex Carol of Ruthland. A Double Grand Victor and top American-bred producer, he did much to establish breed uniformity in America during his time.

Grand Victrix and Ch. Lady of Ruthland by Ch. Pfeffer v. Bern ex Ch. Frigga v. Kannenbackerland. A picture of unsurpassed beauty. American-bred but of imported German stock.

breeding that was repeated several times because of the quality of the off-spring. She was by Ferdl von der Secretainerie, a son of Odin von Stolzenfels, and her dam was Devise von Haus Schutting, a daughter of Dachs von Bern, Pfeffer's sire.

Odin von Busecker Schloss was born in the kennels of Alfred Hahn, who is still breeding and exhibiting fine dogs in Germany today. Odin too was by Dachs von Bern, so Pfeffer and Odin were half brothers. Dr. Sachs, a respected judge in Germany, gave Odin a V1 rating in a large show in Berlin on September 19, 1936, when Odin was two and a half years old. That same

Ferdl v. d. Secretainerie, SchH by Odin v. Stolzenfels ex Tunte v. d. Secretainerie. 1936 and 1938 Holland Sieger. A prominent sire in American, English, and German breeding programs.

Ch. Odin v. Busecker Schloss, a dominant stud force in America, particularly in the Midwest and on the Pacific Coast.

year Pfeffer was shipped back to Germany by John Gans and entered in the Sieger Show in Frankfurt, where he met in intense competition with Odin for the Sieger title. After extensive gaiting Pfeffer was victorious and was declared World Sieger.

On the Pacific coast and in the middle west, Odin became a dominant stud force. Like his half brother Pfeffer, he gave much that was good to his progeny. Used as a factor in linebreeding, he stamped his get with his own strong middle-piece. He was a strong, heavy animal, gray and rather light in pigmentation. He was well balanced and bold, in fact a bit over-aggressive. Alfred

Ch. Nores v. Beckgold by Ch. Quell v. Fredeholz ex Helga v. Beckgold. A top American-bred show dog and a Canadian Grand Victor.

Grand Victor and Ch. Tawnee v. Liebestraum by Judo v. Liebestraum ex Vonda v. Liebestraum, 1951 Grand Victrix. A lovely, American-bred bitch.

Hahn, the breeder of Odin, described the sire of Pfeffer and Odin, Dachs von Bern, and Dachs's sire, Alex von Ebershacken, as: "Beautiful dogs, but no heroes . . . Today they would not pass the temperament test . . . would not be entered in the Koerbook as suitable for breeding. This tight Utz line did not agree with the line of Harras vom Glockenbrink (sire of Alex v. Ebersnacken) in the trait of good character. Further, there appeared tooth trouble, color fading, and so forth."

Chlodulf von Pelztierhof was imported into the United States by Anton Korbel in 1936, and used with great success, mostly on the Pacific coast. He was also gray (what Americans call "sable," and I have no idea why since sable means black or very dark), a large dog with great body depth, heavy bone, and flaunting a tight back and a powerful gait. His pasterns could have had greater spring, but he was an impressive animal. His sire was Edi aus der Leineweberhoffe and his dam Bella von der Lohbrugger-Hohe. Chlodulf also sired some excellent offspring, particularly lending improvement to light-boned, small bitches of unsure temperament.

Other fine German imports brought to the United States were: Quell von Fredeholz, imported by Ernest Loeb (Quell became a champion here with little effort, and sired some nice stock, including Nores von Beckgold, who became Canadian Grand Victor); Atlas von Elfenhain, from Willi Sufke's well-known Elfenhain Kennels, a big, richly pigmented, excellent male who produced well, though some of his get were dysplastic. He was the sire of Frack von der Burg Arkenstede, imported by Ann Mesdag. Frack was a great dog and fine sire. Gray in color, he claimed, in his lower bracket, some of the old and valuable sheepherding families.

Several animals of Heinz Roper's breeding (zu den Sieben Faulen) were imported by Bob Brandenburg who had, as a youngster, exercised many of the Sieben Faulen dogs, for the keenels were near his home in Germany. He also imported the lovely bitch Gisa von Rugereid. A German Shepherd whose name is found several generations back in both German and American pedigrees was Klodo aus der Eremitkenklause, German Youth Sieger. He was the sire in Germany of the excellent Jupp von der Murrenhutte, and was imported to the United States to stand at stud in Florida. Tom Bennett and Fred Becker, Jr., imported Condor von Stoerstrudel, who became Grand Victor in 1963. Fred's father always had a very nice import as a house dog. The author imported V1 Condor von Sixtberg and Della von Devrienthof. Dago von Sixtberg, a younger brother of Condor's, also came to the United States; he became a champion, taking groups and Best-In-Show in the process.

Eric Renner, a good friend of the author's, imported Ch. Harold vom Haus Tigges and the German Sieger Bodo von Lierberg, and Bill Goldbecker brought in Ingo von Burgunderhort. The author owned Ingo's best daughter, Udine von Beckgold, whose dam was Pert von Hoheluft. The sire of the famous Double Sieger Volker von Zollgrenzschutz-Haus, Harry von Donaukai, was imported to the States and became a champion and Canadian Grand Victor. A beautifully balanced gray dog from a top litter, Cito von der Hermanns Schleuse, was imported into the United States and is to be found in the pedigree of Lance of Fran-Jo. Bill von Kleistweg became Grand Victor and is also found in the breeding behind Lance. Katja von Blaisenberg became Grand Victrix in the United States, as did Afra von Heilhortkamp in 1952. Yasko von Zenntal, another import, became Grand Victor.

There have been so many fine imports, including Atlas and Raps von Piastendamm, Astor von Hexenstanz, Grand Victor Brando vom Aichtal, Rasant von Holzheimer-Eichwald. Bart Chamberlain, Jr. introduced Hanko von Hetschmuhle, the Sieger in 1965, to the American way of life, and there was Ulk Wikingerblut, Canadian Grand Victor, and Grand Victor Troll von

Richterbach, grandsire of Lance of Fran-Jo, and the list could go on and on, but in the interest of some tattered remnant of brevity we have to finally cease.

We must remember that all dogs possess faults, even the finest of imports, and we must find out what those faults are, particularly those that are recessive, so that we can breed to eliminate them or cover them and not to double up on them. In Germany the faults of the dogs are acknowledged and openly discussed so that a better knowledge of their breeding value can be arrived at. This information regarding imports must be secured from Germany so that American breeders can have a greater command over the heredity of these dogs. In America there is a tendency to cover up the faults of one's dogs, and some people are less than honest in discussing their animals, the assumption being, "If you can't say anything nice, don't say anything at all." This is certainly not a healthy attitude, nor is it good for the breed.

I must apologize for what to many of you may have been a long and boring litany. But it was necessary to keep the record straight and bring you a clearer picture of what has happened in the breed in times gone by. It was also needed to satisfy students of the breed who desire complete and utter clarity, with no part of the breed's history given cavalier treatment.

These were the imports for which American breeders paid high prices and upon which they hoped to build a staunch foundation for the breed in America. Most of these imported animals became champions and many became American and Canadian Grand Victors, certainly honors that reflect their quality. From them a great many fine American-breds were produced that stabilized the breed basis in America. But we must remember that they carried the faults as well as the virtues of their ancestry.

The impact of the imports on American breeding efforts can be gauged by a perusal of the *Sheperd Dog Review* in 1968. Fully 75% of the advertisements feature either imported dogs or animals that were bred from imports. Those were days of restless anticipation and a striving toward a goal . . . a true American-type of German Shepherd dog. But type was so varied and interpretation of what was wanted so diverse that empirical judgment could not be made. Yet throughout the country fanciers were earnestly striving to produce better specimens, envisioning a rather vague ideal. Then in the Fran-Jo Kennel a propitious litter was born that would, at last, produce the truly American-type of German Shepherd Dog and bring to an end all speculation as to what that dog should be.

THE GERMAN SHEPHERD IN ENGLAND

There is not a great deal of difference between the German Shepherd in England and in America at the moment. There was a time in the past when English German Shepherd Dogs (they were called Alsatian Wolf dogs then)

Ch. Vetter of Dornwald by Ch. Pfeffer v. Bern ex Ch. Fritzie of Gwynllan. A great early American-bred sire and show dog; to his get he gave lavishly of his own superb quality.

Ch. Churlswood Tosca of Brinton. A lovely feminine English bitch who made her championship in top competition.

were not typey enough, except for a few top English-bred dogs, to compete with either the American- or German-bred German Shepherd dog in the ring. This statement will cause a good deal of angry response, but it is true. I think, if I remember correctly, that Mrs. Cole of the Dornwald Kennels was one of the first American breeders to import English stock.

In the eozone period of the German Shepherd in England, after the war, stock was brought to England by returning soldiers who had witnessed the intelligence of the breed and realized their utilitarian worth. It was the era of Rin-Tin-Tin, it was the early 20's, but a stigma was attached to the name German Shepherd, and patriotic Britishers wanted nothing to do with the name so they christened the breed the Alsatian Wolf dog.

Ch. Grandee of Dornwald and Ch. Phoebe of Dornwald, progeny of imported Fels v.d. Rottumbrucke of Dornwald. The male is out of Tammi of Dornwald and the bitch's dam was Ch. Fashion of Dornwald. The genetic dominance of Fels is clearly evident in this photo.

This name did nothing for the breed either. After a group of unfortunate incidents, every animal with erect ears was labeled a German Shepherd and castigated.

But, as the 1970's approached, the popularity of the breed elevated. Some of the faults we witnessed were long backs, a soft coat, lack of shoulder placement and decent croups, and a number of genetic heritable faults that were unseen. Also unseen were the desired, hard temperament wanted in a working dog, a lack of depth in the jaws, as well as jaw anomalies and weak backs.

Now these faults can be found in American and German lines also, particularly in the incipient stage of breeding since the recessive genetic faults cannot be seen and evaluated.

I have seen the residue of such faults in many parts of the world where I have judged, in the West Indies, South America, Hong Kong, and other areas that had been under English influence.

I have many friends on the Islands (Barbados, Trinidad, etc.) with beautiful dogs of English stock, and they have none of the faults listed above. These dogs have been good enough for me to have many times elevated them to Best in Group and Best in Show because of their excellence.

One of these dogs was a grand gray dog of heavy bone and substance, yet with excellent movement and overall soundness, owned by Peter Wupperman who then lived in Trinidad but now resides in Miami, Florida. Richard Rezende of Trinidad, the owner of a bustling guard dog business, also has some fine show dogs. He is leaving for England at present and I am certain will bring some excellent dogs back with him. Today the faults found generally in the English dogs are the same we find in our American-bred dogs.

I find that the English dogs are a bit taller than American dogs generally; they have nice long necks, lack a bit in sex differentiation in the head, and have generally decent bone. They used to be rather long but have adopted the comparative height to length enjoyed by the German dogs apparently. The English do not condemn a slightly larger dog as they do in Germany. There, in Germany, they have made a fetish, under the leadership of Dr. Rummel, of selecting for high show honors, only dogs under 65 centimeters in height.

I do not advocate a monstrous creature, but I do believe the Germans should be a bit more lenient toward a fine specimen that may be just a tad over the wanted size. Now that Dr. Rummel will no longer be judging adult males at the Sieger Show, and Hermann Martin has taken his place, perhaps there will be greater leniency shown the tiny bit bigger dog. Dr. Rummel claimed that the smaller dog was more agile and quick than the larger dog. But the bigger, heavier dog must also be considered because of his stopping power in the protection area of schutzhund work.

The English breeders are doing what the United States did in the 1960's. They are acquiring fine imports from Germany to exhibit in the show ring and to use in the breeding pen.

Ch. Fenton of Kentwood. This is the top English Shepherd (or Alsatian as they are called in Britain) who made breed history by going Best in Show at the famous Crufts show. Fenton is typical of the best of English Shepherd breeding.

This is a very smart step, for the responsiveness of domesticated life-forms are in our hands, when we play God, when we assume the progress of their evolution. The breeding and future of the German Shepherd dog is in our hands and we must take the responsibility of both their physical and mental progress or deterioration. In England they are doing just that; they are bringing in imported stock from Germany to help alleviate faults that their own dogs have.

The English breeder must remember that the German stock also carries faults and they must manipulate virtues and faults to reach the desired results. Many of the faults in both their own stock and the imported stock will prove to be recessive, and they must be eliminated or pushed back by over-riding dominant traits. The breeders of England, with ther acumen and their length of service to the canine race, will recognize and know how to juggle the interlacing puzzle of this genetic breeding.

The pedigrees alone of the native German dogs will grant them information that is not available in pedigrees from other countries (except Holland, Italy, Austria), and inquiries to the SV headquarters in Augsburg, West Germany, will bring them more information and insight into the heritage of the dogs that they purchase from Germany.

Fels v. Rottumbrucke of Dornwald. Fels is both a U.S. and Canadian Champion and is also an R.O.M. sire. Imported and owned by Mr. and Mrs. James A. Cole of Dornwald Kennels fame.

The finest bloodlines in the United States owe their basic value and dominance to German imported stock. Such dogs as Lance of Fran-Jo, whom we have heavily inbred upon over the years, owes his individual beauty and his breeding dominance to excellent imported stock in his pedigree background.   I do not think that there is a dog in America that does not boast of Lance in his pedigree, and generally not once but several times. Of course one cannot continually breed to the same bloodlines, for all dogs have faults and those faults accumulate and become exposed through drastic inbreeding. There inevitably comes a day of reckoning.

In England the breeders live with and for their dogs as they do with certain breeds in Germany. One of those breeds is the German Shepherd dog. This very close association in England brings them a sense of the basic necessities that is almost psychic. They do not live for their Shepherd's success in the show ring, as so many of the breeders do in the United States. No, there is more than that to the association of owner and Shepherd in England.

In the British Caribbean islands they have instituted in several of the specialty shows an interesting added competition. After the classes Shepherds can be entered in an endurance competition, in which they are asked to trot around the ring without stopping, and the dog that exhibits the least distress and does not break stride is the winner. A time limit of fifteen minutes is put upon this endeavor, and a change of handlers can be made, but it is eventually the handlers who find the competition difficult; the dogs, it seems, can keep going all day.

With the new German imports the English breeders are acquiring, they have an excellent chance to shape the breed there to both show and utilitarian perfection. They are certainly using a sounder and more reliable approach, by cannily combining their English bloodlines with the German bloodlines to find an excellent balance. With their new German imports the English breeders can use bloodlines that are completely different from those they have been using and so benefit by incorporating greater vigor and stamina into their strains.

There is a great deal of interest today in German Shepherds as guard dogs in England and on the Islands, because of the increase of crime there and in all parts of the world. A friend of mine in Barbados, (Sugarland Farms, in Saint George) Keith Laurie and his wife Marina, run a very swank guard dog business in that area. Many businesses rent the Lauries' dogs. Another friend, Richard Rezenda, in Trinidad, is the proprietor of the largest guard dog business on the island. He will be leaving soon for England and will undoubtedly return with several more fine German Shepherds. He has a bitch now that is doing very well in the show ring.

Some of the dogs now in England doing well in the show ring and listed in the tabloid magazine *Our Dogs* include those with German bloodlines: Mr. and Mrs. J. Langhorn, with the German stud VA Cito vom Bermannshof, SchH III, VA at the 1982 Sieger show . . . a big dog with no inbreeding. The Bradleys' Norlante Kennels features the fine imports Ch. Fanto von Diemelbergland and Cito vom Konigsbruck. Kenlous Thatcher's import won the working group at the Paignton Champion Show. Jim and Sylvia Haydon have a German import they purchased from Italy, Arci di Casa Solma, and the Kingston Kennels of A. and R. Kallagher own the import Otto vom Nezetstolz, SchH II. The Standahl Kennels of the Haydons also own Standahl's Argus and Standahl's Danzio, lovely English-bred dogs. Other top English showdogs are Ryslinde Lulubelle D'Arlene, Ravenways fine English-bred stock and Elmdahaus's lovely English-bred Shepherds. Kenhope Kennels, Andeways, Renerick's (who own Chieftan and Witchdoctor), Eric and Hazel Newman's Hazelton Kennels all can boast of fine English-bred stock. The Akir Kennels own the lovely Crimson Rose, and the Colorama Kennels

V. Petz v. Zollgrenzschutz-Haus *(above and facing page, above)* by V Raps v. Wasserrad, SchH II ex V Olga v. Zollgrenzschutz-Haus, SchH I. This stallion-type import, linebred on VA Condor v. Zollgrenzschutz-Haus, is siring nice animals and is owned by Elli Matlin and John McDonnell of New York. V Panja v. Zollgrenzschutz-Haus, SchH I *(facing page, below)* is litter sister to Petz and is also owned by Elli Matlin and John McDonnell. This lovely bitch was imported by the author.

are also breeding top English-blooded stock. All these people and many more are breeding top show stock, German- or English-bred, and they are certainly conscious of hip dysplasia, epilepsy and other assorted ills that can come from both the English and German imported stock. In another section of this book you will find a list of anomalies that your Shepherd dog can become heir to—it matters not if it is an American, German or English Shepherd.

The English Show Classes are much different from the United States's or Germany's; there are many more classes. In the Islands the exhibitors use the same numerous classes and the exhibitors are allowed to show in one class; when that class is over, they register for the next class. The only way for a judge to hold onto his sanity under these conditions is to hold the Shepherds he has already judged at one side of the ring, go over the new dogs in his present class, then bring them all together and make his placements after moving them.

Show classes vary in different parts of the world. In areas where the British have had great influence, the classes are the same as they have in England. In other areas, South America, Mexico, etc. the Specialty Show classes are often the same as in Germany, with puppies 12 to 18 months, young dog class 19 to 24 months, and adult class from 24 months and older. There is no intersex competition, and a Sieger and Siegerin are selected from the adult class only. At the last show I judged in Mexico my Sieger was a terrific male imported from Germany, and my Siegerin a beautiful bitch bred in the United States.

The fact remains that England, with her new imports from Germany and her top quality native stock, has a better than good chance of producing superb stock that will rival any in the world. With their deep and abiding love for animals, coupled with their breeding acumen, I am certain that this will come to pass.

I may mention here that I have traveled the world and everywhere I have gone I have seen German Shepherd dogs, and that includes China, Japan, and I saw some fine English-bred Shepherds in Hong Kong, Australia and New Zealand.

I hope that these words give you some idea of what has been done and what is being done with our breed in the British Isles. A report has just arrived on the Windsor Championship Show in England. It is the 34th renewal Show and they had 10,083 entries, a rather large exhibition I would say. The working and utility Group was captured by the German Shepherd Ch. Caljou Angelina Of Parajoy, owned by Mr. and Mrs. Parody, a lovely win indeed.

Chapter 4

Modern Breeding Lines in Germany

Dr. Werner Funk was still president of the SV and major judge of the Gebrauchshundklass Ruden at the annual Sieger Show when the modern breeding lines in Germany came into focus. To be precise the trend began in 1962 with the whelping of the "L" litter Wienerau. Lido was a top V male and a remarkable stud dog and used extensively; Landa was Schutzhund III and German Siegerin in 1965; Leska was a V bitch, as was her sister Liane. The sire of this amazing litter was VA Jalk vom Fohlenbrunnen (by Vello z.d. Sieben Faulen); the dam was Dixie v.d. Wienerau. There are very few dogs in Germany that do not have at least one genetic line back to the "L" litter.

In 1965, when Landa von der Wienerau became Siegerin of Germany, my wife and I were journeying through Europe. We stopped off to visit with Josef Wassermann in Farchant and joined him at the Sieger Show. After the show we went back to Farchant and purchased Condor von Sixtberg from him and had the dog shipped home to Connecticut. Hanko von Hetschmuhle secured the Sieger title that year, and the next year, 1966, Bodo von Lierberg was awarded a VA at the Sieger Show. A year later, in 1967, he became World Sieger and was imported to the United States.

I mention this about Bodo because he too was born in 1962, the same year as the "L" litter Wienerau was born. The "B" litter von Lierberg produced two great dogs, Bodo and his brother Bernd, who earned a high VA rating the year his brother went Sieger. Of the two Bernd was perhaps the better producer. The redoubtable Vello zu den Sieben-Faulen was the sire of the litter "B," and the dam was the top bitch Betty vom Eningsfeld. As a matter of fact this breeding was so successful that it was repeated several times, always pro-

Landa v. d. Wienerau, SchH III, FH by Jalk v. Fohlenbrunnen, SchH III ex Dixie v. d. Wienerau, SchH I. Landa was the 1965 German Siegerin and out of a very successful breeding . . . she is one of the famous "L" litter Wienerau dogs.

Jalk v. Fohlenbrunnen, SchH III by Vello v.d. Sieben-Faulen, SchH III, FH ex Gunda v. Fohlenbrunnen, SchH II. Sired by a famous stud, Jalk in turn gave much to his progeny.

ducing animals of merit. It is interesting to note that Jalk von Fohlenbrunnen, sire of the "L" litter Weinerau, was a son of Vello zu den Sieben-Faulen.

Behind the breeding of Reserve Sieger and many times VA Condor von Zollgrenzschutz-Haus we find his dam, Carmen von Sixtberg (sister to Condor v. Sixtberg), sired by the Double Sieger Volker von Zollgrenzschutz-Haus. Condor is a very important link with the modern breeding lines of Germany, for when bred to V Yoga von der Wienerau he sired one of the greatest producers of superior stock of all time, four times VA and Reserve Sieger Quanto von der Wienerau. Quanto was born in 1967; to this day, he is a factor to be reckoned with in the production of excellent progeny. After many years

Condor v. Hohenstamm, SchH III, FH by Arko v.d. Delog, SchH III ex Asta v. d. Jakobsleiter, SchH II. Sieger and sire of a Sieger, Condor's worth as a stud force in Germany was attested to by the excellence of his get.

at stud in Germany he was sold to Italy for a huge sum and became Italian Sieger. Perhaps his finest son was Youth Sieger and Double Adult Sieger Dick von Adeloga. I saw Dick crowned Youth Sieger, and then Adult Sieger the next year.

This line that produced Dick was truly a fabulous one; Dick, Quanto, Condor, to Sieger Condor v. Hohenstamm, and Double Sieger Volker. Quanto had a fine brother, V Quino von der Wienerau, who was eclipsed by the shadow of his greater brother. Other than Dick a few of the great Quanto sons and daughters were: VA Reza v.d. Wienerau, VA Gundo v. Klosterbogen, VA Lasso di Val Sole, VA Carla v. Haus Hakatherm, VA Freda v.d. Wienerau,

A nice head study *(above)* of Volker v. Zollgrenzschutz-Haus, SchH III. 1958 German Youth Sieger, 1959 and 1960 German Sieger, and World Sieger. Hammer v. Zollgrenzschutz-Haus, SchH I, AD, Kkl I *(facing page, above)* by Held v. Flosserhaus, SchH III, CACIB ex Chuna v. Zollgrenzschutz-Haus, SchH I. From a famous kennel, this big, well-bred, intelligent working dog was imported and is owned by the author. *Facing page, below* is Ubald v. Zollgrenzschutz-Haus by Boris v. d. Burschenpartie, SchH III ex Zilfriede v. Zollgrenzschutz-Haus. This young import is owned by the author.

Eros v. Adeloga, Gundo v.d. Modauquelle, Reza v. Haus Beck, and Basso v.d. Balver Hohle. Dick died after only a short term at stud, but he nevertheless sired many top dogs, among them being: V1 Jalk and Jupp v. Hirtgarten, VA Under v.d. Wienerau, VA Grando v.d. Patersweg, V Daro v.d. Weinerau, VA Herzog v. Adeloga, and a host of other top get. He was a prepotent stud who sired dogs in his own image. Quanto's son VA Reza v.d. Wienerau sired VA Quax v. Bubenlachring, V Valdo v. Gigantenhaus, V Leska v. Tollensestrand and many more fine and productive animals. The sons and daughters of Dick, and their offspring, keep on producing excellent stock. In 1974, while judging a Shepherd Specialty in Mexico, I was happy to hear that Dick had been given the Sieger title again. He was a dog I greatly admired.

The second famous Shepherd of the four mentioned was the top V dog, Canto von der Wienerau, also a tremendously prepotent sire. Canto's most important sons were VA Datscha von Petersweg, Sieger Canto von Arminius, V1 Jago von Baiertaler Strasse, VA Frei vom Höltkamper See, V1 Asslan and Argus von Klammle, VA Erka von Fiemerich and many more dogs and bitches of great intrinsic value.

VA and Reserve Sieger Mutz von der Pelztierfarm is the third member of this important quartet. He sired VA Anderl vom Kleinen Pfahl, VA Atlas vom Dannenwalder Grund, VA Hasso von der Grunen Laterne, VA Kitty von Firnskruppe, VA Jalk von der Rheinhalle, VA Wacker von Eiringsburg, V1 Johnny von der Rheinhalle, VA Dock von der Keiferseck and a long list of other winners and producers.

Sieger Marko vom Cellerland is the last of these four fabulous Shepherds. His three most important sons were VA Eros vom Hambachtal, VA Asko von der Hattsteinburg and VA Kai von Silberbrand. Other fine get were V1 Axel von Hattsteinburg, V Norbo vom Sturmwolke and the excellent bitches VA Xandra von Haus Hanne, VA Zilda Grubenstolz and V2 Ushi von Haus Hanne. The remarkable thing about these four basic studs is that their sons and daughters and the progeny of their sons and daughters continue to produce top stock that carries on the prepotency of their bloodlines.

To chart the genetic backgrounds of these dogs in relation to the older lines is fascinating. We see that Marko vom Cellerland goes back to Utz von Haus Schutting, Canto von der Wienerau to Rolf von Osnabruckland, Quanto von der Wienerau also to Rolf through Condor von Hohenstamm and Mutz von Pelztierfarm to Sieger Alf Nordfelsen.

We have discussed Quanto's male line of descent, but it is of great interest that we note that his dam, Yoga von Wienerau, was by Lido von der Wienerau, of the famous "L" litter Wienerau, whose sister was Siegerin Landa von der Wienerau. Canto's sire was Hein vom

Konigsbruch, who goes back to Rolf von Osnabruckland, and his dam is V Liane von der Wienerau, sister to Lido and again one of the famous "L" litter Wienerau. Mutz von der Pelztierfarm was sired by V Axel von der Pelztierfarm, who goes back to Sieger Alf Nordfelsen through Held von Haus Elkeman, and his dam was the SG bitch Heidi vom Haus Bickert, whose sire was Gero von Haus Elkeman. Kondor vom Golmkauer Krug was the sire of Marko vom Cellerland. Kondor was a dog of excellent conformation and held an HGH (Herding Dog Degree). The good bitch Cilla vom Hunenfeur was Marko's dam. Kondor goes back to Utz von Haus Schutting through Drusus von der Starrenburg and Dux von Haus Schutting.

Quanto was a powerful black and red-tan dog with a tremendous gait, iron back and excellent angulation fore and aft. He possessed superior secondary sex characteristics but was a bit short in croup. He had a strong head and was a bit larger than his sire, Condor.

Canto von der Wienerau was a beautifully balanced black and tan dog, with an easy, reaching gait and a good back; in the aggregate, he was a very impressive and balanced individual. He never made Sieger, but was inevitably highly placed in competition, acquiring a V1 in Sieger competition. Much excellent stock flowed from the loins of this remarkable animal, culminating in the crowning of his son Canto Arminius as World Sieger. The efficacy of the genetic superiority of Canto Arminius has been proven in the stud pen.

At the 1970 Sieger Show, Mutz von der Pelztierfarm attained a VA2 (Reserve Sieger) placing. He was an impressive animal, strong and compact and having good bone and secondary sex characteristics. His head was solid, his back firm and his gait roomy and floating. He could throw an occasional soft ear, sometimes rather light pigmentation and occasionally a roached back. But the best of his progeny were beautiful animals, powerful and impressive. At the 1970 Show where Mutz became Reserve Sieger, Quanto von der Wienerau as VA4, and Marko von Cellerland was VA9.

Deeply pigmented, showing a great deal of black, Marko von Cellerland was an impressive dog. He had good bone, great balance and a ground-eating stride. Marko was all male and was well liked for his working qualities as well as his show attributes. He moved up the ladder of competition at the Sieger Shows to finally become World Sieger. At the 1973 Sieger Show he had not yet reached his full potential; he was late to mature. He was VA4, with the Sieger title going to Dick vom Adeloga and Reserve Sieger to Hero von Lauerhof.

To give you a more vivid picture of the strong productive powers, through the male lines, of these four animals, and particularly Quanto and Canto, consider the following: at the 1981 Sieger show, 47 of the VA and V dogs came

Barry v. Zollgrenzschutz-Haus *(above)* with the Balkan Alps behind him. Olex v. Zollgrenzschutz-Haus *(below)* by Quanto v. d. Wienerau, SchH III ex Nora v. Donauhalle, SchH I. The beautiful type of this 20-month-old solid male is very evident. Olex was strongly inbred on two great sires, Condor v. Zollgrenzschutz-Haus and Lido v. d. Wienerau, and was bred and is owned by Josef Wassermann.

Held v. Flosserhaus, SchH III, CACIB *(above)* by Condor v. Zollgrenzschutz-Haus, SchH III, FH, CACIB, VA ex Balka v. d. Berg Isel Schantz, SchH III, FH. A sire of great quality, Held was Sieger of Austria, Italy, Hungary, and International Beauty Champion of Europe. He is linebred on the famous Double German Sieger Volker v. Zollgrenzschutz-Haus and now resides in the U.S. V Reza v. Haus Dexel, SchH III *(below)* by V Dux v. Vogelsberger Land, SchH III ex V Anja v. Pillingser Bach, SchH III. A fine young male from Richard Dexel's kennels in Germany. Reza was awarded all V scores (286 points or more) in Schutzhund.

Hero v. Lauerhof, SchH II, Kkl I/a by Jupp v. d. Murrenhutte, SchH III ex Celebra v. Lauerhof, SchH I. Several times VA and in the 1972 Sieger Show, Hero made Reserve Sieger (VA2). A top German show dog, his sire dominated all others in winning get at the 1972 Sieger show in Bremen. Hero was bred and is owned by Artur Lauer, Otterberg.

from the Quanto line, 44 issued from the breeding line of Canto, 30 VA and V Shepherds came through Mutz lineage, and ten VA and V harked back to Marko. Of the bitches in the VA and V category, 23 came from Canto breeding, 15 from Quanto bloodlines, 11 through Mutz and three from Marko, whose line is fading.

Of lesser importance to today's eminent animals in Germany was twice Reserve Sieger, VA2 Hero von Lauerhof. He was twice considered for the World Sieger title, but he sported one extra incisor in the front of his mouth, so instead of six he had seven incisors and was therefore put down to Reserve Sieger. He was at stud in an area away from the mainstream of German Shepherd activity and thus had fewer opportunities with top bitches. His best son was VA Arak von der Hollendau, a very impressive animal out of the V bitch Quelle von Bergischen Tal, who was by VA Erko vom Dinkelland. Others of his progeny that have done well are: Siegerin Otti von Trienz-bachtal, a lovely bitch who is a fine producer, V1 Panja von Lauerhof and Ron von Haus Diemert. Hero's sire was the top producer and show dog Jupp vom Murrenhutte, who through Klodo aus der Eremitenklaus goes back to Sieger Klodo von Boxberg.

Among other Shepherd dogs that are producing well in Germany we can list: VA Gauner vom Grundel, VA Reza von Haus Beck, Sieger Arras von

Haus Helma, VA Lasso di Val Sole, Casar Arminius, Eros vom Hambachtal, Kai von Silberbrand, Harko von der Bayernwaldperle, Sieger Heiko von Oranian Nassau, Lardo and Jupp von der Haller Farm, Argus von Aducht, Grando vom Patersweg, Johnny von der Rheinhalle, Jalk and Jupp von Hirtgarten and several more. All of these dogs have achieved either a VA or high V rating at Sieger Shows, and practically all of them are from the bloodlines of the four superb dogs I have earlier written about—Quanto, Canto, Mutz and Marko. (The Marko line is beginning to lose strength, and the top sires today are: Argus Aducht, Lasso di Val Sole, Igor Hylligen-Born, Vello Unterhain, Reza Haus Beck and Watz Kopenkamp.)

Some very fine gray, or sable dogs, as well as black and tans, have originated from Drigon von Fuhrmannshof, Condor vom Momlingtal, Nats von Arolser Holz, Cay von Treiser Hohlen, Arno von Erlenbrunnen, and through the good Busecker-Schloss, Bungalow, Stahlhammer and Itztal lines, specifically in the latter case, through the V dog and Bundessieger (Working Dog Title) Racker von Itztal. These dogs are generally tough, strong, energetic, intelligent animals who manage high scores in Schutzhund competition. Other Shepherds that have contributed to the courage and mentality that shapes a superior working dog are the two Bundessiegers Enno vom Antrefftal SchH III and Falk von der Eichendorfschule SchH III. The exceedingly trainable kirschental (sheep herding and show) stock is valued in this capacity, as are lines to Frie von der Gugge SchH III (an all-black dog who was VA at the Sieger Show), VA Bernd von Lierberg SchH III, V1 Heiko vom Bayersberg SchH III., FH., PSPI II, Lawinenhund, WPO., Sieger Marko von Cellerland SchH III, VA Hero von Lauerhof SchH III, and several other dogs of excellent conformation that also produce good working Shepherds.

The World Sieger in 1980 was Axel von der Hainsterbach, a Lasso di Val Sole son, and Lasso is by Quanto von der Wienerau. The Reserve Sieger was Grando vom Patersweg, who is by Dick von Adeloga, also a Quanto son. Three of the VA dogs that year were by Lasso di Val Sole, who is proving to be a great sire; other of the top dogs were by Casar von Arminius, a Canto von Arminius son, Johnny von der Rheinhalle, a son of Mutz von Pelztierfarm, and Johnny's offspring, Gauner von Grundel. In 1981 and 1982, Natan von der Pelztierfarm was declared World Sieger, one of the few times that a dog in Germany repeated this achievement. He is linebred to Lido v.d. Wienerau (5-3), Klodo a.d. Eremitenklause (5-4), "L" litter Wienerau (5, 5-3), and goes back to Mutz v. Pelztierfarm, Lido von der Wienerau from Alf von Schulweg, and in his male line through Reza v.d. Wienerau he goes back to Quanto. The Reserve Sieger in 1981, Yoll von Adeloga, is linebred to Liane von der Wienerau (4-3), Lido von der Wienerau (4-5). Other dogs in the VA class were by Casar and Canto Arminius, Guaner von Grundel, Lasso di Val Sole, and Mec Arminius, and linebreeding back to Jalk vom Fohlenbrunnen was quite prominent. Of the top bitches in 1981, the Siegerin Anusch von Trienz-

Sagus v. Kirschental *(above)* by V Yasso v. Steppenbrunnen ex VA Xitta v. Kirschental. A fine young 18-month-old male, high SG in Youth Classes, and bred and owned by the Fuller's vom Kirschental Kennels of HGH dogs. VI Watz v. Kopenkamp, SchH III *(below)* by VA Gauner v. Grundel, SchH III ex V Pia v. Kopenkamp. VII at the 1981 Sieger Show and sire of the Reserve Sieger (VA2) at the 1982 Sieger Show, Watz is a respected sire and show dog in Germany.

Can. Ch. Jalk v. Liebestraum, Am. and Can. C.D. *(above)* by Ch. Ravenhaus Noah, R.O.M. ex Dyna v. Liebestraum (by Lance). This handsome red/tan and sable Shepherd was owned by Art Schuetzler and bred by the well-respected Grant E. Mann of the famous Liebestraum Kennels. Hatto v. Zerndorfer-Land, SchH III *(below)* by Kay v. Pathmospark, SchH I, FH ex Bona v. Gravenwald, SchH I. This powerful and handsome stud dog is owned by Hermann Kling of Lampertheim.

bachtal goes back to Mutz von der Pelztierfarm on the male line and to Hero von Lauerhof on the female line. VA2 Ursa von der Wienerau goes back to Canto von der Wienerau, and VA3 Xitta von Kirschental was sired by Lasso di Val Solė, the son of Quanto von der Wienerau. It is quite evident that the top-winning dogs in Germany today come through the breeding lines that we have discussed.

This end result is the fruition of several years of study and shrewd breeding acumen led by Walter Martin of the Wienerau Kennels and his brother Hermann of the Arminius Kennels. What emerged was the fact that by arranging a confluence of the genetic characteristics of Quanto and Canto von der Wienerau, a veritable tide of top-winning dogs could be produced. This was then indulged in by the Wienerau and Arminius Kennels; all the varied combinations, through sons and daughters, backcrossing, linebreeding and utilizing grandsons and granddaughters, have been successfully put to use. From the Wienerau kennels have flowed a veritable tidal wave of top animals, and even those not in the winning classes have proved to be genetically successful as breeding animals. Almost, but not quite as fortunate, has been the Arminius Kennels.

Combining the breeding of Mutz von Pelztierfarm with that of Quanto or Canto (or a combination of both) has produced some excellent results and has proved to be more productive of excellence than combining the Wienerau, Arminius and Pelztierfarm lines, separately or together, with Marko von Cellerland breeding. The combination of Quanto, Canto and Mutz (and particularly Quanto, Canto or Canto, Mutz) at this moment stands supreme in the manufacturing of fine Shepherd dogs. The partners, of course, must be judiciously chosen to counteract each other's faults. But, so well are the faults and virtues of these lines known that it is difficult to envision a breeding of individuals of these genetic lines that will not produce well.

Now, in Germany, the breeders have begun to reach a point where they are beginning to realize that this extensive linebreeding can affect the breed in the future. Cautiously and tentatively they are reaching toward other lines, experimenting, feeling their way. We see animals beginning to emerge that have no linebreeding or inbreeding, that have open pedigrees. We see a leaning toward lines that have almost been phased out: Bernd von Lierberg, whose genetic qualities are held advantageous for working dogs; Sieben-Faulen; Haus Dexel; Sudfeld; Hexenkolk; Murrenhute; Piastendamm; Itztal—not that these lines have disappeared; it is just that they have not been so seriously bred upon as they once had been.

I predict that the lines from Quanto, Canto and Mutz will continue to dominate the show rings through the 1980's, with active competition, but using the same breeding basis, from such kennels as Haus Beck, Hylligen-Born, von Dexel, Adeloga, Kirshental and many more of the aggressive kennels and breeders. American breeders looking for imported stock will want to select from individuals that reach toward the upper limits in size for, as I mentioned, since Dr. Rummel (no longer president) had taken over he had advocated and selected strenuously for a smaller, approximately 63 cm (24.57 inches) to 65 cm (25.35 inches) dog. Many German dogs have roached backs, which are not wanted in the United States. It is a strong back undoubtedly, but it does not conform to the standard. Many German dogs today have excellent angulation behind and short hocks. They can bring to American and United Kingdom bloodlines excellence in balance, fine shoulders, strong heads, excellent character and trainability. They are particularly outstanding in their trainability for Schutzhund work. Selection, of course, must be made for the wanted attributes.

You must remember that the image of the true working dog is always in the forefront of the German breeders' minds. Schutzhund training is a way of life to these people, and there are local clubs dedicated solely to the working qualities of the breed scattered all over the country. Their absorption in the utilitarian purpose of their Shepherd dogs is intense; it is indicated strongly in their conformation shows as well as in their Schutzhund competitions and herding trials. At the Sieger Show in the older class, called the Utility Class, for dogs of 24 months or older (Gebrauchshundklass), only dogs that have at least a Schutzhund II can be shown or reach the VA Select Class. If entered a second time the Shepherd must possess a Schutzhund III award. In Germany the breeders and owners of German Shepherd dogs still remember the Rittmeister's motto, "Utility and intelligence."

Chapter 5

Genetic Heritage in America

Shepherdists in the United States are quite aware of a complete dependence on exports from Germany in years past to supply show and breeding stock, an umbilical cord that stretched across continents and brought life and sustenance to German Shepherd activities. Indeed, where else could Americans find animals of value to nourish their needs? Germany was the fatherland of the breed and its German Shepherds were acknowledged to be the best in the world, so Americans turned to Germans and purchased the finest animals they would send out of the country.

The United States had one comparatively brief moment of independent glory during the Pfeffer era, when it produced some excellent American-bred stock. But, though bred in America, the animals produced were too close to the imports (about which very little was known) to be truly American, and in most instances they produced a variety of type with no clear-cut classic characteristics that could be adhere to.

The breeders here struggled along, occasionally producing truly excellent stock, dogs such as Britmore's Timothy of Lahngold, an impressive Shepherd, linebred on imported Quell von Haus Kilmark; the Celler Schloss champions; Ch. Troytan Faro, by Frack von der Burg Arkenstede; Ch. Juvanko Nemo, by Vox Wilkingerblut; Ch. Hanarob's Imperial Ian; Ch. Falco of Thunder Rock, whose dam was a Cobert bitch; Asslan of Robinsway; Ch. Dopelt-Tays Jesse James; Ch. Philberlyns Iphis; Ch. Troytan's Faro; Ch. Bee Jay's Blitzkrieg, a powerful sable dog; Ch. Santana's Man O'War, who was by Ch. Dot-Wall's Vance; Ch. Dipadon's Dasher; and many more, including excellent animals from Longworth, Liebestraum, Giralda Farms, Waldesesruh Kennels,

Barithaus and Hessian Kennels. Though these dogs and many others of that time were American-bred, they were often sired by imports and lacked uniformity in type.

There was in most instances no particular plan to the breedings made, no thoughtful balancing of genetic traits, because most of the carried recessives were unknown. Earnest breeders put their best bitches to generally top imports that would compensate for the faults they saw in their females. This was actually breeding from dominants for visible aspects, and the complete picture of expectancy was amorphous. There was some gradual improvement but nothing dramatic, with a few exceptions, and no consistency in type was attained.

Then there came a dog from Germany who impressed everyone who saw him. His name was Troll vom Richterbach; his sire was Axel von der Deininghauserheide, and his dam was a daughter of Rosel von Osnabruckerland, sister to the famous Rolf von Osnabruckerland. Troll became an International Champion and United States Grand Victor and in time an R.O.M. (Register of Merit) sire. Troll was eventually bred to a lovely lady named Frigga of Silver Lane, a most advantageous coupling. Frigga's father was the excellent imported gray male Ch. Cito von der Hermannschleuse. The offspring that resulted from this breeding were the legendary "F" Arbywood litter. Of the eight puppies born from this union, six became champions and three R.O.M. sires, and one of the six champions was the outstanding Fortune of Arbywood.

Fran and Joan Ford were exceedingly taken with Fortune or Arbywood, and, after a bit of research, they leased a bitch, Frohlich's Elsa von Grunestahl, to breed to Fortune of Arbywood. Elsa was six years old at the time, and the Fords awaited the appearance of the litter with great expectations. The bitch was a daughter of Ch. Rikter von Liebestraum, who was sired by the imported Grand Victor Bill vom Kleistweg, a truly excellent animal. On her dam's side she went back, in the second generation, to the imported Harold von Schlehenbusche, a son of the famous German sire Hein von Richterbach, who was also the sire of Bill vom Kleistweg, so she was linebred on Hein von Richterbach. But the breeding of Fortune to Elsa was a complete outcross.

The days wore away, and finally the time of whelping came. On February 27, 1964 the litter was born, highlighting the Fran-Jo Kennels for generations to come. One would perhaps expect individual excellence from this outcross breeding, but not the potency that would make Shepherd Dog history and be the beginning of the American-bred German Shepherd as a true and indigenous entity.

In this propitious litter of seven puppies a truly special dog was born, and he was named Lance of Fran-Jo. From his early puppyhood through his teen-age awkwardness he exhibited a profound structural beauty and, as time passed, he developed in his maturity into a magnificent animal. He was a better dog than his progenitors. He was different; he was not a truly German dog but a mutant, and the type that he expressed was destined to become a model for the

Ch. Lance of Fran-Jo by Fortune of Arbywood ex Frohlich's Elsa v. Grunestahl. Lance has greatly influenced American-bred Shepherds of this era. He was Maturity Winner in 1966 and then went on to become U.S. and Canadian Champion and Grand Victor. He is also on the R.O.M. sire list. Bred and owned by Joan D. and Francis L. Ford, Sr.

American conformational standard. He was influenced, it would seem, in genetic type by Troll von Richterbach and Bill vom Kleistweg, but he exhibited in himself a beauty of conformation that was completely individual. It is difficult to describe perfection . . . but Lance was not perfect. He had one missing tooth, and this, perhaps, made his other qualities more precious. His character was impeccable, and in his maturity he was an elegant large black and tan dog with extreme angulation behind, excellent balance, a noble head, good depth of body, fine forechest, good feet, shoulders and back and perfect hips.

But besides these physical endowments he was possessed of a presence, a charisma, that created a gulf between him and any other Shepherd bred in the United States up to his time. No one who saw Lance could be ambivalent in assessing his worth. Needless to say he made his championship with ease. He was not vigorously campaigned yet attained, in excellent competition, 36 Best of Breeds, eight Group firsts, two Best in Shows, and nine Specialty Best in Shows. He reached the apogee of his career when in 1967 he was crowned United States Grand Victor and Canadian Grand Victor while handled by a young Jimmy Moses, whose career as a handler rose quickly with the great dog's wins. Lance's sister Lonie finished her championship on the same day as did Lance. I had just returned from the Middle East and saw Lance being shown for the first time and was captured by this handsome animal, by the aura he emitted and the smoothness of his effortless gait.

Ch. Mannix of Fran-Jo by Lance of Fran-Jo ex Hilgrove's Erle. One of Lance's most successful sons, Mannix was the 1969 Maturity Victor and became U.S. Champion and Grand Victor. Bred and owned by Joan D. and Francis L. Ford, Sr.

Pedigree of Lance of Fran-Jo

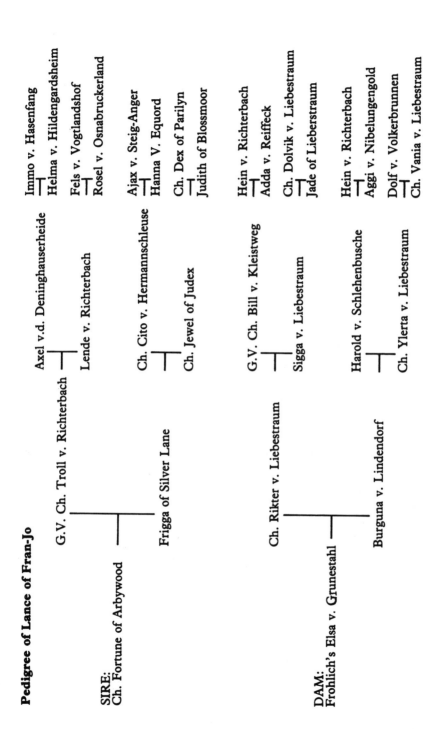

SIRE:
Ch. Fortune of Arbywood

G.V. Ch. Troll v. Richterbach

Axel v.d. Deninghauserheide
Immo v. Hasenfang
Helma v. Hildengardsheim

Lende v. Richterbach
Fels v. Voglandshof
Rosel v. Osnabruckerland

Frigga of Silver Lane

Ch. Cito v. Hermannschleuse
Ajax v. Steig-Anger
Hanna V. Equord

Ch. Jewel of Judex
Ch. Dex of Parilyn
Judith of Blossmoor

DAM:
Frohlich's Elsa v. Grunestahl

Ch. Rikter v. Liebestraum

G.V. Ch. Bill v. Kleistweg
Hein v. Richterbach
Adda v. Reiffeck

Sigga v. Liebestraum
Ch. Dolvik v. Liebestraum
Jade of Lieberstraum

Burguna v. Lindendorf

Harold v. Schlehenbusche
Hein v. Richterbach
Aggi v. Nibelungengold

Ch. Ylerta v. Liebestraum
Dolf v. Volkerbrunnen
Ch. Vania v. Liebestraum

In February 1974 this grand dog passed away, leaving behind him one of the most amazing records in the history of the breed. Again I must reiterate: for the result of an outcross breeding his prepotency was fantastic, because he stamped so many of his progeny with his own symmetry and superb balance. I had been judging a Shepherd Specialty in Trinidad, then went on to Bogota for two International All-Breed Shows and another Shepherd Specialty in Cali, Colombia, and it was there that I was informed of Lance's death. When I returned home I attempted to check his record at stud and found that he had sired approximately 57 champions—and over 100 other of his get had major points toward their championships. Some of his best-known progeny are: Grand Victor Mannix of Fran-Jo, Grand Victor Lakeside's Harrigan, Ch. Cobert's Reno of Lakeside, Ch. Cobert's Golly Gee of Lakeside, Ch. Eko-Lans Morgan, Grand Victor Scorpio of Shiloh Gardens, Ch. Zeto of Fran-Jo, Ch. Bee Jay's Gentle Ben and Ch. Lakeside's Gilligan's Island.

The breeding that produced Mannix was repeated at least twice more, producing Ch. Gailand's Magic of Fran-Jo and Ch. My Molly B. of Fran-Jo. The dam in this service was Hilgrove's Erle, a bitch I knew well since she came from what was in those days my area in Connecticut; she had been formerly owned by John Cosgrove. She was by Ch. Bernd von Kallengarten, a breeding that proved very efficacious, for Bernd, through his sire Watzer vom Bad Melle, goes back to Axel von Deininghauserheide, great-great-grandsire of Lance. Erle was also a great-granddaughter of Alf von Nordfelsen and Rolf von Osnabruckerland. Erle's breeding was purely German.

Mannix was a magnificent animal, but he was slightly overangulated behind and sported a too-short croup. The bitch that when bred to Lance produced the excellent Grand Victor Lakeside's Gilligan's Island, Ch. Cobert's Reno of Lakeside, Ch. Cobert's Golly Gee of Lakeside and Grand Victor Lakeside's Harrigan was Cobert's Melissa, who exhibits two crosses to Ch. Bernd von Kallengarten, indicating a strong influence from Axel von Deininghauserheide. Lance seemed to "nick" with bitches who were descended from Bernd.

In 1971 Gilligan's Island was garnering groups and Best In Shows with great abandon. He seemed to be the dog of the hour. And I must make mention here of Ted and Connie Beckhardt's Reno, a dog that has always been on my list of favorite Shepherds. Ch. Zeto of Fran-Jo and Zeus of Fran-Jo, sons of Lance, were both out of Ch. Mirheim's Abbey, who is a daughter of Lance and goes back to Bernd von Kallengarten, once more indicating a dominant influence by Axel von Deininghauserheide. Zeto, too, was overangulated in the hindquarters.

The magnificent Ch. Eko-Lan's Morgan was another Lance son. Morgan's dam was a great-great granddaughter of Troll and Axel. His most significant son was Ch. Eko-Lan's Paladen, an excellent animal. Ch. Bee Jay's Gentle Ben was sired by Lance, and Ben's dam was by Klodo aus der Eremitenklaus and out of a bitch whose sire was again by Bernd von Kallengarten.

A fine animal in his prime during the early 70's was Ch. Dot-Wall's Vance. Behind him he shows breeding to Ch. Cobert's Ernestine, a daughter of Bernd von Kallengarten, Ch. Treu von Wolfsstork (an import), Ch. Giralda's Deacon and Cobert's Don Juan. This dog, in appearance, is quite like the type exhibited by the Lance family. During this same year we see inbreeding upon Lance already beginning, and in the years since such breeding has been continued and become more intense. His influence is being felt even into the fourth and fifth generations because of intense inbreeding, and unaccountably excellent animals are still resulting from these breedings. For example Wellspring's Howard Johnson in the third generation shows in four male lines, Eko-Lan's Morgan, a son of Lance, and then Lance three times, stopping all male lines. Fran-Jo's Dawn of Gan Edan has all her male lines also going to Lance, and there are many more Shepherds with the same abundance of Lance's heritage.

Lance breeding does well with Yoncalla breeding, perhaps because behind Yoncalla's Mr. America is the shadow again of Bernd von Kallengarten. A touch of the excellent Ch. Caralon's Hein von der Lockenheim can also be brought into Lance's line with good results. It carries on, this bloodlines does, as witness the fact that Lance's son Mannix, a Grand Victor himself, is the sire of Grand Victor Caesar von Carahaus. Another Mannix son, Scorpio of Shiloh Gardens, also made Grand Victor, and the end, I am sure, is not yet in sight.

Cappy Pottle and Gloria Birch, of Covy-Tucker Hills Kennels, have made great strides in the breeding of excellent stock. For many years they produced fine bitches, but in the last several years they have exhibited males of equal quality. Their bitch Ch. Tucker Hills Angelique, by imported Gauss von Stauderpark and out of a daughter of Treu vom Wolfstock, has contributed greatly to the excellence of their stock. They have also brought in Lance breeding to help perpetuate the wanted type. The authority of their breeding acumen has influenced the breeding of the Schocrest Kennels. Their Schocrest On Parade, whom I had selected for his first win as Winners Male in 1977 at The German Shepherd Dog Club of the San Gabriel Valley, went on to Grand Victor in 1979.

Ralph and Mary Roberts, who had such great success with Ulk Wikingerblut, a son of Grand Victor Troll von Richterbach, have also done exceedingly well with Ch. Covy Tucker-Hill's Finnegan, an outstanding animal. At the moment, handled by Ken Raynor, Jr., the excellent male Ch.

Lucas

Kameraden's Crusader has been taking groups and Best In Show with great regularity, a plus for all German Shepherds to have one of the breed win the ultimate placings at All-Breed Shows. Crusader is of Covy-Tucker Hill's Phildore and Carolon's Hein v.d. Lockenheim breeding. Another Shepherd that has had success in garnering top awards in All-Breed Shows is Ch. Beech Hill's Benji von Masco. Joe Poepping's Ch. Bel Vista's Joey Baby, a dog I have judged several times, is an excellent Shepherd who is beginning to make himself felt at stud; and the sables of Waldesruh show merit. Canadian Grand Victor and Ch. Ravenhaus Noah, an impressive sable, is of Waldesruh, Brix von Grafenkrone and Ravenhaus breeding. Grand Victor Yoncalla's Mike breeding should prove of value to offset tightly controlled Lance breeding.

There are a few breeders who still work with top imported stock. Jack Ogren is one; Siegerhaus in California is another; Haus Boland and Monroe Kennels; Heide and David Landau's Von Furstenberg Kennels have been importing and breeding from fine German stock; Bill Fleischer's Fleischerheim Kennels use excellent German stock; Haus Kuhn; Von Holstentor; Oakwood Kennels; Ellie Matlin and John McDonnell are breeding some superior stock; the Haus Sirius Kennels of Paul and Ingeborg Theissen (Paul is an experienced Schutzhund judge who has but recently come to this country); Nordland Kennels; German Shepherd Imports, Inc.; and to some extent Joe Bihari and Frank Lopez's Totana Kennels.

Of course there are the Schutzhund people who import German-bred dogs, usually from proved working lines, to aid them to find better sport and reach greater perfection in their chosen utilitarian aims. They are a very earnest group who are dedicated to the Schutzhund movement and have no desire to compete in the conformation ring.

I feel that I must, in all good conscience, caution American breeders that they must find other, diverse bloodlines that can be used with Lance breeding to gradually phase out the slavish dependence upon Lance and his progeny to control type in the breed in the United States. We know that Lance, despite his superiority, carried recessives for long coats and orchidism and, as mentioned before, he himself was missing a tooth. These are all faults that can be carried for untold generations; they are in many German- and American-bred lines but become visible only when the breeding partner also carries the same recessives. These faults must be guarded against, and bold experimentation in genetic reproduction must be inaugurated by fanciers with the fortitude and foresight to push forward to new frontiers in breeding.

I see some evidence of a tentative reaching toward a greater genetic pool from which to choose by a few breeders who realize that they cannot indefinitely continue breeding upon the same basic bloodlines. But they have only touched the surface of this necessity. They will make mistakes, but they must face this with fortitude and move forward, using whatever knowledge they can gain from genetic truths and from valuable experience.

Select Ch. Covy's Tartar of Tucker Hill*(above)*by Grand Victor Ch. Lakeside's Harrigan, R.O.M. ex Ch. Tucker Hill's Angelique, R.O.M. A gorgeous and substantial animal owned by Cappy Pottle and Gloria Birch. Ch. Covy-Tucker Hill's Triumph *(below)* by Cobert's Sirocco of Windigail ex Grand Victor Ch. Rosemary of Tucker Hill. A bitch with superb type, owned by Gloria Birch and Cappy Pottle.

Chapter 6

The Enigma of Heredity

To solve the enigma of heredity we must study the science of genetics. The word "genetics" need not cause you alarm, for it is linked with the word "science," and science simply means knowledge.

This amazing science of genetics advances with such rapidity that by the time you read this chapter geneticists will have discovered more linkage of the genes and chromosomes (and possibly even other genes) that dictate what we are, who we are, what our dogs are and how we interrelate. The secrets of DNA, the basic life molecule and the central gene control mechanism, have been discovered, and through the knowledge gained from this event a whole new chain of interrelated studies has been released that leads in many new genetic directions.

But we must go back to beginnings to fully understand the awakening theories and hypotheses that led to what we now know of basic genetics and how it applies to the breeding of better German Shepherd dogs.

The initial interpretations of natural phenomena in early days were mythological. But man was, even in those early days, semi-aware of his relationship to all other living creatures on this planet. Such thinking led to more profound deductions, and about 500 years before Christ the Greek philosopher Thales shrewdly concluded that all life originated in the seas that surrounded the continents. Later Aristotle collected all the zoological data known in his time, analyzed it and, based upon comparative anatomy, classified all the recognized species of animals. The process of evolutionary change was acknowledged by the French naturalist Jean-Baptiste Lamarck (1744-1829), who developed the theory that such change was due to exposure to environmental influences, which were then consigned to the succeeding generation through inheritance. This doctrine seemed logical, so it was accepted for a while.

The question of differentiation among species had been a subject for discussion through the ages wherever men of scientific bent gathered. The key was finally found by the eminent Charles Robert Darwin. He theorized that all life-forms were derived from a common ancestor and that they diverged to fit different and changing environments, the adaptation to new surroundings being accomplished through "natural selection." As the species survived and reproduced, the selected individuals changed and progressively fit their environment with greater authority. The process is called *evolution.*

Darwin's theory of evolution was the initial breakthrough toward an understanding of the inheritance of characteristics. But breeders of animals still bred the swiftest to the swiftest, the best to the best, following the rule of thumb that "Like begets like." Acquired characters must be inherited, they argued, and even Darwin was aware that his theory was not all-encompassing. Natural selection produced changes, there was no doubt of that, but how did those changes occur? What was the pattern of inheritance?

While men of science pondered these questions, in a small garden in what later became Czechoslovakia a Moravian monk indulged in quiet experimentation with (after several starts with other living materials) sweet pea plants. He carefully amassed data in an attempt to find the method nature utilized to change the pattern of living, inheritable matter. And he succeeded! The monk's name was Johann Gregor Mendel, and he discovered the units of heredity and how they worked. Using hand pollinization, he selected and studied the results in peas showing many different characteristics. After long and scrupulous experimentation he found that when two plants that differed in a specific trait were crossed, one trait appeared in the progeny and one did not. He called the visible trait a *"dominant"* and labeled it a capital "A." The non-visible or hidden trait he called a *"recessive"* and designated it with a lower case "a." When "A" and "A" were crossed, all the offspring would be purely dominant and therefore "AA." When "a" and "a" formed a union, the result was purely recessive, and therefore labeled "aa." Then Mendel took his experiment one step forward, breeding "A" to "a," or dominant to recessive, and produced a hybrid "Aa" in which the dominant was visible and the recessive carried in hidden form. In his cross-breedings of hybrids he found a persistent ratio of three to one, three dominants to one recessive, and he named this finding the Mendelian Ratio.

Mendel realized that by breeding "Aa" to "Aa" he could produce three different alliances, "AA," "Aa" and "aa." Two pairs of hybrids, "Aa" and "Aa," could produce nine genetically different offspring. Compound this by three combinations in cubic power and the variations are almost infinite. But the combinations in which a single pair of determiners can combine with a similar pair are only six. Mendel named the determiners "units."

Mendelian Expectation Chart

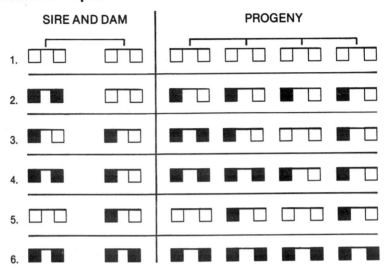

The six combinations that can be formed by a pair of units or determinants. Ratios apply to expectancy over large numbers of progeny, except in matings numbered 1, 2, and 6 where expectancy should be exact. Exceptions can be caused by mutation or cross-over. The black squares on the chart are dominant determiners and the white squares are recessives.

Mendel was, of course, unable to microscopically see his units of heredity, so the results of his experiments had to be considered theory. But he knew the units existed, and he wrote a formula of the biological laws that governed the body of his discoveries:

1. The transmission of heredity factors is accomplished through a large number of independent, inheritable units.

2. If each parent contributes an identical factor, a constant character is passed on to the progeny. When each parent furnishes a different factor, the result is a hybrid. In the reproductive cells formed by the hybrid the two different units are again "liberated."

3. No matter how long the heredity units are in association with other units in an individual, they are completely unaffected and will emerge from any union as untouched and distinct as they were originally.

Mendel, in order to test his hypothesis, indulged in two more experiments with cross-fertilization and then wrote, "In all the experiments there appeared all the forms which the proposed theory demands." The studious monk prepared a paper on his eight years of work and called it "Experiments In Plant Hybridization"; he read it before the local Brunn Society for the Study of Natural Science. The monograph was not understood and was totally ignored. Undiscouraged, Mendel continued his research and eventually discovered another law of heredity: that more than one of his "units" controlled specific traits. This truism explained all the basic laws governing heredity and answered the bewildered questions man has asked for centuries.

Gregor Johann Mendel died in 1884, two years after the demise of Charles Darwin. But unlike Darwin, no acclaim had come to Mendel; his fabulous experiments were lost to the scientific world and it seemed that his theories of heredity would be buried with his human remains. But in 1900 a Dutch botanist, Hugo de Vries, while hunting for data similar to his own experiments in plant hybridization, found reference to Mendel's work and sought out the dust-covered papers that Mendel had published in 1866. By coincidence a German and an Austrian scientist, almost simultaneously with de Vries, discovered Mendel's monumental work and gave it to a grateful world. For the first time mankind gained an insight into one of life's great mysteries. Mendel and his theory of inheritance became immortal and a new science had been born.

By using Mendel's Expectation Chart, the breeder can arrive at a reasonable idea of what to expect from specific breedings. But to know which are dominant and which are recessive traits it is necessary to have some rules that govern these hereditary factors. The following canons give us a reasonably certain approach to the control of such genetic patterns.

Dominant Traits:
1. do not skip a generation.
2. will affect a relatively large number of the progeny in any litter.
3. will be carried only by affected individuals.
4. will minimize the danger of continuing undesirable characteristics in a strain.
5. will make the breeding formula of each Shepherd quite certain.

Recessive Traits:
1. The trait may skip one or more generations.
2. A relatively small percentage of the individuals will carry the trait.
3. Only those individuals who carry a pair of determiners for the trait will exhibit it.
4. Individuals carrying only one determiner can be ascertained only by breeding.
5. The trait must be inherited by the individual through both sire and dam.

In German Shepherds there are several recessives that are controlled by a simple pair of genes. One is eye color. A light eye is recessive, a dark eye dominant. A breeding to a dark-eyed dog possessing two genes for dark eyes will produce all dark-eyed progeny. A long coat is also a recessive, and so is orchidism. Missing teeth are recessive, but a strong, erect ear is dominant over a weak ear.

In 1902, W.S. Sutton of Columbia University, asserted that chromosomes could very well be the vehicles or containers of Mendel's "units." And in 1933, Thomas Hunt Morgan, a biologist working with millions of fruit flies *(Drosophila melanogaster)*, proved that Mendel's "units" were carried by the chromosomes, changed the name of the "units" to "genes" and became known as the father of modern genetics. In recognition of his experiments Morgan was awarded a Nobel prize.

With this brief background on the science of genetics and how it came into being, we will now plunge into the exciting application of this knowledge to canine breeding and explained how it can be used to breed better German Shepherd dogs.

But first we must, once and forever, destroy old beliefs and superstitions that have come down through the ages and can only cloud the truth.

The inheritance of acquired characteristics is a falacious theory that still surfaces as a scientific fact. A Russian agronomist, Lysenko, embraced this doctrine and caused havoc in Soviet food production for years. It is simply a reiteration of Lamarck's false doctrine that environmentally controlled changes were inherited, which Mendel and the many geneticists who followed him proved to be completely wrong.

Another untrue theory predicates that *birthmarking* is a fact. The dog's genetic material cannot be influenced by its environment (with a few exceptions, but birthmarking is not one of them). Isolated incidents of this bogus belief must not be considered "proofs."

Telegony advances the hypothesis that the sire of one litter can influence the progeny of all future litters out of the same bitch. Only true if the same sire is used again. This ridiculous theory is akin to the concept of *saturation,* which postulates that if a bitch is bred a number of times to the same stud she will be *saturated with his blood,* and unable ever to produce progeny unlike that stud even when bred to another, completely different dog.

The most widely held theory is that *blood* is the vehicle that passes inheritable material from the parents to the progeny. Though discredited as a doctrine it still endures in the phraseology we use in terms such as *"pure blooded," "new blood," "blue blooded,"* and *"bloodlines."*

Your dog is a mammal and is made of organs which are fashioned by tissues that are created by cells. Each of those myriad cells contain a specific number of chromosomes. The dog possesses 39 pairs, or 78 chromosomes, 32 more than are inherited by man. We refer to chromosomes always as being paired because the dog receives half its chromosomes from one parent and the other half from the other parent. The chromosomes pair off like twin strings of beads, appearing to be exactly alike, but in reality being slightly diverse, yet quite different from the adjacent pairs.

The dog, even as you and I, is programmed by its genes, and the genes (Mendel's units) are packed inside the chromosomes; each has a specific "locus" or location, and is linked so that it will be passed on to the next generation as a unit. There is an exception to the concept that all the chromosomes are paired, for one of the thirty nine chromosomes is not . . . the sex chromosome. The female chromosomes are exact, and paired, and we specify this pair XX. But the partner chromosome possessed by the male is a Y chromosome, so we designate the male pair of sex chromosomes XY. If the male Y sex chromosome unites with the X chromosome of the female, the resulting pup will be a male, XY. But if the male X chromosome fertilizes the female egg, uniting with her X chromosome (remember she has two X chromosomes) then the resulting offspring will be a female.

Like the chromosomes, the genes are also paired, and a gene that affects a particular characteristic has a mate that influences the same characteristic. When both these genes are identical and exert the same influence, the dog is genetically *homozygous* for that specific characteristic. A gene pair can be recessive or dominant, and a gene pair which differ in their influence makes the animal *heterozygous* for that characteristic. When the genes differ, one dominant and one recessive, they are termed *alleles*. The recessive allele is carried unseen in the dog's germplasm, while the dominant allele is visible and affects the dog's appearance. An *allelomorphic series* is a group of alleles that affect a specific trait.

A complete set of chromosomes and genes is carried by every cell in the body. They constantly multiply to replace dying cells or to produce growth. The cells themselves multiply by dividing, a process called *mitosis*, and when they divide the chromosomes split lengthwise into halves called *chromatids* and form two separate *nuclei*. Each half has a complete set of chromosomes and is capable of splitting again. When this occurs the cells are termed *somatic* cells to differentiate them from the sex cells. In the sex cells, called *gametes*, a different division, *meiosis*, takes place. Each male sperm and each female egg receives only *half* of the chromosomes and their genes. Then when the sperm fertilizes the egg, the halves of each, male and female, join to make a complete whole, a new individual, one that has been given half of the sire's package of heredity, and half of the dam's. During the mating that produces this effect, the sex of the offspring in the litter is a matter of chance, since sperm is capricious and fertilization is random.

The sex cells can also carry sex-linked characteristics, though in the dog not many of these traits have been discovered. When they are recessive they can be detrimental. An example of such a character is orchidism. This trait is a simple recessive and so must be carried by both sire and dam to affect the progeny, but in the female the trait would not be visible and, if the male also carried it as a recessive, a percentage of the male puppies would have one or two

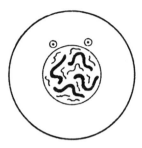

Mitosis beginning. The chromosomes are becoming thicker and more obvious in the nucleus of the cell.

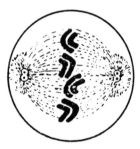

The spindle, which has been forming, now covers the middle of the cell. The nucleus has disappeared and the centrioles (cores of the asters) have divided into separate pairs. The chromosomes have split and will separate and move along the spindle to opposite sides of the cell as the cell prepares to divide.

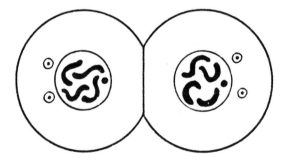

The cell is about to complete division and become two cells. The spindle has vanished, its job done. A nucleus appears in each of the cells in which there now is a complete set of chromosomes and two centrioles (for each cell). Each cell is now complete and perfect in itself, capable, and soon ready to divide again.

testicles that failed to descend into the scrotum, and some of the females would again carry the recessive for orchidism.

Let us now examine the genes, those tiny bits of material that are the "all" of life. Environmental modification of the individual (acquired characteristics) due to illness, accident, deficiencies, lack of proper diet and so on cannot have any affect upon the dog's genetic structure; its inheritable material remains inviolate.

The exact chemistry of the gene was unknown until a series of clever experiments opened the door to an understanding of new areas of inheritance. The genes, it was known, contained chemical messages that allowed them to control the metabolism of the cell. Now, it was discovered, the genes, coupled with chemical regulators in the cell called enzymes, totally control the organism in which they reside, in this case, the dog.

Genes can also mutate and, in so doing, express a trait that is entirely alien to the hereditary design of the individual. Many mutations are hidden within the body of the dog, or are so small in effect that they are not discernible. If they are visible sometimes we select for these mutations if they benefit the breed, but a mutated gene is capable of mutating again, and sometimes in another direction. Most mutations are detrimental, and some even lethal, but mutation keeps the gene-pool from becoming stagnant and so becomes the essence behind evolution, for these alien, mutated traits can either advance the recipient or retard it. Recombinant genes, allied to sexual reproduction, bring mutated genes into new unions. These fresh combinations are tested by natural selection and either kept or discarded, according to whether they damage or aid the species.

We know that change can be achieved by breaking genetic equilibrium and can be caused by four factors: mutation, selection, migration and genetic drift. In the controlled environment of German Shepherd dog breeding only the first two factors are valid. The last two can be replaced by a single factor, environment. Change can also occur immediately before the chromosomes divide in the sex cells. Opposing members of the chromosome pairs twist together, allowing a gene or genes to relocate on another chromosome. The result is a change in the inheritable material that is passed on to the progeny. This effect is labeled *crossing over* and, not unlike mutation, it causes a variance in genetic effect by changing the Mendelian balance.

Another change seldom encountered is the *triploid,* an individual who has been influenced by a triple chromosome phenomenon, caused by chromatic change. A dog can possess too many chromosomes *(polyploidy)* or too few *(aneuploidy),* and in some instances the effect of any of these phenomena can be lethal. The *phenotype* is the animal you see, the visible outward appearance of the dog. The *genotype* is the complete animal encompassing all of the Shepherd's genetic inheritance, that which you see and that which you don't see, the individual's complete heritage.

Every German Shepherd that stands before you is not one but two Shepherds, the *shadow* and the *substance*, the *phenotype* and the *genotype*. It behooves the breeder to know both the shadow and the substance if he wishes to improve the breed. Only when you do can you pair your animals intelligently and with certainty as to the outcome. We must search for the genetic composition of every animal we contemplate using in a breeding program and weigh our findings against the dog's producing ability until we know our pair, male and female, for what they are genetically so that we can actually chart the heritage of this union. We must be coldly analytical and consider each partner as a vessel, a custodian, of a specific hereditary pattern that can be molded toward an envisioned end.

When recessives link and come to the surface so they can be seen, remember they do not become dominant simply because they are visible. They are still recessives and affect the dog as recessives. They can be pushed back to invisibility in a single breeding by a pure dominant that affects the same area of the dog. Some dominants have varied penetrance and do not express themselves fully in every individual.

Cells are in a constant state of chemical modification and the genes, combined with cell enzymes, govern the speed and sequence of these chemical changes. Genes are therefore also cell regulators and direct the development of the cell in which they are contained. This function is not really important to the dog breeder; it is mentioned here simply to complete this area of our genetic exploration.

Our Shepherd dogs are the result of selection by man over a long period of time so, as a breed, its inheritable material has been shaped to certain specifications and blocks of genes selected and balanced to constantly reproduce an animal of specific physical properties, a certain kind of temperament, trainability for particular purposes, and limited to a definite size. Working from this broad basis the breeder attempts to modify individual sections of the dog's conformation to reach greater species perfection. How can this objective be accomplished?

The answer to that question is not easy. The breeder must make a completely objective study of both of the dog's parents, investigate their littermates, what they have produced when bred to certain partners and, if possible, make test matings of the dogs they have considered pairing. If you are able to acquire a four-generation picture pedigree of both animals, check the faults and virtues seen in the photographs and how they are passed down to each generation. Did the littermates show these same faults? How were they eliminated (if they were), or pushed back to recessive invisibility? The more you know the easier your endeavor will be. I warned you it would not be easy, but nothing that is worthwhile is easy, and from what we know of the random selection of the thirty-nine pairs of chromosomes before reduction division, that are ready to produce the full complement of seventy-eight chromosomes

Chromosomes in the nucleus of a cell *(left)* and arranged in pairs, showing partnership *(right)*.

through chance selection, it would seem mathematically impossible to control any genetic factors.

But don't give up. You have the Mendelian Expectation Chart for reference and the rules that are applied to dominant and recessive traits. With this knowledge and some diligent detective work you can bring the genotype Shepherd into much sharper focus. Remember, too, that some dogs are prepotent and stamp their progeny with their own type, and that sometimes the lesser brother of a famous champion stud can produce better progeny because of a happy confluence of genetic factors which he is heir to.

It would be easy, given exact knowledge of the genotype of each partner of a mating, if all characteristics were governed by simple Mendelian factors, but this is not true. Any complex of cells, chromosomes and genes of any section or small part of the body of the dog is, in order to function correctly, dependent upon many other adjacent parts of the body, so we are dealing with interlocking blocks of cells, chromosomes and genes in a life pattern of chain reaction. But, by using what you have learned in this chapter, you can make giant strides forward. You cannot lean upon guesswork, intuition, or hope. If you wish to breed better dogs you must depend on knowledge, truth, and scientific observation.

Though it will not aid you in the production of better dogs, I feel it imperative that you should more fully understand the intimate chemistry of genes and the tremendous impact the science of genetics will have in time to come. The chemical material of the gene is a fantastic molecule called DNA *(deoxyribonucleic acid)*. It differs chemically from all other cellular tissue. RNA *(ribonucleic acid)* is a similar molecule, but it is created by DNA for the specific purpose of aiding DNA in its tasks, which are regulating body chemistry and cell specialization, directing growth and dictating what all the living cells shall be and shall do. DNA and RNA make proteins by putting amino acids together, and they are constantly reproducing themselves. They are the material of life, the basis of heredity, the marvelous molecules that have complete domination over all life processes.

DNA is a spiral molecule that boasts two coils and is linked by four interlocking, chemical composition, subunits. The heredity of any life-form, including the German Shepherd dog, is determined by the sequence in which these chemical subunits are arranged. The carrier of the inheritable "code" is RNA, which assembles the essential chemicals to manufacture the proteins, synthesizes them (aided by electrical forces), and completes the pattern it has received from DNA.

DNA is so small that only through the use of powerful electron microscopes can it be seen. Yet it possesses a creative diversity that molds unbelievable billions of configurations and has access to an infinite variety of life-forms. Does DNA independently utilize all living things, including man and dog, simply as vehicles for the constant reproduction of ever more DNA? This is a moot question, to which science has yet to find an answer.

Geneticists surge forward in their scientific endeavors. Legislative pressures have been brought to bear upon geneticists who are engaged in recombinant DNA research involving *Entamoeba coli,* (a type of protozoan). In the laboratory men of scientific vision are combining segments of *E. coli's* DNA with the DNA of other animals and plants and attempting to create new forms of life unlike any that we have ever before seen. The furor this research has caused finds a parallel in anything man has ever done to scientifically reach beyond the mundane to a dream of great tomorrows. With gene-splicing a new alchemy has been born that creates new drugs, vaccines, foods, fuels, industrial chemicals and a great variety of raw materials.

Through gene-splicing man has acquired an unparalleled tool for examining and changing the involved machinery of heredity; it will aid in the appalling job of locating and analyzing each of the hundreds of thousands of genes in a Shepherd's cell. It can give to a living entity a characteristic from an alien species, and the new trait will be passed on to future generations. James Watson and Francis Crick won a Nobel prize for disentangling DNA's double helix structure and making recombinant DNA possible. To them we may, in all probability, owe the brave new world of the future.

Chapter 7

The Tools of Breeding

Man has a great need to be creative, to conceive and fashion something new and better, something that is the product of his imagination, his dream, rather than accept what has been done before. In this day and age of computers, Pacman, Atari, robots, and spaceships, the instinctive need to originate a lasting concept that is of the heart, the hands, and the mind, is almost smothered by a mechanistic sci-fi world. But the breeders of dogs are exceedingly lucky, for they can indulge in this creativeness, this need to design something entirely of the imagination. They can express human inventiveness in living bone, flesh, and blood, to create a creature fabricated in a mental fantasy that only they can see, deep in the recesses of their inspiration.

The tools necessary to reach this plateau of creativeness are the units of inheritance and the art of manipulating their infinite combinations. Think first of the physical aspect of the dog. Imagine the skeletal structure, the bones, for they are the basic edifice that you will wish to manipulate. How would you evoke change? To begin with, what is a bone? The cells could have adopted any of the more available raw materials of the earth to produce a bone; iron, silica, rock, but instead the bones of all the animals on this planet are made of calcium, carbonate of lime. Why? Because all earthly creatures come originally from the sea. So, if you wish to change the shoulder angulation of a German Shepherd, you must breed to change the angle of two pieces of calcium. And to get the 90 degree angulation between the scapula and humerus (shoulder bones), you must breed for recessives, for the straighter (and more natural) shoulder is dominant. Again, there are rules that must be followed to gain the best results from the tools of breeding.

From the chapter on heredity you have gained a more intimate knowledge of the genes and how they perform. Now you will learn how to use the tools by which they can be manipulated to the fullest extent. The techniques which are described here have been tested with marked success in many forms of production and reproduction in both the laboratory and the field, but knowledge and care must be utilized by the breeder who uses these techniques to change or perpetuate wanted characteristics. Great variation occurs in the design of the germplasm, but due to specific breed boundaries variation is limited and controlled by breed type. Within this breed boundary there is a norm which the great majority of German Shepherds mirror. If you will draw a straight horizontal line on a piece of paper and label it *"Norm,"* and above it draw another line and call it *"Above norm,"* representing the top, excellent dogs, you will find this latter line to be much shorter than the "Norm" line. Below both these lines draw yet another line and label it *"Below norm."* This represents Shepherds that possess faults that you do not wish to perpetuate, and this line will be shorter than the "norm" line and longer than the "Above norm" line. In your breeding endeavors your objective is, with each litter, to lengthen the "Above norm" line and to shorten the "Below norm" line.

Once you have accomplished this your next objective will be to raise your "Norm" line up to the "Above norm" indicator. With each breeding season your "Above norm" stock should be more numerous, and the line should be higher than the "Above norm" of the season before. Select for breeding animals always from those in the "Above norm" bracket, assess them carefully, and breed to accent their virtues and correct their faults.

Breeding in this manner is termed *"upgrading"* and is a basic breeding procedure. Over a period of time, so many people have bred German Shepherds without access to elemental breeding knowledge (in the early days of the breed such knowledge was not even available), that the dogs bred from such haphazard practices could have dangerously lowered the norm. Often in a pedigree we find a weak line that causes us anxiety. It behooves the breeder to nullify the effect of such a line by strengthening the virtues of the other lines.

Four important characteristics must be incorporated in your breeding lines if you wish to gain the greatest good from their potential:

1. *Vigor:* Loss of hardiness or vigor with its allied ills such as lower resistance to disease, appetite loss, finicky eating habits, etc. must be diligently guarded against.

2. *Fertility:* This is an essential, the lack of which must not be tolerated. All Shepherds in the line must have a high fertility rating, be easy whelpers, and facile breeders.

3. *Longevity:* An individual who exhibits many virtues and great prepotency must be useful as a breeder for many years so that full opportunity is taken of his or her breeding potential.

4. *Temperament:* The sum total of the German Shepherd's utilitarian status must be realized in the breeding individual. Lack of this character statement can nullify any advances in physical virtues reached in your breeding program.

Regression toward the average is normal, and it is a constant battle by the breeder to continue to upgrade his stock. Occasionally, below average stock will produce an excellent, above norm individual, but inevitably such an animal will reproduce the faults of his family and few of the virtues he himself displays. It is much safer to use an average dog from a fine family as a breeding partner than an excellent animal from below average stock. There is an ancient Swedish proverb to that effect, "Marry not the only good maid in the clan."

It is also true that sometimes a great show dog will produce only average get, while his brother, obscured by the champion's eminence, is capable of producing better young. Often this tendency is not recognized because the better bitches are sent to the champion to be bred. Consider the fact that the individual is the custodian of its inheritable material, and it is this germplasm that is handed down to its progeny, and the truth of the statements made above become obvious.

If used with intelligence and understanding, the categories of breeding techniques which follow will aid you greatly in your breeding endeavors. You must be the one to choose which method will best advance the worth of your stock. But you will find that there will come a time when you must incorporate other forms of the methods outlined here to introduce new genetic values, or to concentrate wanted inherited traits.

LINEBREEDING

Linebreeding is a form of inbreeding that concentrates the genetic qualities of a valuable individual on both sides of the pedigree (sire and dam). It preserves genetic characteristics of that individual by concentration, and allows the breeder some control over his or her familial type. The breeding formula is not extreme and is therefore recommended to novice breeders.

Through this method a kennel can build a strain that is recognizable as such under the kennel name. But it must be remembered that, to successfully linebreed, selection is imperative, for the individuals you designate to carry on your breeding in succeeding generations must be prototypes of the animal you are linebreeding upon and exhibit his or her virtues, for this is inbreeding of a more remote type.

The breeder must also make certain that he does not eventually select his breeding partners on pedigree alone, and ignore breeding individuals and all gathered data to use in conjunction with the pedigree study. If the dogs used in linebreeding exhibit prepotency, and if the breeding is quite concentrated, the mating can evidence all of the intense power of inbreeding. The following pedigree of Doppelt-Tay's Hammer is an excellent example of this type of intensified linebreeding.

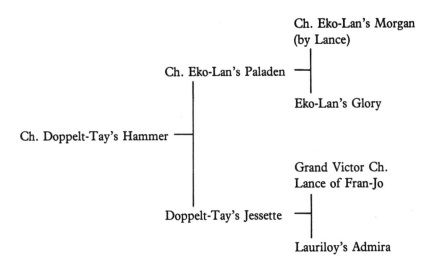

Ch. Doppelt-Tay's Hammer

Ch. Eko-Lan's Paladen

Ch. Eko-Lan's Morgan
(by Lance)

Eko-Lan's Glory

Doppelt-Tay's Jessette

Grand Victor Ch.
Lance of Fran-Jo

Lauriloy's Admira

In this example of close linebreeding on a prepotent male, Lance would definitely stamp the line with his own type for, as you see, he is also the sire of Eko-Lan's Morgan.

Not quite so heavily linebred is the Shepherd whose grandparents were litter brothers and sisters. If the name of a specific dog, perhaps coupled with a litter brother or sister, is repeated approximately three times in the fourth or fifth generation of the pedigree, it indicates more remote linebreeding. In Germany linebreeding, generally fairly remote, is used considerably to hold type and intelligence. Linebreeding can be found most often there on such animals as Jalk v. Fohlenbrunnen, Hein v. Richterbach, the "L" litter Wienerau, the "B" litter von Bern, and Quanto and Canto v. Wienerau.

To create a strain through linebreeding within the breed the following recommendations predicated upon the advice of Humphrey and Warner and Kelly and Whitney can be useful.

1. Determine what characteristics are essential to the success of your linebreeding venture. Fertility, vigor, longevity and temperament must be included. Decide also what faults cannot be tolerated and breed to eliminate them.

2. Corresponding to your goals, develop a system of scoring and tally wanted traits and unwanted characteristics. Evaluate them (faults and virtues) on a 1 to 10 basis, stressing particularly faults that need drastic improvement.

3. Consistently linebreed on the best individuals you produce that most closely resemble the Shepherd upon which you are linebreeding. To establish a definite and worthwhile strain, every Shepherd used must be firmly assessed for breeding superiority and the ability to pass wanted virtues on to his or her progeny.

94

INBREEDING

Consistency and stability of inherited characteristics are the results of inbreeding, which is interpreted through matings of brother and sister (the closest of all inbreeding), father to daughter, half brother to half sister and son to mother. Inbreeding will concentrate defects and virtues, will bring recessives to the surface where they can be evaluated, and will give added strength to dominant heritage. Through inbreeding the breeder has the most thorough control he can possibly possess over homozygosity, prepotency and the most intimate access to the selection of inheritable factors.

Fallacious reasoning preaches that inbreeding produces faults, but this is not true. Inbreeding will only bring to the surface virtues and shortcomings that are inherent in the germplasm of the animals used in the union, where they can gain visibility and be kept or eliminated by the proper breeding procedures.

The most significant properties to remember when inbreeding are:

1. Partners with the fewest defects and most virtues must be chosen.
2. The resulting litter must be ruthlessly culled.
3. Faults produced by this type of breeding must be specifically noted. Crippling or lethal defects and congenital disease syndromes must be particularly noticed and guarded against. Any animal indicating such anomalies should be put down and its healthy siblings reassessed.

Inbreeding delivers to the breeder a much simplified formula, for specific results can be expected from the inbred dogs. In scientific fields where laboratory animals are utilized for experimental purposes, the use of inbreeding is a recognized fact, for the reaction of the creatures to experimentation must be exact, and this can only be achieved if all the animals react exactly alike (an identical twin reaction). Often these animals are the result of hundreds of generations of brother to sister matings. In genetic experiments with plants and animals it was found that when two inbred lines from divergent basic parentage were crossed the result was larger and more vigorous progeny exhibiting, to an enormous degree, what we know as *hybrid vigor,* which will enable the resulting young to thrive even under negative environmental circumstances. We call such breeding *heterosis,* because it is the most drastic form of *heterozygosity.* We will learn more about this type of breeding a bit later.

We Shepherd breeders are aware that very drastic inbreeding was espoused during the formation of the breed by Max von Stephanitz in an attempt to quickly form specific type, and he knew that inbreeding was the tool to use for such an endeavor, for it can give you the best and the worst to select from and often in the same litter. If the specimens selected are above average, inbreeding can be very effective. It was done with Pfeffer and with Lance. Pfeffer was bred to his sister to produce the "C" litter of Da-Rie-Mar-Hill, and a bitch from that litter, Cita, was the granddam of Grand Victor Ch. Valiant of

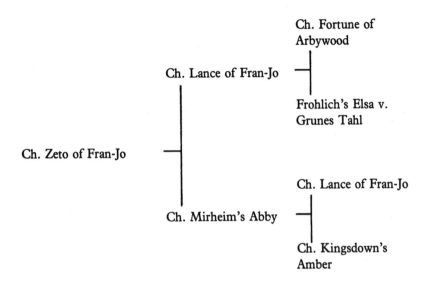

Ch. Zeto of Fran-Jo

Ch. Lance of Fran-Jo

Ch. Fortune of Arbywood

Frohlich's Elsa v. Grunes Tahl

Ch. Mirheim's Abby

Ch. Lance of Fran-Jo

Ch. Kingsdown's Amber

Draham. Above is one classic example of Lance inbreeding. This breeding produced Ch. Zeto of Fran-Jo and the R.O.M. sire Zeus of Fran-Jo.

Inbreeding is generally not practiced in Germany. The breeders there are aware that there are too many latent faults in the breed that can be accentuated by inbreeding, faults particularly of character and the breed's ability as a working dog. Such faults of temperament and the inability to train well for the myriad tasks a Shepherd must perform cannot be seen as physical defects often can, because they are of the mental makeup of the dog. German breeders are also fearful that they will destroy the breed's vigor and longevity by close inbreeding.

Half brother and half sister mating has been indulged in quite frequently in the United States. The 1951 Grand Victor Jory of Edgetowne was the product of such a breeding. Inbreeding can have very drastic results and literally destroy a line if many imperfections of a serious nature become obvious. Yet such is the nature of this avenue of breeding that one cross to an outcross line can bring the inbred strain back to normalcy.

Facing page: Classic head study of Highland Hills Tarter by Blitz vom Farbenklecks, SchH II ex Highland Hills Quinora. Bred and owned by Elli Matlin of Highland Hills German Shepherds.

96

During a few seasons I was asked to act as civilian advisor to the hush-hush. Armed Forces Super-Dog Program, stationed at Edgewood Arsenal, Maryland. My job was to check all dogs and puppies every two months, record on tape conformational information about them and recommend breedings. There were generally about four hundred dogs that I had to assess, then engage in "think tank" discussion with the officers in charge (mostly veterinarians) in reference to proposed breedings and temperament tests.

We relied heavily on inbreeding to reach results as quickly as we could. It was necessary to soon wash out several of the American-bred lines because of temperament faults and lack of working ability. One or two of the American-bred lines survived after outcrossing to German strains. Several of the German lines endured and the best was inbred on Bodo and Bernd von Lierberg. The animals became slightly smaller and more wiry with each inbred generation until they reached a plateau. Their color became richer black and red tan, they developed a nick behind the withers, they lost angulation behind and their shoulders became straighter. But they were intelligent and willing and their training quotient was high. At three months of age most of them were hitting the sleeve with tenacity and courage.

The best chance of success with an inbreeding program is to start with linebred or inbred animals that seemingly have not been affected by the close-up breeding. The breeder must have an absolute understanding of inbreeding to use the program to best advantage. You must realize that inbreeding does not create defects or virtues; it merely fixes them and makes them visible. Prepotency and similarity of type results from inbreeding—prepotency because there are fewer animals used to deliver their inheritable factors to the line. The hidden, recessive faults that are brought to light can be selected against by proper breeding procedure. Complete stability of the breeding material is the end result of inbreeding, yoked to obdurate choice.

The average progeny that results from inbreeding is generally equal to that produced by any other kind of mating, but the extremes of good and bad are generally of a much greater range than those created by any other form of breeding. Inbreeding is capable of producing the best and the worst in the extremes, and sometimes in the same litter.

BACKCROSSING

This is another kind of inbreeding which we equate, to the greatest extent, to the stud dog. In backcrossing we select a stud dog with as few imperfections as possible and of magnificent type, who prepotently produces excellent progeny. Basically what we hope to accomplish is to infuse our entire breeding line with the genetic qualities of this fine male. A good bitch, who will correct any of the slight failings the male may have, is bred to him and from the ensuing litter the best female puppy that in appearance is most like her sire is selected, kept, and at the proper time bred back to the male. It is generally advisable to keep two female pups in case something drastic occurs that results in the elimination of one of the bitches. The second choice bitch can then be used. Again, after the bitch has whelped, the best bitch puppy that mirrors the male's excellence is saved and bred back to her sire when she reaches maturity.

This form of incest is continued again and yet again until a time arrives when the alpha male can no longer reproduce, or until physical or psychological debilities become apparent (if they do) that make it inexpedient to continue the experiment. If the male dog seems to have acquired much of his virtues from his dam, then the initial breeding should be to her. If the stud dog's sire seems to have lent him most of his fine traits, then the first breeding should be, if possible and if she fits the breeder's needs, to the sister of the male's sire.

By backcrossing the genetic worth is consolidated and the germplasm fashioned into a wanted mold. This conformation that you have wrought by backcrossing will continue to prevail for several generations after the alpha male can no longer produce, if breeding continues within the confines of the linebred family.

OUTCROSSING

This breeding technique can be considered a counter-measure to any kind of linebreeding or inbreeding. Outcross breeding means that for at least five or six generations there has been no common ancestry, that no individual appears more than once in the pedigree. Actually it is impossible to engage in true outcross breeding with German Shepherds, for the breed was initiated through intense inbreeding and no matter how open a pedigree seems to be it will eventually go back to linebreeding or inbreeding. True outcrossing cannot be achieved, therefore, unless a different breed is introduced as one of the breeding pair.

The only control the breeder can have over the get of an outcross breeding is if one of the mated pair is inbred or linebred. The other partner should be dominant in any needed type or temperament compensations. Outcross breeding generally brings greater vigor and new and needed characteristics to a strain, and usually a lack of prepotency and uniformity in the progeny. It

Overleaf: Import SG Vargus vom Busecker Schloss, SchH III, FH Int., IPO III, KKL 1 "a." Owned by Gene and Joan Fetty, Henryhill German Shepherds (*left*). Ch. Hedgemeer's Chimo, C.D.X. taking Second in Group at Hochelaga Kennel Club show. Photo courtesy of Raymond Filiatrault of the Canadian kennel Chenil Vondiray (*right*).

will also help cover up recessives that may be detrimental to the stock. The statement regarding prepotency and uniformity in the progeny does not always follow. There have been quite a few excellent animals that have been produced by outcross breeding that have also been prepotent, as witness Lance of Fran-Jo.

Animals of outcross breeding frequently, but not always, indicate a lower breeding worth because favorable genetic factors have not been clustered and inheritable material has been dispersed. In America we see some few outcross Shepherds throwing sterling young, and in Germany there are many outcross studs consistently siring excellent progeny. If one of the mated pair is linebred or inbred and the other an outcross, the breeder assumes that the inbred type will be dominant. But this does not always follow, and often with a prepotent outcross stud it is the outcross stallion that will govern the litter type.

Generally outcross breeding is utilized to correct some obvious failings and to bring new genetic attributes to the strain. But when you attempt corrective or compensative breeding you must not breed to extremes to arrive at a middle effect. For instance, one must not mate a dog with a very roached back to a bitch with a sway back in the hope of producing progeny with normal backs. Most of the whelps will probably display either roached or sway backs, and this is especially true when both sire and dam are from lines that have always exhibited these faults. If your dog is defective in some respect, or lacking in some desired trait, breed it to an animal that is extremely normal in that respect; then, in the progeny, you can hope to find some that will show improvement in the area needing correction.

Two examples of outcross breeding appear in the following pedigrees, one American, the other German. The import is owned by the author.

American Pedigree

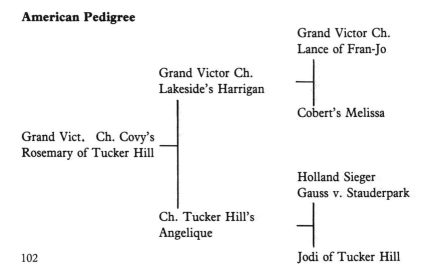

Grand Victor Ch.
Lance of Fran-Jo

Grand Victor Ch.
Lakeside's Harrigan

Cobert's Melissa

Grand Vict. Ch. Covy's
Rosemary of Tucker Hill

Holland Sieger
Gauss v. Stauderpark

Ch. Tucker Hill's
Angelique

Jodi of Tucker Hill

German Pedigree

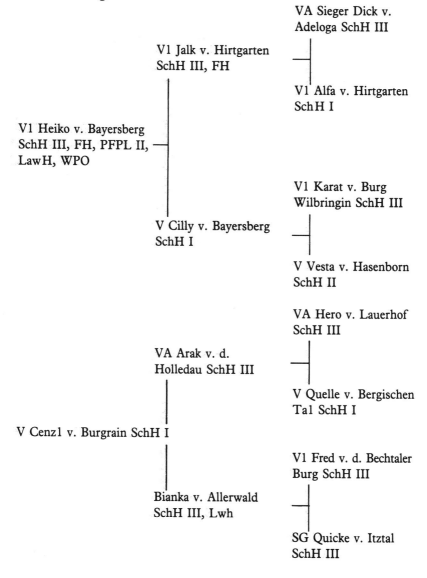

V1 Heiko v. Bayersberg
SchH III, FH, PFPL II,
LawH, WPO

V1 Jalk v. Hirtgarten
SchH III, FH

VA Sieger Dick v.
Adeloga SchH III

V1 Alfa v. Hirtgarten
SchH I

V Cilly v. Bayersberg
SchH I

V1 Karat v. Burg
Wilbringin SchH III

V Vesta v. Hasenborn
SchH II

V Cenz1 v. Burgrain SchH I

VA Arak v. d.
Holledau SchH III

VA Hero v. Lauerhof
SchH III

V Quelle v. Bergischen
Tal SchH I

Bianka v. Allerwald
SchH III, Lwh

V1 Fred v. d. Bechtaler
Burg SchH III

SG Quicke v. Itztal
SchH III

Overleaf: 17 x V-Jupp vom Fehntjer Meer, SchH III, KKIa "a" in action. Owned by Shirley Lewis of Shirhaus Kennels *(left).* The beautiful Shepherd pups in this vom Linderhof litter *(right),* bred by Bob and Ute Santella of the vom Linderhof Kennel in New York, will go on to be faithful working-dog companions when they mature.

Perhaps the most important improvement that outcross breeding can bring to the kennel is in its ability to return virility, vitality and hybrid vigor back to a line that has acquired weaknesses due to close breeding. Abnormalities, congenital ills and anomalies that have been brought to the surface by linebreeding or inbreeding can be arrested, corrected or terminated. In Germany many outcross dogs are always waiting in the wings to come onstage and rescue strains that have gone too far in close breeding and are reaping the disasters that sometimes follow in its wake.

BACKMASSING

Three or four generation pedigrees are sometimes completely open, indicating no evidence of any close breeding. But if we go deeper and extend our inquiries to greater pedigree depths, we sometimes find a massing of the name of one particular prepotent stud dog. I have termed this type of breeding "backmassing," the aggregation of the genetic factors of a specific dog, his name appearing numerous times in the extended generations of a pedigree.

The first three generations of a pedigree are generally the most important, influencing the progeny to a greater extent than later generations. But when those initial generations indicate no close breeding, allowing various genetic factors to consolidate and affect the young, then the influence of the backmassed animal will be felt. Backmassing can bring merit as well as flaws to a bloodline, but we can only be cognizant of the cause if we search further back in the animal's ancestry.

HETEROSIS

In the sphere of basic genetic research, heterosis has been utilized mostly in the agricultural field and in experimental work with fowl and swine. Research is still continuing and since such research can vary greatly in end results with varied genetic sources, it should, perhaps, not be included here because it has not been used in conjunction with the canine species. But to completely cover the subject of the tools and techniques of breeding, I am including it here, for I am reasonably certain that it could become a genetic tool to use in dog breeding if it had meritorious application.

The basis of heterosis is the breeding together of siblings that have been selected for type, strength and the absence of detrimental imperfections. This is continued for many generations to arrive at a completely homozygous family strain. Due to genetic variation, crossover and mutational effects, it is actually rather doubtful that complete homozygosity can be attained, but the brother to sister breeding must continue for enough generations to arrive at the most homozygous result possible. Several breeding lines must be begun simultaneously for there can be loss of a strain or strains at any time during the experiment. As you can see space and cost would eliminate this experiment from becoming seriously considered by dog owners unless the animals used were Chihuahuas.

Test crossings between several of the strains are tried to determine which lines will bring the greatest improvement. The lines that do are maintained and the brother x sister inbreeding continues. After approximately ten to twelve generations of sibling inbreeding the strains are again crossed. The results should be dramatic, resulting in progeny that are healthier, larger, possessing hybrid vigor and having a great deal more vigor than the original stock that you began with. These end result animals can also be used to establish new strains.

I experimented with heterosis using Budgerigars as my genetic material. After the fifth generation the inbred strains showed degeneration. By the eighth generation some improvement was indicated, but several of my lines had lost their ability to care for their young or to reproduce, and in other families the chicks were eliminated due to lethal factors. In the surviving lines, in succeeding generations, improvement took place and when they reached the twelfth generation they had returned to nearly normal. I then began to breed the remaining strains together and the results were dramatic. The progeny were bigger and better than the stock I had used to begin the experiment. The birds were vigorous, with brilliant plumage, very large and excellent breeders and feeders.

Suffice it to say that the birds that I bred from this experiment won innumerable Best In Show honors at large shows for the next several years. I also applied heterosis to the breeding of fancy guppies (originally from Paul Hahnel stock) with the same success. Both birds and fish were easily kept in an aviary and in tanks. The aviary was outdoors, but I must confess my wife was not exactly pleased with the twenty or more tanks I had in various parts of the house. I advised her that she would really have cause to worry if my interest became attracted to elephants.

FROZEN SEMEN

As you are probably aware, about four million cattle in the past two decades have come into being through the agency of frozen semen. The author has always reasoned that frozen semen could be the answer to better genetic control. If one had access to the spermatozoa of a fabulous, prepotent stud dog, how much easier it would be to bring advancement to a strain and produce a line of super dogs. There is that dream again. But, in the past, the American Kennel Club would not recognize a litter that was the result of frozen semen injection. Even the common artificial insemination is only recognized by the A.K.C. if accomplished under very controlled conditions. And secondly, ear-

Above: A promising stud, pictured at five months, is Onaway's Bronze Warrior with his owner Sue Nugent. **Facing page:** Onaway's Cambrian Crystal, a seven-week-old female by Langenau's Scout of Brasban ex Ch. Klearview's Aurora of Onaway. Bred and owned by Jack and Sue Nugent of Onaway Kennel, Ontario, Canada.

ly efforts to freeze canine semen failed due to its extreme fragility. Now, through the use of liquid nitrogen vapor, or solid carbon dioxide and liquid nitrogen, dog semen can be frozen and kept viable for several years, and through this method genetic control can be established. Progeny born of frozen semen injection have at last been approved for registration by the A.K.C., a monumental step forward in dog breeding.

I have recently read of a scientific experiment in which a growth gene was transferred by surgery from a rat to a mouse. The result was a litter of mice more than twice their normal size. One of the female littermates was bred; she also produced a litter of mice well beyond normal size. This demonstrates that genetic information can be transmitted from one mammalian species to another and that cross-species genetic manipulation can effect subsequent generations. There could be an easy approach to conformational improvement through this method.

As experimentation continues there will be, in the future, other methods of breeding propounded that will bring us closer and with less effort to what we wish to accomplish . . . the production of superb Shepherd dog specimens. That which you have read in this chapter is what we now know of the subject. We have no way of knowing what will happen in the future. We cannot, in one restricted lifetime, know all that we hunger to know. But here, on these pages, you will discover something that a prowling mind has found, something that is made of those elusive elements of which the human dream is fashioned for both you and me.

There is an ancient Asian proverb that was told to me in China: "The restless see today, the patient see eternity."

Chapter 8

The World Sieger . . .
Show of Shows

It is an awesome, overwhelming sight, the prestigious World Sieger Show in the country of the breed's nativity. It is early morning on Friday as you approach the show grounds, and it's a bit chilly but clear and bright. You peer up at the slow-moving clouds and keep your fingers crossed with the hope that the skies will smile on this, the Show of Shows, the Mecca of all who are true believers of the German Shepherd dog. And all around you there are people and dogs, German Shepherd dogs . . . wherever you look there are German Shepherd dogs. There are people from Japan and China, and gentlemen from Pakistan, the Philippines, Sweden, Holland . . . and there are German Shepherd dogs. Americans and Englishmen are here, Austrians, Italians, Norwegians . . . and German Shepherd dogs. I see avid shepherdists from East India, France, South America, and the Netherlands . . . and German Shepherd dogs tied to trees, to fences, walking, trotting, running, German Shepherd dogs.

My wife and I had been traveling in Australia, New Zealand, Tahiti, and Fiji, and now to Germany for the Sieger Show, and this, to me, was the best part of the entire trip. It happens this way with us. We plan to go to the Sieger Show and then we begin to think of other places we want to see, and soon geographic spread sets in and we end up in some remote part of the world on a month's safari. But now we are here in Germany at the Sieger Show, and everything is exactly as it should be . . . we are completely surrounded by German Shepherd dogs.

The scene is one of bustle, preparation and anticipation. As one enters the show grounds the booths first draw your attention. Most of them display the

Ch. Noroda's Fuego Rojo, a Top Twenty German Shepherd Dog in 1982. Bred and owned by Rosemarie Davis, Noroda Ranch.

accoutrements of Schutzhund work, the padded and leather sleeves of many varieties, the overalls and full armor, the muzzles, leashes and collars of various kinds. Then there are the dog food booths featuring colorful packaging displays to catch the eye and sell the product. Under separate cover, in another section of the grounds, is the vast display of beautiful trophies, huge, intricately engraved cups, gleaming in the light, accompanied by the brilliantly hued rosettes and handsome plaques. And outside there are small stands where all manner of sausages and wursts are sold, with sauerkraut and thick slices of homemade bread, and cognac, beer, kirshwasser, schnapps, or soft drinks.

Now let me guide you through the "Eingang" sign and into the area where the huge rings are located. Overhead the clouds group and part and scurry away, mimicking the movement of the excited, expectant, earthbound spectators below. And every which way you turn there are dogs, strong, richly-colored, powerful, conditioned and perfectly obedient dogs, a feast for the eyes. And each time you veer to view another specimen it is the one you want to take home. You don't see the people attached to the other end of the leash; they are amorphous, accompanying ghosts, and only the dogs lure your eyes. The handlers wear numbered bibs, and as each dog attracts your gaze you hurriedly leaf through the catalogue you have purchased on your way into the grounds for the dog's identification. This is a fabulous smorgasboard of Shepherd delicacies, and you are the gourmet who views it all with titillating taste buds.

To avoid the heady excitement engendered by the dogs and return to essentials, there are German Shepherd dogs from about twenty-five countries entered in the show, generally of German breeding and, of course, most of the dogs are the finest bred and owned in Germany. Each year the Sieger Show is held in a different big city, a metropolis that has a large race track, industrial world's fair complex or a sports arena large enough to hold this big event, for there is a vast influx of people from all over the world—approximately twenty-five hundred—and every one of them a dedicated Shepherd dog fancier; all manner of people, speaking in many tongues.

In the classes at the show there are over fifteen hundred Shepherd dogs entered, and there is an air of excitement in the streets of the city itself, for on the thoroughfares, in the restaurants, hotels and parks, one sees a host of German Shepherds. For the next three days, here in the city, the German Shepherd dog is king.

The most important gentleman at the Siegerhauptzuchtschau is the president of the Verein für Deutsche Schäferhunde (SV), the Club for German Shepherd Dogs, for he will officiate in the Gebrauchschundklasse Rüden (Utility Class dogs), which is similar to our Open Class. The Shepherd that emerges victorious from this vast class will be crowned World Sieger (VA1), his stud book will be full, (at least sixty breedings a year, and approximately

$15,000 or more a year in stud services) and his genetic worth will influence the breed for the next several years, for he will have sired approximately three hundred and sixty progeny a year.

The show begins on a Friday at 8 A.M., and will continue for three days to Sunday at roughly 6:30 P.M. The dogs will be shown in three separate rings at the same time, three rings for male classes and three for bitch classes. There will also be a separate class for Herding Dogs *(Herdengebrauchshunde)*. At no time during the show will there be intersex competition. The classes at the show will be the *Jugendklasse Ruden* (Youth Class for dogs of from twelve to eighteen months); the *Junghundklasse Ruden* (Young Dog Class for dogs from eighteen to twenty-four months); and the *Gebrauchshundklasse* Ruden (Utility Dog Class) from twenty-four months and older who have achieved at least a Schutzhund I degree (working dog degree). There are three parallel classes for bitches *(Hundinnen)*: Youth, Young and Mature.

When Dr. Rummel became the principal arbiter of the Sieger Show he had advocated a smaller dog than had previously been shown, philosophizing that a smaller animal is a faster animal, lithe and more fit to do the myriad jobs a Shepherd has been bred for. I do not agree with this rationalization. There must, of course, be a limit to the height at the withers, but limiting it to this extent can retract from the breed some of the essence of nobility. As a result of Dr. Rummel's ruling we see most of the mature males measuring approximately 63 centimeters, or under this size (24.57 inches), to a maximum measurement at the withers of 65 centimeters (25.35 inches).

Only in the *Gebrauchshundklass Rüden* (Utility Class Males) and the corresponding class in bitches can the *Vorzuglich* (Excellent) award signified by a "V", be given. In the *Jugend* (Youth), and the *Junghund* (Young Dog) classes the highest award is a *Sehr Gut* (Very Good) and the abbreviation is "S.G." To be permitted into the Utility Classes the animal must have, besides the Schutzhund degree, a grading of *Vorzuglich* (Excellent) or at least a *Sehr Gut* (Very Good) at a *Landsgruppen* (Regional) show, or a previous Sieger Show. Foreign dogs must have passed a working dog test, according to International Working Dog rules. The Youth and Young Dog and Bitch entries need not have been given a previous show rating of Very Good to be entered.

Show ratings are called *Zuchtbewertung* (ZB) and are presented at both Specialty and All-Breed contests. To be recommended for breeding a dog must have a minimum ZB degree of "G" (Good). The complete awards at the Sieger and other shows are: V, *Vorzuglich*, (Excellent); SG, *Sehr Gut*, (Very Good); G, *Gut*, (Good); A, *Ausreichend*, (Sufficient); M, *Mangelhaft*, (Faulty); and U, *Ungenugend*, (Insufficient). All dogs are placed consecutively in the order of their worth, no matter how many Shepherds there are in the class, and each dog is given a critique outlining its faults and virtues.

From the Utility Class at the Sieger Show a small number of dogs are chosen as being outstanding and are given a *Vorzuglich Auslese* (Select) rating,

A lovely portrait of two sisters, Ch. Onaway's Imperial Amethyst and Ch.
Onaway's Tawny Agate, by Ch. Wynthea's Gallant Jason, C.D., T.D.X. ex Ch. Klearview's Aurora of Onaway. Bred and owned by Jack and Sue Nugent.

12 MONTH
PUPPY
DOG
WARE VALLEY
G.S.D.C.
ELDES PHOTO

in both the male and bitch classes. These are the finest Shepherds exhibited at the annual Sieger Show; the top male is named World Sieger VA1 and the best bitch is given the title of Siegerin VA1. Behind them, similar to our Select Class at the National, are from ten to fifteen dogs and bitches placed in numerical order from VA2 down. After them the V dogs and bitches are listed in the order in which they placed, V1, V2, V3 and so on. In the Youth and Young Dog Classes, the SG (Sehr Gut) is given according to the animal's merit, and listed SG1, SG2, SG3, etc.

To be selected for an Excellent Select rating a dog must have at least a Schutzhund II training degree; if entered a second time in the Select Class Excellent and if three and a half years old or older, the dog must be *Angeköert* (Surveyed). The Sieger or Siegerin title will not be conferred on a dog or bitch unless they possess a *Koerklasse I/a,* which means they have been surveyed, recommended for breeding and their hip X-rays indicate that they are either "normal," "near normal," or "still permissible." All dogs in the Utility Classes are brought to a special section of the grounds and are tested in attack work, close up and at a distance, and must bite with a full mouth and show courage, pronounced aggressiveness and fighting spirit. This section is well attended, and the crowds give vent to their appreciation of the performance with boos or loud clapping. In the conformation rings the steadiness of the dogs, while they are being judged, is tested with gunfire.

The class for Herding Dogs dictates that only Shepherds of at least twelve months of age, with normal coats, and which are active herding dogs with a Herding Trial qualification can compete. They are rated on their conformation and physical fitness. Some lovely animals are seen in these classes. Kirschental dogs usually dominate this class.

To reach the high echelons in the Utility Classes a dog or bitch must also come from a "good,family" and must possess a scissors bite and a full complement of teeth. When a stud dog is old enough to have mature, or almost mature progeny, if he has not sired animals of merit, he will not be further considered for a top rating. In the center of the huge conformation ring for males, Utility Class, there is an orange-colored tent erected, and inside the tent are the Kor books which list every dog with an interpretive critique and pedigree, going back to the beginning of the breed. If the judge sees a fault in a particular dog or strain, he can check back through the Kör books, pinpoint it, find out where it originated and recommend that the dog displaying the trait not be bred to specific lines that also carry it.

Each class begins with the dogs being examined in a standing position. The gun test is utilized during this inspection and the dogs are very carefully scrutinized. Teeth and testicles have been previously checked, and a report submitted to the judge or his secretary in the ring. Following this part of the judging, at a signal from the judge, the dogs begin their seemingly eternal trotting around the huge ring. With experienced eye the judge now evaluates the movement and functioning of the bones and muscles that flow together in a tapestry of litheness: the firmness of joints and ligaments, the power of the thrust in movement, the quality of coat, secondary sex characteristics, pigmentation, the aura which emanates from the animal as he cruises the ring, the steadiness of back, the suspension in flight. During the course of the three days, handlers are often changed, for the two legs of man cannot compete with the dog's four.

Much attention is paid to temperament. If even the smallest shadow of a doubt is felt in this area the dog is dropped down. No concessions are made, and a deficiency in nerves or character is severely penalized. First and foremost, this is a utilitarian breed and as such, its character must be exemplary and indicative of the ability to perform many tasks with the innate ability that is at the core of the Shepherd breed.

The schedule for the three days of the show is as follows: Friday; judging of all classes begins in the morning and continues throughout the day, testing of courage begins. Saturday; class judging continues, judging of Herding Dogs is accomplished. In the evening the welcoming party for exhibitors and spectators is held. Sunday; class judging continues and the top dogs are finally selected and graded, kennel group competition takes place and trophies are presented with a ceremony honoring the winners.

The judging of the progeny groups is highly exciting and tense, for through them can be judged the prepotency and genetic worth of all the sires represented. It is an extremely important class and is judged by the second Chairman Dr. Beck and Hermann Martin, who is the Chairman of the Board and who traditionally judges the Utility Class Males. Kennel Group competition is also quite interesting as the many handlers, one to each dog, move abreast before the judges. The dogs are of course magnificent, and the handlers of each kennel group are attired in the same clothing like a team.

All this that you have read are cold facts and have nothing to do with the glamor, excitement and suspense of the show. Let me attempt to give you a more intimate knowledge, a glimpse of the moving tapestry of color, the inner feeling of the show. For instance, when the luncheon break is announced, you hurry to the crowded restaurant on the grounds or close by. You finally find a table to share with cheerful Germans and under the table at your feet lie two German Shepherds, chins on paws, unmoving. You make conversation through the medium of charades and the meager German you possess, which

Overleaf: The German Shepherd Dog is a working dog, as evidenced here by "Prince" (*above*) who served eleven years with the London, Ontario Canine Police Force and who had over 200 arrests to his credit and "The Khan" (*below*) who is hitting the sleeve during Schutzhund training. Prince was bred by Joanne Chanyi of Hoof Print Farm, and Khan (also known as Highland Hills Tarter) was bred and is owned by Elli Matlin. A beautiful male head study of Issac Preussenblut, C.D., imported from Germany for the vom Linderhof Kennel, Bob and Ute Santella, owners (*right*).

generally leads to much hilarity. After a hearty luncheon and a delightful brew in this place of good cuisine and the mingled odors of warm, enticing food and beer, you hurry back to the show grounds. You don't want to miss a thing, even though your eyes seem to be swiveling on stalks like a great bug in an attempt to watch six rings, the herding dog judging and the courage tests at one and the same time.

Someone calls your name. It is a German friend, and you embrace and chatter happily in fractured German and English. During the conversation you mention the hotel you are staying at, and he asks you why you didn't write him you were coming to the show; he would have made a reservation for you at the pension where he and his friends are staying for eight dollars a night, with breakfast. You smile and change the subject, not wanting to divulge the fact that you are paying sixty-five dollars a night at the hotel sans breakfast. You meet more friends, German and American, and you wander with them from one ring to the next, watching the judging with avid eyes.

Finally the judging is done for the day. Night moves in on raven wings, and long shadows paint the ground with prussian blue and purple. You hurry back to your hotel, shower, shave and change clothing, then hurry to the Festhalle for the welcoming party. There you sit at a large table with your friends and drink beer until you are afloat and talk at great length about German Shepherd dogs, the day's judging and speculate about who will be the Sieger, the chosen one, this year.

You are up early the next morning, answering the tocsin call of the clock alarm you set the night before. A shave, shower and breakfast with friends. And then another day of dog watching. It never bores, never does less than thrill you with its tapestry of movement, its drama and thrills. But all things that have a beginning must finally have an end, and so the World Sieger Show eventually reaches its climactic conclusion. The World Sieger and Siegerin, flanked by the VA2 and VA3 dogs and bitches, stand on an Olympic-type platform in front of a colorful background of many national flags, and the awards are presented to the staccato sound of much enthusiastic applause. The handlers stand tired but straight and proud with their charges sitting at their sides and accept the awards with stiff and formal bows. It is over, the éclat of a fine achievement, another glamorous page added to canine history . . . and now we must go home. You say goodbyes to friends you might see next year, or may never see again, and your eyes fill a bit as you turn away.

As you leave the amphitheatre with the flowing throng, you are handed a mimeographed copy of the catalogue number of every Shepherd in the show and the rating it was awarded during the show, a last gesture of Teutonic efficiency. Back at your hotel you sit at the bar emotionally and physically exhausted. And 'round and 'round in your head, behind your tired eyes, German Shepherd dogs march and trot . . . 'round and 'round . . . 'round and 'round . . . .

Titus v. Eschenzweig, SchH III, FH Kkl I/a by V1 Enno v. Haus Pari, SchH II ex V1 Inken v. Eschenzweig, SchH III. A handsome, stallion-like male, Titus has been V1 and V over 30 times; in the Sieger shows of 1971 and 1972 he was V7 and V8. His breeding is a study of the intelligent use of knowledge to produce type, temperament, movement, and good hips. Owned by Heinrich Janszen, Germany.

Overleaf: Can. Ch. Select Vondiray Sam Jr. *(left, above)*. Taking Best of Opposite Sex and Best of Breed respectively are Am. Ch. Select and Can. Ch. Stuttgart's Sundance Kid, owned by Inge Vyprachticky, and Can. Ch. Select Vondiray Santa Fe, owned by Raymond Filiatrault and Huguette Daviault *(left, below)*. Family portrait of Pela Preussenblut, C.D., Issac Preussenblut, C.D., and Lahngold's Charm pictured with Elizabeth and Richard. Dogs owned by Bob and Ute Santella, vom Linderhof Kennel *(right, above)*. A champ at rest—Can. Ch. Poplar Valley's Sinbad by Can. Ch. Poplar Valley's D'Artagnan ex Bet n' Dals Daiquiri. Bred by Cherie Sobieralski and Betty Phares and owned by Liv Mc Lea of Leeven Rob Kennels, Ontario, Canada *(right, below)*.

Chapter 9

The National . . .
America's Premier Show

It has been named "The Greatest Show On Earth," and it could very well be so. The National is a moving, many-colored pageant, a tribute to the German Shepherd dog in America. It combines all the glamor and excitement of an opening night on Broadway, and it is truly and wholly American in its concept. The rosettes awarded the winners are multi-colored, magnificent and huge beyond belief; and the silverware, gleaming and shimmering under the lights, is splendid in its modelled intricacy and size, superb examples of the silversmith's art. These are pieces to treasure like ancient heirlooms, for their own beauty, the high awards they represent and the intensity of the competition that will attempt to win them.

It happens every year, the National does, and the finest German Shepherd dogs from all over America (and from Canada) from the north, south, east and west gravitate to this great show wherever the host city happens to be. Venue is generally changed each year, but no matter how far away the host city may be, the dogs, their owners and handlers converge upon the area by plane, car, station wagon and van to be exhibited in this premier show.

What handsome animals these are that are to be exhibited here in the National! Coats full and gleaming, groomed to perfection akin to the entrants in the Miss America pageant, with not a hair out of place, tails like medieval plumes, and fluid in movement as they walk or trot by. The males, a macho lot, swagger a bit and flex their muscles; the females, dainty but substantial, move with the litheness of ballet dancers performing in *Swan Lake*. They take your breath away, these magnificent animals, and this is as it should be, for the German Shepherds entered here are the most beautiful in the whole, wide world—over 700 magnificent animals.

The rings, no matter where the show is held, are huge, and it is mandatory for the rings to be seventy-five feet by one hundred feet in size, ample room for large classes to move around in without crowding. The show is an exercise in expert planning and execution. Nothing has been left to chance, and from the beginning to the absolute end it runs smoothly and efficiently.

I might mention here, just to give perspective to the National event, that the first dog show ever held occurred in the year 1859, and only English pointing breeds were entered. At that time it became evident that specific breed standards were definitely needed if a judge was to officiate with any degree of expertise. So the standards came into being prodded by "Stonehenge," the pseudonym of the editor of *The Field*, an extremely prestigious magazine of the day in England. That is how it all began and this, the National, is the epitome, the end result, as it were, of that meager, rather haphazard show that was held in Britain one hundred and twenty-four years ago.

Let us first consider the mechanics of a show of this size. To begin with, it differs markedly from the German World Sieger Show in that it is held in an indoor arena, while the Sieger Show is always presented outdoors. The National is planned so that the weather need never be a problem and that the dogs, handlers, judges and spectators will not be made uncomfortable or be inconvenienced because of inclement weather conditions. Another very noticeable difference between the National and the Sieger Show is that a very large percentage of the dogs being shown at the American show are accompanied by professional handlers, while in Germany there are actually no individuals that are designated as professional handlers.

The classes too are dissimilar. The National has eight basic classes for dogs and bitches: Puppy Class, 6 to 9 months; Puppy Class, 9 to 12 months; a new class, 12 to 18 months; Novice class; Bred By Exhibitor class; American-bred class; Open class; and a special class for Veteran dogs. There are several different judges, one to adjudicate the male classes, another for the bitch classes, still another for Best of Breed. We have a judge for Intersex and two more judges for the National Futurity Sweepstakes, which are also divided into two

Overleaf: Magnum's Major Event, son of German import and Magnum foundation stud Fello von Widenberg, SchH III, TT-162-GS. Bred by Art and Wanda Mandala (*left, above*). The young Fero vom Shirhaus, bred by Shirley Lewis of Sirhaus Kennels (*left, below*). Bennie v. Kirschental by Sieger Natan v. d. Pelztierfarm, SchH III ex Victrix Inka v. Pflaunbachtal. This beautiful young bitch was the first get of the 1981 and 1982 Sieger to be brought to the United States. Owned by Allyn H. Weigel (*right*).

classes, Futurity and Maturity. There is an arbiter for Best In Futurity and Best of Opposite Sex in Futurity, and another for Best in Maturity and Best Opposite Sex in Maturity. There are also, of course, the various unsung, wraithlike stewards whom we never notice, but who do yeoman duty with no recognition. Theirs are the unnoticed hands that guide the show smoothly throughout its course.

There is a Winners Male and a Reserve Winners Male, and a Winners Bitch and a Reserve Winners Bitch, and a Best of Winners which is selected by the judge when the Winners Male and Winners Bitch compete. Both Winners Male and Winners Bitch then compete against the Specials (Champions) for Best of Breed and Best of Opposite Sex. The Shepherd selected for Best of Breed becomes the Grand Victor or Victrix, and the dog chosen for Best of Opposite Sex becomes Grand Victor or Grand Victrix according to its sex. The United States Grand Victor is named Select Number 1, and there follows approximately six to twelve other dogs, also Select, that are numbered in their designated order: Select Number 2, Select Number 3 and so on. The same order is followed in the bitch classes. The Grand Victrix is Select Number 1, followed by Select Number 2, etc. The dogs selected as Futurity and Maturity winners generally place rather well among the Select animals. This is particularly true of the Maturity Male and Bitch winners. Recently adopted is a class for Best Junior Handler.

The obedience people work in three rings of at least 40 feet by 50 feet, separate from the conformation section. In the obedience classes one judge officiates in Novice B and Open A, and the second judge does Novice B and Open B, while a third adjudicator works Utility, Graduate Novice and Team classes. There is a prize for the highest scoring (in obedience) conformation champion, and there is a Tracking Test, which takes place in a special open area outside which is conducive to this activity, usually an approxiamtely two hundred-acre field. During breaks in the program of the conformation rings there are team hurdle races which elicit a good deal of excitement.

One of the most captivating of all the events programmed is the Parade of Greats. Led by a runner bearing a banner on which the name of the dog is inscribed, the great dogs of the breed are announced over the loudspeaker system and out they trot, one by one, behind their banners, the famous ones, the great Champions who have given so much to the breed. In all their glory they gait proudly around the ring as though aware of their contribution to Shepherd dog history. It is a nostalgic moment, one that brings a lump to the throat and a bit of mist to the eyes to see these grand old dogs, the pillars of the breed in America. One encounters somewhat the same feeling when viewing the classes for Veteran dogs and bitches.

During each day of the show you sit with people here and there and share a little time of close association as you watch and comment on the dogs and the judging, and you meet friends that you haven't seen in years, and you think how pleasant it is to see and speak with them again. Then there are the acquaintances you meet almost every year at the National who smile with you and speak of family, friends and dogs. You are pleasantly surrounded by a loose net, a shimmering spider's web of familiar faces and voices, the German Shepherd crowd, and it all makes you feel content, as though you have come home again.

At luncheon and dinner, after the judging is finished for the day, you share a table with other fellow Shepherdists and speak of years gone by and times to come, of dogs and people, some gone now never to return and others still active and participating. It is a kaleidoscopic way of life, of many-colored prisms that began in a time before we were born and will continue beyond our limited share of years.

Leading up to this event, the Futurities have taken place. They were originally conceived as breeders' shows, and the dogs that are exhibited are the results of breeding programs indulged in by kennels and breeders to see which progeny projects are the most successful. There have formerly been nine separate shows in that many key sections of the country, but this number will probably, in the future, be cut to six Futurity shows. They generally employ three judges, one for dogs, one for bitches and a third for intersex competition. Because an accepted A.K.C. arbiter is not necessary, quite frequently the judges employed are well-known handlers such as Jimmy Moses, Doug Crane, Lamar Kuhns, Joe La Rosa, Fred Olsen, etc. The classes for this competition are: Junior Dogs, Teenage Dogs, Intermediate Dogs, Senior Dogs and Maturity Dogs, with similar classes for bitches.

Because entries have been slackening there has been a move to employ a lesser number of judges to officiate at the Futurities. There are some lovely animals presented, as evidenced by the high placings at the National of the winning Maturity dog and bitch, who are generally Champions of record.

The Futurities are an exciting and colorful part of the tapestry that is the German Shepherd dog fancy. The breeder nominates a litter within ninety days of whelping and in the geographic region in which it was born. The breeder or co-breeder must be a member in good standing of the G.S.D.C.A. A puppy may be shown in any one of the nine regions, but must not be entered in more than one region. Points toward a Championship are not awarded at the Futurities.

When the Futurities were first inaugurated as a breeder's show, entire litters were exhibited, allowing breeders to view the best and the worst that specific studs could throw from different bitches, and the dogs were handled by their breeders or owners. Today the youngsters, handled by professionals, are the selected cream of several litters, individuals of great promise, and they are shipped to other areas to be shown under judges who favor their type. The fundamental reason for the holding of Futurities has been lost in a mad scramble for recognition and ribbons.

Above: Select Ch. Covy's Tarragon of Tucker Hill by Grand Victor Ch. Lakeside's Harrigan ex Ch. Tucker Hill's Angelique, C.D. Handled by Gloria Birch and being put up by the author. This lovely bitch is owned by Cappy Pottle, Gloria Birch, and J. Stevens. **Facing page:** K-9 Officer Basko v. d. kleinen Laber taking a respite from work.

I would very much like to see the clock turned back to the time when whole litters were shown and handled by their breeders and owners. But alas, time marches on, and my medieval wishes will find no acceptance in the frantic and competitive aura of today's Futurities.

The Victory Dinner at the National is a pleasant affair, and the individuals who mount the podium are generally the Chairman of the Board of Governors of the German Shepherd Dog Club of America, who introduces the judges who have officiated at that particular National. It is a friendly get-together, the atmosphere relaxed and congenial. The show is over and it is time to relax. It is a tribute to those people who have been so fiercely competitive over the last few days, that they can find equanimity and tranquility in good company when the competition has ceased. The speakers hold your attention when they discuss the exhibits and the prevalence of any specific faults that they have observed this year. The highlight of the evening is the filling of the huge trophies with champagne by the owners of the Grand Victor and Grand Victrix, and the quaffing from the great cups by everyone present at the ceremony. I inevitably think of this traditional custom as a rather interesting way to spread cold germs.

The National has ended, and the greats have been crowned and honored and received our homage, and we who have attended leave with a feeling of satiation. We are tired and, at the moment, we tend to think of ourselves, as do all men who are egomaniacs, as quite ordinary people who have just indulged in an interesting and satisfactory experience. Not so. What we have experienced is a spiritual revelation, for we who are of the so-called German Shepherd fancy are special people who live in a special world, with its own vocabulary, its own species of knowledge, its own dreams and aspirations. We have become one with another life-form, and through this close canine association have enlarged our horizons, seen our own visions and interpreted in our own way the messages we have received from whatever gods there be. Man is mortal, but the spirit is immortal.

Chapter 10

A Comparison . . . American-bred v. Import

There is much that is different between the best of the American-bred Shepherds and the fine import dogs, but there is also a great deal that they have in common. To arrive at a comparison it is necessary to weigh all the differences and balance what we find against the qualities of both breeding and exhibiting systems, German and American. Actually it is difficult to find a beginning, to pinpoint one area from which we can move to reach our conclusions.

Let us first appraise overall type: it is perhaps the best place to begin our search. The type arrived at in the American-bred Shepherd dog is infinitely beautiful—of that there can be little doubt. Due to inbreeding and strong linebreeding, the best American-breds exhibit a general sameness of type, each one a lovely interpretation of the American German Shepherd dog standard. The long neck, high withers, length of bone and angulation in the hindquarters, low hocks and sloping but level backs, lend the American-bred an elegance unmatched in the Shepherd world. An abundance of American-breds do exhibit a less than perfect croup.

The German-bred dog generally has an excellent shoulder assembly, a neck shorter than the American-bred, a stronger head with parallel planes, less angulation behind, but a more powerful rear thrust and greater soundness going away. Many of the top dogs in Germany flaunt a roached back and also fail in croup. They are strong, athletic dogs in hard physical condition. Some German dogs, but not as many as formerly, display a round eye which distracts from the facial expression. Feet are generally compact and tight, in keeping with the picture of a true working dog, but type varies a bit because the dogs are usually remotely linebred or completely outcross bred.

Above: Futurity Winner, Select, American and Canadian Ch. Covy-Tucker Hill's Monte Alban, U.D., Can. C.D.X. by Cobert's Sirocco of Windigail ex Ch. Covy's Rosita of Tucker Hill. This impressive animal has done it all, both in the show ring and obedience! Shown here at the National with Ralph Roberts judging and George Collins standing by. Owned by Freeman Spencer, Gloria Birch, and Cappy Pottle.

Facing page: Officer R. K. Galloway of the Opopka Police Department shown with his canine working partners, Basko v. d. kleinen Laber, SchH II and Billy v. d. kleinen Laber, both German imports.

Van Cleve's Edge *(above)*, handled by Don Kille and owned by Carmen Battaglia, is pictured at 14 months of age and is seen taking Best of Breed over Specials from the American-bred Class . . . he won 3 days in a row. Dick v. Holtkamper See, SchH II, KKI I/a *(below)* was a fine young stallion by the great Canto v. d. Wienerau and out of V Hexe v. Holtkamper See. Imported by the author.

In movement the American-bred has a lithe and agile profile trot, but the exaggerated angulation and long bones in the hindquarters bring unsureness to the very low hocks. Indeed, some of the animals appear to be almost plantigrade, like a bear, or a man, or the ancient sabre-toothed feline *Homotherium*. Nevertheless, in profile the American-breds who are not grossly overangulated behind move well. The German dog moves with great propulsive strength and sureness, and the powerful thrust from his hindquarters is transmitted through the strong back (a roached back *is* a strong back though unsightly) to the forehand. The American-bred often displays less than the wanted angulation in the shoulder (90 degrees), and the dogs that lack in this area cannot reach forward as far as necessary to accept the drive from the hindquarters. To compensate they lift the front upward slightly. The straighter shoulder allows them a high wither and a downward slope in back when standing and posed.

The German-bred dog has generally the necessary angulation in the shoulder and can therefore reach well before him. He consequently moves with his head and neck held lower than does the American-bred dog. The best of both the American-bred dog and the German-bred boast excellent middle-pieces and good fronts.

From what we can learn by comparison, the American-bred is the more beautiful animal and the German-bred the sounder dog. This is as it should be, for the German dog has been bred from its conception to be a working dog, the utilitarian animal supreme, while the American-bred has been selected solely for its beauty. Each dog, the American-bred and the German-bred, therefore fulfills the destiny for which it has been bred.

Both German- and American-breds sport unwanted recessives. Through both we can carry unwanted inherited faults of orchidism, missing teeth, long coats, overshot and undershot muzzles and other lesser cosmetic faults as well as inherent medical problems. In both Germany and America we have critiques by judges we can study that can present us with a word picture of most of the prominent dogs. In the pedigree area the Germans have developed a far superior document than that utilized here. This is due to the firm and unique hold the SV has over the entire German Shepherd dog venture in the Fatherland. In the mother country of the breed the German Shepherd dog has its own puissant, self-governing body, the *Verein für Deutsche Schäferhunde,* that is an imperial entity, answering to no higher source.

Overleaf: Ch. Covy's Mazarati of Tucker Hill by Cobert's Sirocco of Windigail ex Grand Victrix Ch. Covy's Rosemary of Tucker Hill, R.O.M. A handsome, powerful stallion. . .the essence of nobility. Owned by Gail Sprock, Gary Cook, Cappy Pottle, and Gloria Birch.

In America we have the German Shepherd Dog Club of America and its Board of Governors, on which I had the elected pleasure to serve for two years. But the G.S.D.C.A. has to answer to, and is governed by, the American Kennel Club, a completely autonomous entity that controls all dog activity of all breeds in the United States. Therefore, the G.S.D.C.A. does not have the jurisdiction over the breed in the United States that the SV enjoys in Germany.

The offices of the *Verein fur Deutsche Schaferhunde* in Augsburg, West Germany, is the heart of the Shepherd dog fancy in that country. There are kept and labelled with Teutonic efficiency all the documents that pertain to the breed since 1889. From this central office all pedigrees; registrations; Körsheim reports; show ratings; Schutzhund records; whelpings; herding, avalanche, disaster, police degrees; etc., are kept and issued. The yearly stud books, the names of local breed wardens, endurance and tracking tests, and all the other records and documents are studied, classified and, if necessary, distributed. Here, too, the monthly club magazine is printed and dispersed. This complete dominion over the fate of the breed in Germany allows the governing body absolute dictatorial authority, which is a great deal more jurisdiction than the board of governors or the membership of the German Shepherd Dog Club of America have over the destiny of the breed in America, due to our necessary compliance with the sovereign authority of the A.K.C. It is, at times, quite frustrating for the Board of Governors of the G.S.D.C.A. not to be able to make necessary decisions without having first to consult the powers that be at the A.K.C. for permission.

The pedigree of a Shepherd in Germany is a four page document emblazoned at the top of the first page with the logos of the SV, the VDH, FCI *(Federation Cynologique Internationale)*, and the WUSV *(World Union)*. On this first page we also find the name of the dog, sex, coat quality, markings and color, tattoo number, date of birth (also written out in German), breeder and address. If linebred, the dogs he is linebred upon are listed and where they are in the pedigree, or if outcross-bred, this too is noted, the names, colors, and coats of his siblings are listed, and the number of pups in the litter. Below are the breeder's signature and the dog's registry number and date. When the pedigree is opened we find a four generation pedigree. The first two generations list the sire and dam and the four grandparents, the registration numbers of the sire and dam, their Schutzhund degrees, the years they've been recommended for breeding, their hip condition, Körsheim or show rating, color (abbreviated), a complete description of the animals from their Kör reports, and a list of their siblings, their color and Schutzhund degrees.

The four grandparents are given exactly the same attention. The last two generations on the pedigree, the great-grandparents and the great-great-grandparents, supply us with the names, Schutzhund and any other degrees, and the registered number of these twenty-four animals. There is also a space

Rasse-Echtheitszertifikat

Herausgegeben vom Verein für Deutsche Schäferhunde (SV) e. V., gegründet 1899

Gründerverein der Rasse und für den Standard Deutscher Schäferhunde zuständig

| Anerkannt von | Verband für das Deutsche Hundewesen e. V. | Federation Cynologique International | Weltunion der Vereine für Deutsche Schäferhunde |

Körzucht-Leistungszucht-Ahnentafel

für den Deutschen Schäferhund .... **Reza vom Haus Dexel** ....

Geschlecht: ..... **Rüde** ..... Haarart: ..... **stockhaarig** .....

Farbe und Abzeichen: .... **schwarz, gelb-braune Abzeichen an Kopf und Läufen** ....

Besondere Kennzeichen: .... Tätowier-Nr. ...... **F-K 1181**

Wurftag: ..... **2.Juli 1979** ..... Wurfjahr: **Neunzehnhundertneunundsiebzig**

Züchter: ..... **Richard Dexel**

Anschrift: .... **Auf dem Schilk 9, Hemer-Becke**

Inzucht auf:	Geschwister:
-ohne-	**Rio sgbAKL Rani sgbAKL**
	Rona sgbAKL Roxi sgbAKL

Erläuterung über Wurfstärke: ...... **Wurfstärke 2,3** ......

Die Verwendung der Ahnentafel und der Eintragungen in ihr, die Anfertigung von Abschriften, Auszügen oder Übernahme in andere Zuchtbücher ist nur mit ausdrücklicher Genehmigung des SV zulässig. Eintragungen und Einstempelungen in die Ahnentafel dürfen nur vom Zuchtbuchamt des SV vorgenommen werden. Ausgenommen hiervon sind die Eintragungen des Eigentumswechsels und über Ausbildung des Beurteilungs- und Bewertungsheftes sowie Eintempelung der HD-Röntgenstelle. Die Ahnentafel hat nur Gültigkeit, wenn sie vom Züchter eigenhändig unterschrieben ist; sie gilt als Urkunde im juristischen Sinne! Wer Ahnentafeln fälscht oder mit solchen Mißbrauch treibt, wird von SV strafrechtlich verfolgt. Die Ahnentafel ist der schriftliche Nachweis über Rassereinheit, Name und Abstammung des Hundes, sie gehört somit zum Hund und ist beim Verkauf dem neuen Eigentümer unbedingt auszuhändigen. Beim Eingeben des Hundes ist sie an das Zuchtbuchamt einzusenden.

Deutscher Schäferhund-Zwinger

Bemerkungen: .... *vom Haus Dexel*

Besitzer: Richard Dexel

Für die Richtigkeit vorstehender Angaben: (Unterschrift des Züchters) .... HEMER-BECKE

Telefon. Hemer (02372) 10621

Eintragungs- und Prüfungsbestätigung: Der oben bezeichnete Deutsche Schäferhund ist in das Zuchtbuch für Deutsche Schäferhunde (SZ) eingetragen worden. Die Ahnentafel wurde ausgefertigt vom Verein für Deutsche Schäferhunde (SV), Mitglied des Verbandes für das Deutsche Hundewesen (VDH) in der Fédération Cynologique Internationale (F.C.I.). Die Abstammungsangaben sind nachgeprüft, und ihre Richtigkeit wird hiermit bestätigt.

SZ Band ...... **78** ...... SZ Nr. ..... **1475830** ..

Augsburg, den **18.Dezember 1979**

Das Zuchtbuchamt des SV i. A.:

Neugestaltung gültig ab Januar 1979

A page from the pedigree of the great V Reza v. Haus Dexel.

Overleaf: Ch. Covy-Tucker Hill's Zinfandel, R.O.M. by Grand Victor Ch. Lakeside's Harrigan ex Ch. Tucker Hill's Angelique. This Shepherd is a Lance of Fran-Jo grandson on his sire's side. Owned by Cappy Pottle and Gloria Birch.

on the right hand side for abbreviations of all the various awards, colors, and titles and their German meanings. Below this section is a space reserved for the veterinarian's stamp indicating the condition of the animal's hips. On the back page is the triangular stamp with the "a" in the middle indicating the dog's hips are normal (if not there will be no emblem). The German owner of the dog is listed, and his or her address and signature. There is a notary stamp and sixteen regulations of the SV. If the pedigree is pink, the breeding that produced this dog was sanctioned as a good and advantageous mating. If the pedigree is white it indicates that the Breed Survey did not pass the parents as "good" partners. Would that we in America were supplied with a pedigree as comprehensive as this!

The next important document a German dog receives is the *Körschein.* The Körmaster is inevitably a well‑respected judge, whose integrity and knowledge of the breed is impeccable. This report contains the date on which it was accomplished, the Körmaster's name, the dog's name, registry number, Schutzhund degrees, tattoo number, date of whelping, the sire's name and his sire and dam, and the dam's name and her sire and dam, and the owner's name. The main body of the *Körschein* report is an extremely detailed description of the dog standing and in motion, beginning with the animal's size, weight, circumference, color, testicles, followed by a short, concise but exceedingly accurate description of the animal.

Every part of the physical animal is examined and described, as is also the dog's temperament, character, and courage. At the end of this report a recommendation is made regarding the mate this dog should be coupled with. We in America have nothing similar to this document as a guide. The *Körschein* has been tried here with German Körmasters, but has not been successful. The *Körschein* could be invaluable, particularly for the novice, but most American breeders would not accept such a dictatorial document by a single individual who, it would be argued, might or might not be correct in his assumptions.

In Germany, to be allowed to be used for breeding by the SV, a dog must have been entered in a show and have received a minimum rating of "Gut" (Good), and obtained a working qualification.

On the opposite side of the coin, in America there are the Futurities which enable breeders to appraise the young stock as it appears and evaluate the genetic breeding value of the various stud dogs and brood matrons. Another plus is the Register Of Merit (R.O.M.), where points are accumulated by dogs and bitches through the winnings of the progeny. It allows an insight into the breeding value of the top Shepherds in the U.S.

For a male to become qualified for R.O.M. listing he must have a total of 100 points or more. Ten or more of his progeny must have earned the points, and the title of Champion must have been bestowed upon five of those offspring. For a bitch to qualify for R.O.M. status, she must have achieved a total of 40 or more points, which have been earned by four or more of her progeny, and the title of Champion must have been attained by a minimum of two of her get. Futurities can also add to the points garnered by an R.O.M. animal. Best in Futurity and Best of Opposite Sex can bestow three points each upon the winner's sire and dam. Best in Maturity and Best Opposite is worth four R.O.M. points, while Best in the National Futurity and Maturity and Best Opposite is worth five points each.

One can also earn R.O.M. points for obedience titles, a very important consideration, but the points can only be won if the dog has achieved a minimum of a Reserve Winner in a major (three point or more) show. The points given are for either sex: C.D. Title—five points; C.D.X. Title—ten points; U.D. Title—fifteen points; T.D. Title—five points; O.T. Champion—five points. All R.O.M. point data is collected from the official show results published in the American Kennel Club *Gazette*. In Germany a similar system of tabulating is done and published each year after the Sieger Show in the SV magazine. The records are of the prominent sires, successful or not.

Breeders in America should, as Erich Renner has so often suggested, utilize the tattoo method for normal and O.F.A. identification. It should be made mandatory. It is my considered opinion that every German Shepherd dog in this country should have attained a minimum of a Companion Dog (C.D.) in obedience before it is graced with the title of conformation Champion. This would, to some extent, guarantee the animal's temperament and intelligence. The temperament test inaugurated by the German Shepherd Dog Club of America, and in use now, is a rather vapid and unorganized approach to a true test of temperament, but it is a good beginning.

In reference to intersex competition both in America and in Germany, I feel that it serves no eminent purpose. It does allow us, however, a bit of extra glamour at our shows and adds another winning dimension.

As you know inbreeding is not allowed in Germany; only linebreeding is practiced, and many dogs are completely outcrossed. This can be a blessing and a curse. In the chapter on genetics (The Enigma of Heredity) you have learned that inbreeding brings faults to the surface where they can be evaluated and eliminated. But German breeders feel that they will lose vigor, intelligence, longevity, and breeding vitality, and increase the possibility of the appearance of hereditary diseases.

All of these prospects can accompany inbreeding, but without this breeding tool we are covering up all the faults. They recede within the germplasm and lie dormant and we are not aware that they are there until the proper mating is made, and then to our dismay they come to the surface. In America inbreeding occurs with great abandon and an airy belief that it certainly is the thing to do since everyone else is doing it and getting fantastic results. Yes, Americans do keep that beautiful type, but at a price. Longevity has been lost; too many dogs reach an untimely end when they should be in their prime. A lack of basic vigor permits too many animals to become victims of

Ch. Covy-Tucker Hill's Tecate by Cobert's Sirocco of Windigail, R.O.M. ex Ch. Covy's Rosita of Tucker Hill. This lovely group-winning bitch is owned by J. and S. Davenport, Gloria Birch, and Cappy Pottle.

disease, of bloat, hip dysplasia, parvo, and an accumulation of congenital diseases that the animals are almost helpless to combat.

Throughout the rest of the world German Shepherd governing bodies have accepted the German method of hip X-raying at a year of age. In America the Orthopedic Foundation For Animals (O.F.A.) will not assign a breed registry number for hip X-ray to a dog under twenty-four months of age, though radiographs of animals between eighteen and twenty-four months will be read by the O.F.A. and non-dysplastic classified as "excellent" or "good" (incidentally, the O.F.A. definitely approves of identity tattooing). Evaluation at two years of age is much more important for a precise reading. I know that American representatives at the World Union meetings after the Sieger Show in Germany (notably Dr. Joe Giardina) have attempted to induce the other nations to bring the radiographic age up to eighteen months, for this would give them a higher accuracy percentage, but so far they have not succeeded. I have known dogs of German ancestry that have been given an "a" normal stamp who, by the time they were from two to three years of age, had developed a slight dysplasia in one hip. German dogs seldom show any outward evidence of dysplasia because of their hard muscular condition and tight, strong ligamentation.

In the S.V. magazine each month there is a list of German dogs that have disqualifying faults. The name of the dog is published, its sire and dam, linebreeding if any, the owner and breeder. Dysplasia is dominant in these reports, but also listed are shy and timid dogs, monorchids and cryptorchids, Shepherds too large or too small, animals that are undershot, overshot, or have missing teeth, or any other fault.

There have been some attempts to bring German Shepherd dogs out of East Germany. For many long years these animals have been bred apart and have had no common ancestry with West German or American-bred dogs. They could prove to be valuable outcrosses for both German and American stock, if they were of the wanted type. I have heard of one or two of these dogs finding homes in the United States.

Through judicious crossing of the genetic lines of selected imports into the best of the American-bred strains, selecting from the get and then outcrossing again the same way, and finally breeding back to selected American-breds of the wanted type, we would see some improvement in the areas that need correction without losing type. It would take many small, intelligent steps in this direction to finally arrive at what we want. After all, when one looks back into the pedigrees of the great American-bred Shepherd dogs, one must inevitably recognize the dramatic genetic influence of the fine imports from whose loins they came into being.

The prices of puppies and grown dogs have risen sharply in the United States, in show kennels and particularly in those kennels which house German imports and cater to the Schutzhund people. Stud fees for imported dogs that

Otti v. Uesener Werk by Quanto v. d. Wienerau, SchH III ex Yana v. Uesener Werk, SchH II. This lovely young Landsgruppen Youth Siegerin shows the quality imparted by her sire, the great modern stud and Reserve Sieger Quanto, son of the famous Condor v. Zollgrenzschutz-Haus. Otti was imported from Germany by the author and is shown here with handler Richard L. McMullen.

Ch. Howard's Troleway, handled by Scott Yergin, wins Best of Breed out of the Open Class to finish his championship. By Ch. Lost Hills Bold Legend ex Howard's Misty of Cenway and owned by Doug Crane and Libby Cameron.

Facing page: Select Ch. Lochwood's Sundance v. Stutgart by Ch. Doppelty's Hawkey ex Ch. Backwood's Csacsa. This very successful show dog taking the group is handled by Doug Crane.

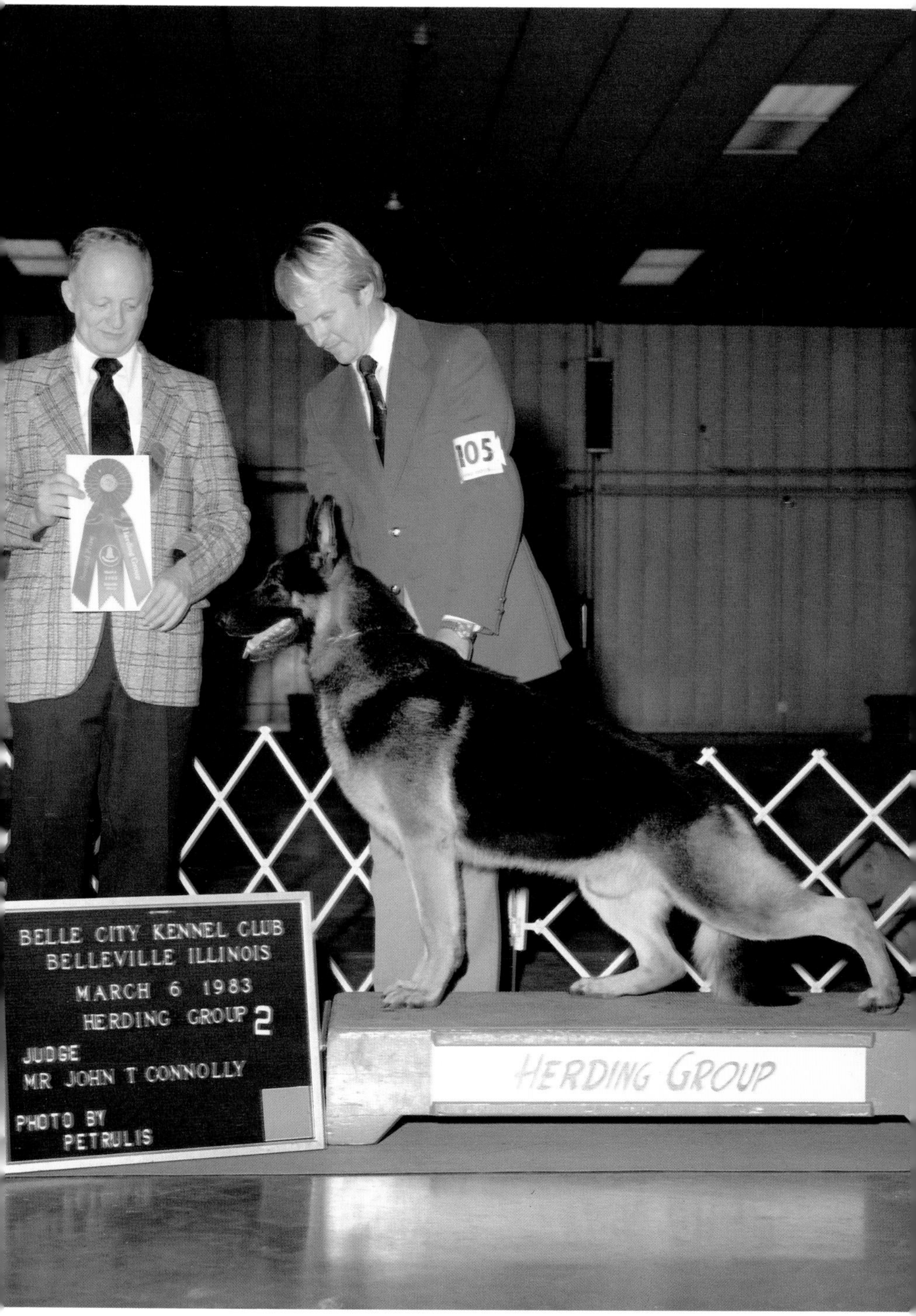
BELLE CITY KENNEL CLUB
BELLEVILLE ILLINOIS
MARCH 6 1983
HERDING GROUP 2
JUDGE
MR JOHN T CONNOLLY
PHOTO BY
PETRULIS
105
HERDING GROUP

are bred from working stock are also high in kennels that are Schutzhund-oriented. The price of imports today is astonishing. Top show dogs are usually priced the highest assuming they can be purchased at all. They are fully trained, Schutzhund III dogs and trained to protect the house, kennel, car and children. Nice animals of excellent breeding with a Schutzhund I, perhaps, and an "a" stamp on hips can be bought for much less than a top show specimen, if you know where and how to find them and have good contacts in Germany. If a German dog is sired by a Sieger or a VA-rated dog, the price is generally higher. A fine Schutzhund-trained Shepherd from Germany is a joy to own and will soon be rated beyond intrinsic value by the family it lives with. To acquire such an animal is a unique experience in canine ownership.

To sum up what you may have learned from this chapter, it would seem that there is a fairly equal number of reasons to select either an import or an American-bred dog. One can generally view the parents and siblings of the American-bred, while selection of the German dog must be made from a photo and the breeder's description. The complications of purchasing an import: where to look, who to trust, how much to pay, is also a detriment to buying. On the other hand the significance of the import's training and intelligence is of obvious value.

One would, of course, never purchase a German-bred puppy and have it shipped over when an American-bred can be bought with so little trouble. A German import should be at least over a year of age, sixteen to seventeen months and older is even better. It should have its "a" on hips and have or have well started on a Schutzhund education. I generally advise friends who come to me to purchase an import for them, if it is a bitch they want, to leave the animal with the breeder to be bred to a top, recommended stud in Germany and then have her shipped to the United States. The sale of the resultant progeny could, with any luck, pay for the cost of the bitch.

If your dream is to import a fine dog from Germany or to purchase an excellent American-bred youngster from top show stock, go for it. Remember, life is short and dreams are difficult to come by. Get the best your wallet will allow and then sit back and enjoy the fruits of your decision.

Chapter 11

A.K.C. Standard of the German Shepherd Dog

GENERAL APPEARANCE

The first impression of a good German Shepherd dog is that of a strong, agile, well-muscled animal, alert and full of life. It is well balanced, with harmonious development of the forequarter and hindquarter. The dog is longer than tall, deep-bodied, and presents an outline of smooth curves rather than angles. It looks substantial and not spindly, giving the impression, both at rest and in motion, of muscular fitness and nimbleness without any look of clumsiness or soft living. The ideal dog is stamped with a look of quality and nobility—difficult to define, but unmistakable when present. Secondary sex characteristics are strongly marked, and every animal gives a definite impression of masculinity or femininity, according to its sex.

CHARACTER

The breed has a distinct personality marked by direct and fearless, but not hostile, expression, self-confidence and a certain aloofness that does not lend itself to immediate and indiscriminate friendships. The dog must be approachable, quietly standing its ground and showing confidence and willingness to meet overtures without itself making them. It is poised, but when the occasion demands, eager and alert; both fit and willing to serve in its capacity as companion, watchdog, blind leader, herding dog, or guardian, whichever the circumstances may demand. The dog must not be timid, shrinking behind its master or handler; it should not be nervous, looking about or upward with anxious expression or showing nervous reaction, such as tucking of tail, to strange sounds or sights. Lack of confidence under any surroundings is not typical of good character.

Above: Note the alert expression of our beloved breed, here portrayed in Ch. Van Cleve's Colombo, C.D., owned by Dr. Carmen Battaglia. **Facing page, above:** Kaiserberg's Ruffian Hey Jude shown winning in the class at the Santa Clara Valley Kennel Club under judge Battaglia. **Facing page, below:** Ch. Destino's Pleasure Mine by Ch. Zete of Fran-Jo, R.O.M. ex Ch. Shadyhaven's Glory, C.D. Handled by Scott Yergin under judge Carmen Battaglia.

The old ideal German Shepherd male.

The modern ideal German Shepherd male.

Any of the above deficiencies in character which indicate shyness must be penalized as very serious faults. It must be possible for the judge to observe the teeth and to determine that both testicles are descended. Any dog that attempts to bite the judge must be disqualified. The ideal dog is a working animal with an incorruptible character combined with body and gait suitable for the arduous work that constitutes its primary purpose.

HEAD

The head is noble, cleanly chiseled, strong without coarseness, but above all not fine, and in proportion to the body. The head of the male is distinctly masculine, and that of the bitch distinctly feminine. The muzzle is long and strong with the lips firmly fitted, and its topline is parallel to the topline of the skull. Seen from the front, the forehead is only moderately arched, and the skull slopes into the long, wedge-shaped muzzle without abrupt stop. Jaws are strongly developed. *Ears:* Ears are moderately pointed, in proportion to the skull, open toward the front, and carried erect when at attention, the ideal carriage being one in which the center line of the ears, viewed from the front, are parallel to each other and perpendicular to the ground. A dog with cropped or hanging ears must be disqualified. *Eyes:* Of medium size, almond shaped, set a little obliquely and not protruding. The color is as dark as possible. The expression keen, intelligent and composed. *Teeth:* 42 in number—20 upper and 22 lower—are strongly developed and meet in a scissors bite in which part of the inner surface of the upper incisors meet and engage part of the outer surface of the lower incisors. An overshot jaw or a level bite is undesirable. An undershot jaw is a disqualifying fault. Complete dentition is to be preferred. Any missing teeth other than first premolars is a serious fault.

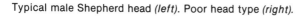

Typical male Shepherd head *(left)*. Poor head type *(right)*.

Covy's Oregano of Tucker-Hill, R.O.M. by Grand Victor Lakeside's Harrigan ex Ch. Tucker Hill's Angelique. This breeding combination was very successful for Covy-Tucker Hill Kennels, owned by Cappy Pottle and Gloria Birch.

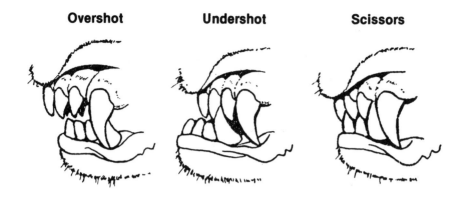

Overshot **Undershot** **Scissors**

Examples of jaw and teeth conformations resulting in various bites.

NECK

The neck is strong and muscular, clean-cut and relatively long, proportionate in size to the head and without loose folds of the skin. When the dog is at attention or excited, the head is raised and the neck carried high; otherwise typical carriage of the head is forward rather than up and but little higher than the top of the shoulders, particularly in motion.

FOREQUARTERS

The shoulder blades are long and obliquely angled, laid on flat and not placed forward. The upper arm joins the shoulder blade at about a right angle. Both the upper arm and the shoulder blade are well muscled. The forelegs, viewed from all sides, are straight and the bone oval rather than round. The pasterns are strong and springy and angulated at approximately a 25-degree angle from the vertical.

FEET

The feet are short, compact, with toes well arched, pads thick and firm, nails short and dark. The dewclaws, if any, should be removed from the hind legs. Dewclaws on the forelegs may be removed, but are normally left on.

PROPORTION

The German Shepherd dog is longer than tall, with the most desirable proportion as 10 to 8½. The desired height for males at the top of the highest point of the shoulder blade is 24 to 26 inches; and for bitches, 22 to 24 inches. The length is measured from the point of the prosternum or breastbone to the rear edge of the pelvis, the ischial tuberosity.

BODY

The whole structure of the body gives an impression of depth and solidity without bulkiness. *Chest:* Commencing at the prosternum, it is well filled and carried well between the legs. It is deep and capacious, never shallow, with ample room for the lungs and heart, carried well forward, with the prosternum showing ahead of shoulder in profile. *Ribs:* Well sprung and long, neither barrel-shaped nor too flat, and carried down to a sternum which reaches to the elbows. Correct ribbing allows the elbows to move back freely when the dog is at a trot. Too round causes interference and throws the elbows out; too flat or short causes pinched elbows. Ribbing is carried well back so that the loin is relatively short. *Abdomen:* Firmly held and not paunchy. The bottom line is only moderately tucked up in the loin.

TOPLINE

Withers: The withers are higher than and sloping into the level back. *Back:* The back is straight, very strongly developed without sag or roach, and relatively short. The desirable long proportion is not derived from a long back, but from over-all length in relation to height, which is achieved by length of forequarter and length of withers and hindquarter, viewed from the side. *Loin:* Viewed from the top, broad and strong. Undue length between the last rib and the thigh, when viewed from the side, is undesirable. *Croup:* Long and gradually sloping.

TAIL

Bushy, with the last vertebra extended at least to the hock joint. It is set smoothly into the croup and low rather than high. At rest, the tail hangs in a slight curve like a saber. A slight hook—sometimes carried to one side—is faulty only to the extent that it mars general appearance. When the dog is excited or in motion, the curve is accentuated and the tail raised, but it should never be curled forward beyond a vertical line. Tails too short, or with clumpy ends due to ankylosis, are serious faults. A dog with a docked tail must be disqualified.

HINDQUARTERS

The whole assembly of the thigh, viewed from the side, is broad, with both upper and lower thigh well muscled, forming as nearly as possible a right angle. The upper thigh bone parallels the shoulder blade while the lower thigh bone parallels the upper arm. The metatarsus (the unit between the hock joint and the foot) is short, strong and tightly articulated.

GAIT

A German Shepherd Dog is a trotting dog, and its structure has been developed to meet the requirements of its work. *General Impression:* The gait

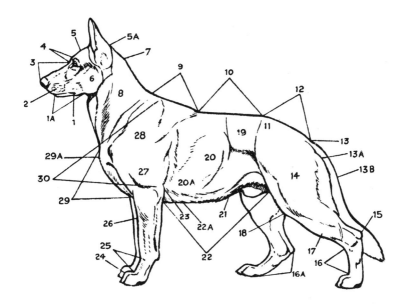

Parts of the German Shepherd Dog: 1—Lip corner (flew). 1a—Jaw (lower). 2—Muzzle. 3—Foreface. 4—Stop. 5—Skull. 5a—Occiput. 6—Cheek. 7—Crest (of neck). 8—Neck. 9—Withers. 10—Back. 11—Hip. 12—Croup. 13—Tail set. 13a—Point of haunch or buttocks. 13b—Tail or stern. 14—Thigh (quarter, haunch). 15—Point of hock. 16—Metatarsus. 16a—Hock. 17—Lower thigh. 18—Point of stifle (knee). 19—Loin. 20—Ribs. 20a—Chest. 21—Abdomen. 22—Bottom line. 23—Elbow. 24—Feet (paws). 25—Pastern. 26—Forearm. 27—Upper arm. 28—Shoulder blade. 29—Forechest. 29a—Prosternum (breastbone). 30—Shoulder.

is outreaching, elastic, seemingly without effort, smooth and rhythmic, covering the maximum amount of ground with the minimum number of steps. At a walk it covers a great deal of ground, with long strides of both hind legs and forelegs. At a trot the dog covers still more ground with even longer stride, and moves powerfully but easily, with coordination and balance so that the gait appears to be the steady motion of a well-lubricated machine. The feet travel close to the ground on both forward reach and backward push. In order to achieve ideal movement of this kind, there must be good muscular development and ligamentation. The hindquarters deliver, through the back, a powerful forward thrust which slightly lifts the whole animal and drives the body forward. Reaching far under, and passing the imprint left by the front foot, the hind foot takes hold of the ground; then hock, stifle and upper thigh come into play and sweep back, the stroke of the hind leg finishing with the foot still close to the ground in a smooth follow-through. The over-reach of the hindquarter usually necessitates one hind foot passing outside and the other hind foot passing inside the track of the forefeet, and such action is not faulty unless the locomotion is crabwise with the dog's body sideways out of the normal straight line.

TRANSMISSION

The typical smooth, flowing gait is maintained with great strength and firmness of back. The whole effort of the hindquarter is transmitted to the forequarter through the loin, back and withers. At full trot the back must remain firm and level without sway, roll, whip, or roach. Unlevel topline with withers lower than the hip is a fault. To compensate for the forward motion imparted by the hindquarters, the shoulder should open to its full extent. The forelegs should reach out close to the ground in a long stride in harmony with that of the hindquarters. The dog does not track on widely separated lines, but brings the feet inward toward the middle line of the body when trotting in order to maintain balance. The feet track closely but do not strike or cross over. Viewed from the front, the front legs function from the shoulder joint to the pad in a straight line. Viewed from the rear, the hind legs function from the hip joint to the pad in a straight line. Faults of gait, whether from the front, rear or side, are to be considered very serious faults.

COLOR

The German Shepherd Dog varies in color, and most colors are permissible. Strong, rich colors are preferred. Nose black. Pale, washed-out colors and blues and livers are serious faults. A white dog or a dog with a nose that is not predominantly black, must be disqualified.

COAT

The ideal dog has a double coat of medium length. The outer coat should be as dense as possible, hair straight, harsh and lying close to the body. A slightly wavy outer coat, often of wiry texture, is permissible. The head, including the inner ear and foreface, and the legs and paws are covered with short hair, and the neck with longer and thicker hair. The rear of the forelegs and hind legs has somewhat longer hair extending to the pastern and hock, respectively. Faults in coat include soft, silky, too long outer coat, wooly, curly, and open coat.

DISQUALIFICATIONS

Cropped or hanging ears. Undershot jaw. Docked tail. White dogs. Dogs with noses not predominantly black. Any dog that attempts to bite the judge.

Chapter 12

Interpreting the Standard

Precisely what is a standard? A conformation standard is a document agreed upon and written by a committee of our peers. It is not the "word," a declaration by God, nor can it be compared with the Ten Commandments. It is, in fact, the written expression of what the breed should be. We can hope that our standard has not been shaped by what we have rather than what we hope to achieve. It should reach toward a better animal than presently exists, an animal not yet born. "Hitch your wagon to a star"; this should be the purpose of a standard.

A standard must not be vague or too short, allowing many areas to be interpreted by the idiosyncrasies of a judge or breeder. And it must not be so long that it is boring or repetitious. For no matter how long and precise it may be, in the last analysis, the written word is never so accurate that it does not lend itself to a variety of interpretations. This is the inadequacy of all language.

The German Shepherd Dog Standard is quite long but not too long. It attempts to present us with a word-picture of an excellent and typey specimen. It is faulty as all written analysis is faulty, by being open to a variety of interpretations. We cannot correct this in any foreseeable way so we must live with it. In the criticism that follows I will admit that I am being inordinately censorious, but the corrections I discuss should be considered and would give us a better grasp of the breed standard.

In the first paragraph, "General Appearance," we have a description that is fairly accurate but, if you were not thinking in terms of the German Shepherd dog in particular, it would conceivably be representative of several other breeds. To allow the description better identification the size, hair coat,

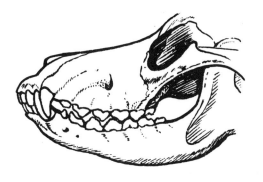

Correct scissors bite.

bushy tail and erect ears of the Shepherd should be mentioned. In reference to the sentence, "The ideal dog is stamped with a look of quality and nobility – difficult to define, but unmistakable when present," let me quote von Stephanitz in his introduction to the 1930 Kör book. He wrote an article entitled, "What Is Nobility?" and stressed the fact that, "Nobility has nothing in common with the worthless shell of surface beauty." Rather does it lie ". . . in the complete suitability of structure for the purposes demanded of it; this includes firm nerves, willingness to accomplish, even if it be only to accomplish the reproduction of its kind." He mentions bitches that are "too noble," referring to over-refinement, which gives point to his classification of "nobility of appearance," as a combination of "robust health, strong constitution and typical expression." As stated in the standard, nobility is definitely difficult to define. To me it is beauty, strength and fearlessness, blended into an aura of complete poise and "breediness." This is the essence of nobility.

The standard states that "Secondary sex characteristics are strongly marked . . ." I see no reason to belabor the point by the additional "and every animal gives a definite impression of masculinity or femininity, according to its sex," a section that should be deleted. In the sentence, "It looks substantial and not spindly . . . and nimbleness without any look of . . ." the words "not spindly" should be changed to "strong" and the word "nimbleness," in the rest of that sentence, changed to "quickness." Added should be mention of the "solid bone" the ideal Shepherd should possess. A mention of color ("Generally black and tan or sable in color") would then give us a much more definite picture of the "General Appearance" of an excellent German Shepherd dog.

The second paragraph is quite comprehensive but could have added in the middle of the sentence that begins with "Any dog that attempts to bite the judge . . ." the qualifying words, "through fear or viciousness," and continue as written in the standard "must be disqualified."

166

The section on "Head" is very good. When it declares "Jaws are strongly developed," it might be well to add, "the bottom jaw is rather deep to give added strength to the bite." When the dog bites, only the lower jaw moves (the upper jaw is stationary), swiveling on the hinge it forms with the skull. The amount of pressure it exerts comes, therefore, from the power engendered by the lower jaw. In reference to teeth, I would like to make an observation here. I have seen an occasional German import with a missing molar or other tooth, which was plucked from its mouth by an overzealous agitator when, at a young age, the dog attacked the sleeve during Schutzhund training.

The "Neck" segment is fine as is. Under the heading "Forequarters" I would add the correct skeletal nomenclature for the bones of the shoulder blade (scapula), upper arm (humerus) and pastern (metacarpus) to give them exact definition. Otherwise this section is without comment, as is the section labelled "Feet."

In the "Proportion" segment the ideal proportion of length to height is assessed as being 10 to 8½. During the scientific experiments with Shepherds, undertaken by Humphrey and Warner, it was concluded that to attain the greatest degree of breed utility, the structural proportions of the dogs should be 10 to 9 and no more than 10 to 8.8. In Germany, where utility is of prime importance, it is significant that these are also the wanted proportions of length to height, though it has been my observation that most of the German dogs are longer than their ideal length-to-height ratio.

The Shepherd should, undoubtedly, be longer than it is high, but it should be compact enough so that the center of balance in motion is not too far from the extremities that provide thrust and momentum. During the act of propulsion the dog that is too long in body finds it difficult to recover from each propulsive movement and therefore labors and lacks endurance. There have been, and still are, many fine Shepherds in the United States who have attained high show honors who are noticeably short in body. Such animals as Doppelt-Tay's Hammer, Titan or Nordlicht, Alpinebeach-Baobab Clouseau, come to mind, and there are other dogs of beautiful type that do not exhibit the 10 to 8½ body proportions. Most of the American-bred dogs will measure out to the proportions wanted in the standard. Incidentally, German dogs are, on the whole, slightly longer in leg than American-bred animals.

Under "Body" no fault can be found with the description of "Chest," "Ribs," "Abdomen," but there should be a mention of "false fronts." This occurs when the area of the forechest is extremely well filled, lending an appearance of a well laid-back shoulder when in fact the correct shoulder angulation is missing. No mention is made of the position of the withers in relation to the position of the elbow. With the wanted 90-degree shoulder angulation and the correct wither length, a plumb line, dropped from the center of the withers to the ground should, in profile, touch the elbow and run down the back of the front leg to the back of the pastern hinge.

Shoulder Assembly Angulation

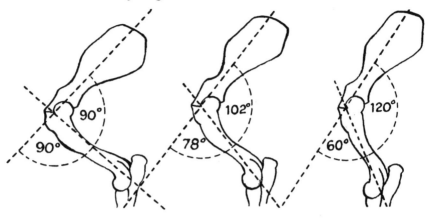

Excellent, or correct, *(left)*, fair, or incorrect, *(middle)*, and poor, or incorrect, *(right)*. Extension of reach is indicated by broken lines.

A long upper arm (humerus), suspended at the correct angle, is necessary for a complete reach, for this is the section of the shoulder assembly that swings forward and propels the leg in front of the body when the dog trots. Incidentally the shoulder assembly, the scapula and the humerus, are not attached to any other bones as are all the other parts of the dog's skeletal structure. They are held in place by muscles and ligaments.

Also, in discussing the body, relative proportions of the front and middle-piece are not mentioned. The front section of the middle-piece that includes the withers and front legs should, from the withers to the elbow, constitute 45 percent of the measurement from the withers to the ground. The remaining 55 percent measure from the front leg elbow to the ground. From the withers to the chest (or bottom) line of the dog, these figures are reversed; 55 percent from the withers to the bottom of the chest beyond the elbow, and 45 percent from the chest bottom to the ground.

Under the heading "Topline" and the subhead "Withers," nothing can be added or subtracted. But the section labelled "Back" tells us ". . . but from over-all length with relation to height, which is achieved by length of forequarter and length of withers and hindquarter, viewed from the side." It should read ". . .achieved by width of forequarter, length of withers, width of hindquarters, and position and length of croup." The rest of this section is entirely acceptable, and so is the section referring to "Hindquarters," except for the fact that no mention is made of the comparative lengths of the bones of the femur, fibula and tibia, which gives us the angulation so wanted in our Shepherds. Also, it is my contention that overangulation should be mentioned and considered a fault. Coupled with short hocks it can affect movement. The end result of overangulation is sickle hocks.

Gait is one of the most important elements of the German Shepherd's physical being. Every breed manufactured by man enjoys a specific gait that is the essence of that breed indicating its structural balance. This is particularly true of the German Shepherd because it is a working breed and must move with an economic and floating gait that is tireless if it is to perform the tasks wanted of the breed.

Of all breeds, the northern sled dogs and the German Shepherd are closer in conformation to the basic family Canidae. For true economy of movement I recommend the gray or timber wolf, *Canis occidentalis.* Note how closely he travels behind so that he can reach under to his center of balance and propel himself forward on his large, heavily-padded, symmetrical feet. As it is with dogs, the wolf's front feet are larger than his rear feet because they must support the neck and head, added appendages. A gait that is considered taboo in Shepherds is pacing, yet I have never seen a well-balanced Shepherd that, at a specific rate of speed during the trot, did not pace. Look again at the wolf. He paces constantly as will most wild felines and canines. Analyze the structural beauty of the wolf; it is in all ways completely economical, and from it we can recover some of the basic functional values that become lost or mislaid in the maze of fads and fancies that eventually encompassed every breed.

Overangulation *(left).* This was drawn from an actual photograph of an advertised stud dog ... actually this dog exhibits sickle hocks. Correct proportion of leg length and body depth to total height at withers *(right).*

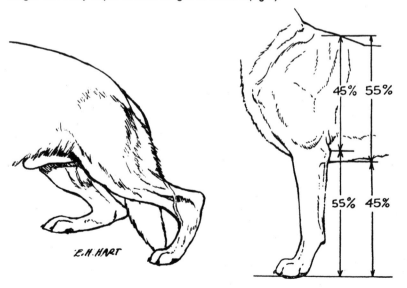

The "unlevel topline" mentioned under "Transmission" means that the dog, when gaiting, falls on its forehand. No mention is made of the fact that all the thrust and power of movement is executed by the hindquarters, while the front assembly is utilized almost solely for balance. It should also be noted under "Gait" that there is a difference between the movement of a male and a female Shepherd. The male moves with great power, planting his feet with authority and surging forward with dynamic grace and energy, while the female moves much like a ballet dancer, floating and light yet with authority. The standard does not assert that the Shepherd's movement is a four-beat gait of ground-covering economy that is the sum total of the animal's harmonious structure.

During movement there is a period of suspension when the dog reaches a gait that brings into balance all his parts and he moves without effort. When this occurs it is truly a beautiful sight; the animal seems to be actually floating in an alien time sphere that is akin to slow motion. Shy dogs often gait beautifully, as though trotting on eggs; they exhibit light and graceful movement. But this floating gait as they spurn the ground is merely a manifestation of their inner uncertainty and fear.

Many breeds offer a point scale to arrive at a more accurate appraisal of the dog. Each part of the dog is given a specific number of points according to its importance to the breed type, all of the points adding up to a total of 100. It presents a judge with a definitive yardstick for computing the value of every dog that comes before him. It could be an important aid, I think, to be utilized in the German Shepherd Dog Standard. I suggest the following point system for the German Shepherd Dog.

Falling on the forehand, or unlevel topline.

GENERAL CONFORMATION
& APPEARANCE

Proportions . . . . 6 points

Bone and substance . . . . 6 points

Temperament. . . . . 8 points

Nobility . . . . 3 points

Condition . . . . 3 points

HEAD

Shape . . . . 4 points

Teeth . . . . 4 points

Eyes . . . . 2 points

Ears . . . . 4 points

NECK

Length, crest . . . . 2 points

BODY

Withers, backline, loin,
croup . . . . 10 points

Chest, brisket, ribs. . . . . 8 points

Shape and proportions. . . . . 3 points

FOREQUARTERS

Shoulder. . . . . 5 points

Legs, pasterns, paws. . . . . . . 2 points

Angulation . . . . 5 points

HINDQUARTERS

Thigh, stifle, hocks. . . . . 3 points

Angulation . . . . 5 points

Paws. . . . . 2 points

GAIT

Walk and trot. . . . . 10 points

COAT

Color, texture, markings. . . 5 points

Total—100

This is an arbitrary example of the point system and can be changed with a point or two taken from one area and added to another.

Specialists in all fields and breeds tend to allow themselves to become obsessed with exaggerations, assuming that if overstatement of a particular part adds to the animal's all-around beauty, that part can be stretched to caricature for even greater beauty. When such extravagance is allowed to proceed unchecked, balance and function are destroyed and the fanciers lose contact with natural essentials. In some few Shepherds, occasionally seen, we have overangulation of the hindquarters that permits the animal to almost walk on its hock, and is a manifestation of such an approach.

In Germany a dog may rise above the competition of a more perfect animal in conformation if it exhibits the valuable attributes of strength, nobility, balance and tireless gait, evidences great working ability, and comes from a "good family." These can be nebulous qualities and the ability to balance them against more obvious attributes on the judicial scale is not always recognized by some American judges; if they were aware of such qualities

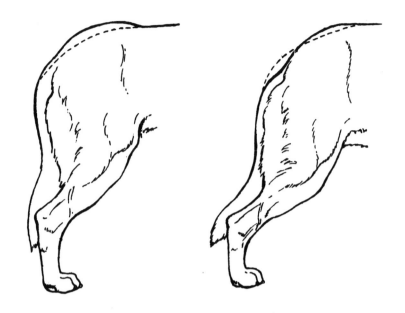

Overbuilt, high hock, (*left*). Steep, short croup (*right*).

Balanced, extended trot.

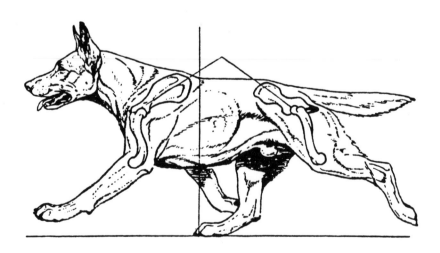

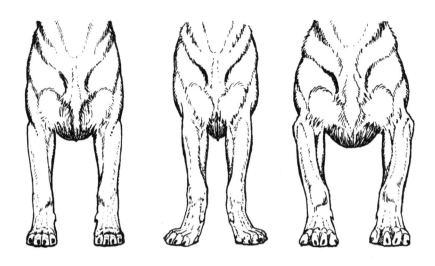

Excellent front *(left)*. East and west, pinched elbows, too narrow *(middle)*. Barrel-legged, loaded shoulders, out at elbows, poor feet *(right)*.

Excellent rear *(left)*. Cowhocked, dewclaws *(right)*.

Examples of Structural Faults

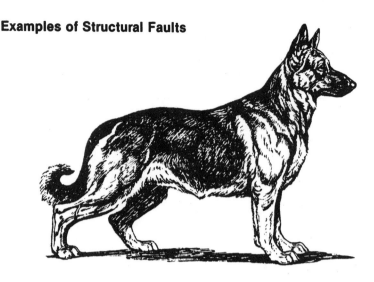

This bitch displays the following faults: sway back, false front assembly (filled forechest disguises lack of proper shoulder angulation, too long in body, too long in loin, legs too short and bone spongy, weak pasterns, too short in neck, sickle hocks, tail curled and too high set.

This male has a poor head, snipey in muzzle and with apple skull, wet in neck, roach-backed, shallow in body, and too high and square. He lacks bone and depth of body and his pasterns are too straight. He shows flat, mutton withers, too much tuck-up, too little angulation both in shoulder and hindquarter. He lacks forechest, his croup is too level, his tail too short, and he lacks pigmentation. These faults are typical of the Kriminalpolizei bloodlines.

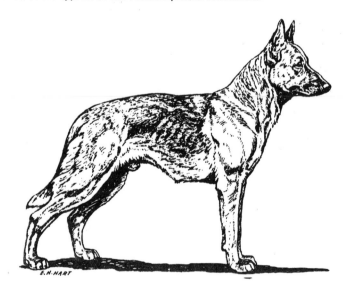

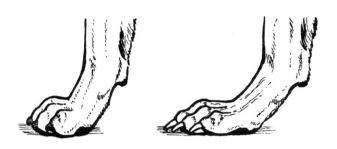

Excellent foot and pastern *(left)*. Hare foot, weak pastern *(right)*.

they would probably be censored if they judged in this manner. With these few succinct words von Stephanitz summed up the German attitude: "I have often urged that judging should not confine itself to mere details, and in particular not allow itself to be misled by false interpretations of beauty. Our Shepherd dog happens to be a working dog, and shall continue as such."

Words are not cohesive enough to present us with a standard that is mathematically correct; they are too open to varied interpretation. The authors of our standard have striven to present us with a workable document, and for the most part they have succeeded. Actually, the only way to make the standard completely understandable is to indicate the faults, virtues and proportions on living dogs. This being impossible to do with words, the only other way to accomplish this visibility is by accompanying the text with carefully rendered illustrations.

There will probably come a time when scientific research will enable us to chart correlations between physical manifestation and linked genetic sources. Then we can rewrite our standard to incorporate such findings and draw a blueprint of the perfect German Shepherd dog. But until that day arrives, if it ever does, we are very much thrown on our own resources.

Chapter 13

The Art of Judging the German Shepherd

Judging is truly an art, for it is a creative interpretation of a mass of words that is called the standard. The dogs themselves, as living entities, are the result of genetic sculpting by the breeder's art, and some of them are indeed masterpieces of bone, muscle and sinew formed into a thing of beauty. The judge must find and blend in his mind the flowing lines, the chiaroscuro, the delicate shades and nuances that together form the symmetry of the German Shepherd dog and, like an art critic, he then awards with highest honors the animal that comes closest to the portrait of the perfect German Shepherd.

The judge at a dog show in the United States has absolute control of the ring in which he is to adjudicate, and authority over all the persons in it. So it is decreed by the American Kennel Club and is an iron-clad rule. But despite this absolute jurisdiction over your assigned domain it is not a comfortable occupation to be a judge, for in the ring you can sway interpretation of the standard by your placings and in so doing exert pressure that can lead to change, for good or ill, in the breed.

The mechanics of becoming a judge are not terribly complicated. You must make application to the American Kennel Club and they investigate your standing in the dog community and your general character. They then send you a set of forms to fill out and return and upon their decision that you can fulfill the duties of a judge with knowledge, dignity and integrity, you are asked to perform three (or possibly more) assignments as an apprentice judge. An American Kennel Club representative observes your performances in the ring and advises the American Kennel Club as to your ability, or lack of ability, to adequately represent that august body in the nation's dog show rings. If the report is positive you will be informed by the A.K.C. that you have been accepted as a qualified judge of German Shepherd dogs and your name will be published in the American Kennel Club *Gazette* indicating your new status.

The mechanics of judging is fashioned of many small but important things and of the one big element—the judging of the dogs. In the ring you will eventually emerge with one Winners Male, a Winners Bitch (both of whom will be awarded championship points), a Best of Breed and a Best of Opposite Sex. If you have the good fortune to have the full complement of Shepherds which a judge is allowed in a large Specialty Show, one hundred and seventy-five animals, you will have four happy people and possibly one hundred and seventy-one rather frustrated and probably unhappy owners and handlers. The percentages for popularity are certainly not in the judge's favor. There are, of course, several classes where the owner is joyous to merely acquire a first place ribbon, but exhibitors do not enter their animals in a dog show to lose; they enter to win, and when they don't, they are generally not pleased with the judge's decisions.

The A.K.C. publishes numerous booklets, and among them is a pamphlet entitled "Guidelines For Dog Show Judges." It is but one of many relating to all activities within the A.K.C.'s wide sphere of authority governing the dog world in the United States. In this invaluable little book the A.K.C., in no uncertain terms, delineates the responsibilites, deportment, procedure, authority and all the activities of the judge before, during and after the show.

An arbiter is allowed to examine and place one hundred and seventy-five animals a day, no more. Judges who have had at least ten years of experience and who, because of age or ill health, wish to limit their assignments to one hundred dogs a day may notify the A.K.C. and be granted this privilege. A judge generally examines approximately twenty to thirty dogs an hour. When one considers the necessary time expended on gaiting, it leaves little time for an evaluation of temperament, so very important in the German Shepherd dog.

Every dog entered under the judge is entitled to a complete examination; the owner has paid for it and they must have it, even though the animal is a poor specimen and you know it will not place in competition. It also behooves the judge to withhold a ribbon from a dog that is so poor a specimen that it does not deserve recognition, or it is the only animal in that particular class and you do not want it to appear in the Winners Class. The arbiter must mark his judge's book and hand out the ribbons himself.

I like to have the dogs I am to judge enter the ring in catalogue order. I indicate with a hand gesture where I want them to line up. When the class is completely in I mark my judge's book, checking for absentees, and then, as the handlers set their dogs up, I walk down the line for my initial inspection. I then request the handlers to move their dogs around the ring at a reasonably slow trot and on a loose lead. After they have circled two or three times (more

Competition for Best of Breed *(above)*. Handler Doug Crane trots around the show ring with puppy bitch Tapferhaus Rosie *(facing page)*.

if the class is quite large), I bring them to a halt. I have now seen them standing and moving and they are ready for a closer scrutiny.

I examine each dog individually in profile again, then approach him from the front and move in. The shape of the head is first assessed, the ears, eyes, planes of the head, then the teeth and depth of jaw. I then view the front legs and feet, move to the side and check the prosternum, shoulder angulation, slope of pastern, depth of body, neck, withers, loin, spring of ribs, back, croup and hindquarter assembly, then hocks and hind feet. I run my hand down the tail to check for any deformity and stand behind the animal to see how the neck fits into the withers and shoulders and how the body and ribs shape back to the loin. Lastly, if it is a male, I check the testicles to feel if both are down in the scrotum and of the proper size and in the proper place. Actually all of the examination I have just described can be accomplished without touching the dog except for the three "T's": teeth, testicles and tail.

Now it is time to move the individual dog immediately after completing the inspection and test its movement behind going away, in profile once more, and coming toward me to assess front movement and elbows. I have the handler take the dog away in a straight line from me at a trot to the end of the ring, turn directly left and cross to the other side of the ring, then bring the dog back to me straight in, angling the ring. I halt him on a loose lead as he reaches me and view the animal when he is not stacked. Then I ask the handler to move the dog at a smarter pace circling the ring and back to the end of the line. If, for any reason, I decide the ring is too small or narrow and I wish to change it, it must be done before I have finished judging my first class.

After I have gone through the class I move the dogs around the ring at a trot and then a walk and a trot again and I begin to place them, occasionally calling for a faster trot from one or two, and sometimes halting the class so that I can watch two dogs move away from me and back, to once again check movement of hocks and elbows. Each time I shift the dogs to other slots in the line I stop the class. Finally I have my first four dogs selected. The rest need not be placed in their order of designation; only the first four are important. I signal them into the markers and point to each indicating my order of choice, then walk to the table, retrieve my judge's book and enter my selections therein, peering at the armband numbers of the handlers. Back at the table with my precious book, my steward or stewardess hands me the ribbons and I mete them out to the lucky winners.

When I select my Winners (dog or bitch), I mark by book, award it the ribbon, excuse the animal from the ring and call in the animal that was second in the class from which my Winners came, and gait this dog around the ring with other class winners to choose my Reserve Winner.

The Winners Dog and Winners Bitch appear in the ring to compete with the Specials (Champions) for Best Of Breed. The judge must now assess every Special since he has not examined them before. After several minutes of gaiting, the decision is made and I award ribbons and prizes for Best Of Breed, Best Of Winners, and Best of Opposite Sex to Best of Breed. Then the tedious posing with trophies, ribbons, handlers, and dogs (and occasionally the recalcitrant dog) to catch this triumphant moment on film for posterity takes place, and you must smile and bear with it.

Late arrivals, or a change of handlers is allowed at the judge's discretion, but only up to the time when the dogs in the class have been examined but *not* placed. During the process of adjudicating, the procedure one uses to find the winners is to compare the individual dogs against the mental picture the judge has of the standard; then, when addressing himself to the entire class, his selections must necessarily be by comparison of one dog with another. The decisions of one judge may not be the same as those of another simply because a dog may not look or show as well in one show as he did in another, and also because the adjudicator's findings are subjective and interpretation of the standard varies. An animal must be judged as he appears on the day you judge him, not by the quality he exhibited in some previous show. When judging particularly large classes, the judge can divide them into separate units and

My Winners Bitch in the Dominican Republic Specialty Show. The owner and handler is Monsignor Agripino Nunez C., Director of the Universidad Catolica Madre y Maestra and a keen Shepherd fancier.

select the outstanding dogs from each group; these are then brought together for final judging of the class. It is not wise to keep only four dogs in the ring from which to make your final placements. One may become suddenly lame, or indicate a sudden fault of temperament or other defect, leaving you with three dogs to place at four markers. An amazing trick if you can do it. It is best to hold six dogs from which to choose your four placings.

I do not attend many shows during any given year except those at which I am judging. I have no desire to become familiar with specific winning dogs or aware of what the judges may be putting up. I enjoy entering the ring to adjudicate with no preconceived visions of the animals to be shown under me and to make my own decisions as to their value.

A scene in the show ring; shown here is the Open Dogs Class.

Judging varies greatly in different sections of the globe. I judge many shows each year outside the U.S.A. and all over the world under Federation Cynologique Internationale (F.C.I.) sponsorship, and I judge All-Breed Shows as well as Shepherd Specialties. In many places (South America, Mexico, etc.) German Shepherd Specialties are judged as they are in Germany: six classes, three each for males and females—12 to 18 months, 18 to 24 months, 24 months and older, and no intersex competition. The dogs are all placed in the order of their merit down to the last animal in the class, and some classes number from twenty to forty animals. After handing out the ribbons I have the dogs walk around the ring, for I have to write a critique on every dog and I need to see the dog to accomplish this chore with accuracy. This critique is published in the breed magazine and is used on the animal's pedigree, which is much like a German pedigree. Incidentally, I dictate my observations about the dogs to a secretary who translates them into the language of the country in which I am judging.

In these shows the dogs are not handled by the judge. As each class enters the ring a document is handed the steward from two veterinarians outside the ring who have examined the animal's teeth and testicles and supply you with this information on every dog in the class. You test the stability and temperament of the dogs with gunshots. I use a gunshot for every three dogs as I walk down the line about three feet from the dogs and watch their reaction. Actually there is no real reason to touch the dogs. The coat of a Shepherd is not so heavy that the dog's basic structure cannot be clearly seen, and gaiting will tell the judge all else he needs to know.

The Federation Cynologique Internationale, under whose auspices I judge in all parts of the world other than the United States and her territories, is the recognized guardian European organization in the world of dogs with complete jurisdiction over all dogs, shows, owners, etc. Under the F.C.I., to become a Champion of record, a dog must receive a Certificate of Beauty and Aptitude (CACIB) four times at four different shows in three countries and under three judges. The CACIB can be compared to the Winners Dog and Winners Bitch points given in the United States, but it is also given to the Best of Breed. There are no Specials. Champions must compete in the Open Class. When the dog has won its four CACIB's under the F.C.I. rules mentioned above, it becomes an International Champion. CAC's are also bestowed upon winning dogs in many countries. If an animal accumulates three of these certificates at different shows, under different judges, he becomes a Champion of that particular country, i.e., Champion of Spain, Champion of France, etc.

The Federation Cynologique Internationale is the most prestigious European organization in the world of dogs. It was formed in 1932 with headquarters in Brussels. To become a judge under its banner one must pass an extensive written and oral test that encompasses the field of genetics and husbandry, as well as the standards of all breeds it recognizes.

Sometimes it is necessary to keep your dogs gaiting a bit more than is usual. I have done this when I have felt a lack of stability in an animal's balance. It is something not so much seen as subconsciously sensed. Under such circumstances I will keep the class moving in an attempt to break the dog down and, if there is something physically at fault, the dog will begin to pound in front, fall on its forehand, or lose drive behind. I must confess that I have a reputation (unfounded of course) of moving the dogs a bit more than do most judges (until the handlers have their tongues hanging out, it is unjustly said). But I earnestly wish to be assured that the German Shepherd dogs in my ring are not soft and flabby but are in hard athletic condition as a working dog should be. The handlers should also be in good condition.

A judge does not have time to do an in-depth evaluation of temperament when he is judging approximately twenty-five dogs an hour, which allows the judge about two minutes and forty seconds per dog, without extended gaiting and awarding of ribbons. He must appraise temperament in that short period by the expression in the dog's eyes (not always a totally certain test), and by closely watching the animal's reaction to a loose-leash examination. I generally test by walking very close to the dog so that I am in contact with the right side of his body, and then I run his ear gently through my fingers as I move to his rear.

Ch. Steinhuegel's Siggo V Lord v. Elingswiese ex Rackoda's Quia v. Steinhuegel. A strong, solid Shepherd with excellent conformation, an iron back, and working-dog structure. Owned and bred by Anne C. Given.

In places such as Barbados and Trinidad in the West Indies, where I have frequently judged, the impact of British dog show ideology is quite evident. A huge variety of classes is provided, and the exhibitors make multiple entries in different classes with the same dogs. The only recourse for a judge under these circumstances is to inform his steward to gather all dogs previously judged at one side of the ring and examine the new dogs in the class on the other side of the ring. The dogs are then brought together for some final gaiting and the selection for awards made. There are so many classes and repeats of entries that long before the classes reach completion it is quite obvious who will be the winning dog and bitch.

At every show in the United States there is a representative of the American Kennel Club who monitors the show. They are usually reasonable individuals who are there only as observers, or to aid in any way they can, if necessary, in reference to A.K.C. rulings.

I must make mention here of a very disquieting habit that has become prevalent in German Shepherd rings—double handling. I do not mind very discreet and quietly performed double handling, but when it interferes with other spectators and with the judging it is not to be tolerated. Believe me, it is no way to make friends and influence people—or the judge. I have seen the most ridiculous performances indulged in during double handling than I have ever witnessed before, *with* shouted directions from the handlers in the ring. I have witnessed wild-eyed, grimly determined owners outside the ring, rushing to and fro like maniacs, bumping into other spectators, lurching into trophy tables, whistling, calling, causing pandemonium in general, and

Van Cleve's Never On Sunday by Stencil Me of Billo ex Van Cleve's Celeste. This lovely young bitch is owned by Carmen Battaglia and is handled here by Kevin Reynolds.

agitating the dogs in the ring until they are almost wild. I have stopped judging many times to admonish exponents of double handling and have threatened to move their animals to the end of the class unless it was stopped. In Mexico last year, in the Sieger Show during the Adult Male Sieger Class, I found it necessary to call several men to ringside and tell them in no uncertain terms that they must quit the double handling or I would stop the show; the dogs were lunging instead of gaiting and becoming almost unmanageable. They apologized and discreetly withdrew. It is my considered opinion that no judge should have to tolerate such deportment outside or inside the ring.

Exhibitors must be tolerant and realize the difficult chore the judge faces in adjudicating large and arduous classes of excellent animals in the short time allotted to him or her. The responsibility is great and most judges earnestly want to do their best, but sometimes, not very often, they may make a small error in judging, for "To err is human, to forgive divine." So don't doubt the judge's integrity, good taste or ability; simply "be divine" and forgive him his small lapse into error.

Most exhibitors present their dogs for competition in the best condition possible, using natural means to reach their goal. But there are a few who resort to any kind of deception, even to cosmetic surgery, to win. Tails are fixed (a practice also indulged in in Germany); ears receive surgery; testicles altered or added; braces are affixed to teeth to correct bites; "uppers" and "downers" are administered, whichever are necessary for the specific dog; other medications are utilized for performance correction; spayed bitches are shown; and other devices used to rectify faults. All of these transgressions are directly opposed to A.K.C. rules and also to the canons of good sportsmanship. Of course the word "sportsmanship" would scarcely be a part of the vocabulary of individuals who indulge in any of these practices.

We all dream of owning the truly great dog that no judge can ever ignore, who can never be defeated, who is a living vision of the standard. But we must never lose sight of the realities that afflict the dream, that define and sometimes distort our vision. You must realize that there has never been a perfect dog, but faults that make him less than perfect must not be eliminated by artificial means. Live with the imperfections and love your dog despite or because of them. Our love for the dog makes us blind to all but what we want to see, and this is the better of two avenues of thought . . . and is as it should be.

Chapter 14

Training

There is no breed of dog in the world that can execute all the many tasks that canines are capable of accomplishing, not even our beloved German Shepherd dogs, as versatile as they are. It would be ridiculous for us to attempt to train a Shepherd to point or course game when we can use any one of the many pointing or hound breeds for such work. They are genetically fashioned for pointing and coursing game and the Shepherd is not, and it would be a waste of time to attempt to educate a German Shepherd to perform these tasks.

But every dog should be trained to be a good citizen, and it is the duty of every dog owner to expose his pet to basic training to ensure good conduct and gentlemanly deportment. An uncontrolled dog can become a nuisance or a menace and bring despair to its owner and censure to its breed.

There are many worthwhile books that can be purchased in book stores or pet shops that instruct in the intricacies of training. Or you can join a training class—there are thousands of them across the country—and work with an experienced instructor and with other novices like you and your dog. There are myriad ways to give your dog an education that will make him a better dog to live with, and so add to the esteem you will accord him and the rapport you will reach with him.

The dog is a pack animal; that is, his heritage is based upon a carnivorous propensity to run down his game in the company of a pack of his peers. So when he comes to you and lies on his back or side waiting for you to acknowledge his existence, he is psychologically accepting you as his pack leader and is according you obeisance. You are the master, and he loves you and wants to please you. Your Shepherd is a responsive and willing pupil with a high intelligence quotient and it is your responsibility to reach and mold this intelligence into basic training channels. Incidentally, when referring to the pupil from now on I will use the masculine gender for simplification.

Let us assume that you are about to train a puppy you have just purchased. To keep harmony in the home, stains off the rugs and odors from accumulating, your first chore of training will be housebreaking. To begin with you should purchase the puppy on a Friday so that you can spend the whole weekend at this chore. He should be kept at night, and when he is left alone at any time, in the bathroom, which is easily cleaned if the floor is of tile or linoleum composition.

You must constantly remind yourself to be cool, calm, and collected during this trying period. Remember Shepherds are intelligent, and if you spend the weekend without taking your eyes from the pup, chances are that by Monday he will be almost completely housebroken.

Puppies that are raised on earth-surfaced runs are easily housebroken. When they want to relieve themselves, they feel the need of familiar material under their feet. and realize happiness and relief going on the ground in your back yard. The trick to quick housebreaking is to watch the pup constantly, and particularly after he has been fed and watered, and rush him outside to go *before* he urinates or defecates on the floor. Praise him extravagantly when he performs outside, and sternly admonish him when he makes a mistake inside the house. When he is left alone in the bathroom at night, cover the floor with newspaper; then retrieve the paper he has soiled, remove the rest of the paper, and use only the soiled paper as bait for the next night. Dogs prefer to utilize an area that they have soiled before, and the soiled paper serves this purpose.

Soiled paper can also be carried out into the yard, anchored with stones, and used to bait the dog into relieving himself outdoors. Day by day cut down on the size of the paper until it is completely gone and the dog is using only the ground. The key word to remember for quick and easy housebreaking is "vigilance." Watch the dog constantly over a long weekend and rush him outside the moment he shows any indication that he is about to relieve himself. Feed him at regular intervals and supply him with water only after meals until he is completely housebroken. By this method you will become aware of the intervals between feeding and drinking and their natural results, and bring the puppy to its toilet area in time.

The use of baby suppositories is another way to control the time of the puppy's voiding. Injecting the suppository will result in almost immediate reaction. If he has recently eaten use the suppository, then rush him outside to his toilet area. The result will be gratifying. If you follow these directions you will shortly have a housebroken dog and a clean, odorless house—I hope.

Training actually begins with the first meal that you supply to your puppy. You put the bowl of food on the floor and call the puppy by name to you. You are, by this gesture, teaching him his name and to come when you call, promising him the reward of food if he obeys. During this period of feeding you can also accustom your dog to loud noises or gunshots. After allowing a few days for him to become accustomed to the house and you, while he is voraciously immersed in his food, stand a few feet behind him, take the top of a garbage can and drop the top to the floor. The floor should, of course, be either cement or tile, not rug, which would muffle the sharp sound and nullify what you wish to accomplish.

THE BASICS OF TRAINING

The most important element in training, basic or advanced, is *control*. You must control the dog and you must control yourself. By the latter I mean never allow yourself to become exasperated due to frustration. Keep calm and cool. If the dog does not react to your command it is your fault, not his; you are not getting through to him on his plane. You must try again—and again, and again, until he understands what it is you want him to do.

Next to control, *consistency* is your most important training aid. Always use the same word of command for the same action in the same tone of voice without any variation. Do not call your pupil to you by using the word *"Come!"* one time and *"Here!"* the next time. Use one word or the other, and continue this practice with all the words you use in training.

The third and last prerequisite to training is *patience* and *firmness*. Patience is truly a virtue in training, for without it you will lose the most important tool of training, control. Firmness must be brought to every mandate you give to your Shepherd. Be firm and, if you are sure he understands what you want him to do, make him obey. I do not mean that you should punish your dog should he not obey. Never punish him unless he maliciously bites.

Be firm by repeating the exercise over and over again in the same way and using the same commands until he obeys; then praise him lavishly. Instead of punishment, you patiently go through a specific maneuver over and over again until your pupil understands and accomplishes it. Then praise him.

Other laws you should follow in training are to keep your training periods short, no longer than about ten or fifteen minutes in length, particularly at the beginning of training, and *always preface each command with the animal's name* to get his undivided attention. Never begin instructions immediately after feeding; your dog will be lazy and lethargic when you want him sharp and willing. Praise him profusely when he obeys, and scold him when you know he understands but does not obey. Never strike him with anything: your hand, the leash, a rolled newspaper, or a switch. The dog is not for beating! Please remember that.

YOU AND YOUR PUPIL

Now let us examine the two individuals involved in this process of training—you and your pupil. You are to be the teacher and your dog, the pupil. You love your dog and may be inclined to be lenient. Don't be. It will just take you longer to accomplish what you could have in much less time, and your dog will never work for you with the precision he should.

Perhaps you won't be lenient. Perhaps you have a short fuse and will become angry when he doesn't obey. Shouting and angry reprimands that lead to physical chastisement only confuse and frighten your pupil. If he does not obey he needs *teaching*, not punishment, and you need control over your own vagaries of temper. Training should be a serious yet pleasant time that brings you both closer together.

Now let us assess your pupil, the dog. He depends on his keen scent and hearing to know his world. His eyes are not as keen as yours, but he is quick to detect movement. His olfactory sense is astonishingly more acute than man's. A German Shepherd has from 220 to 230 million olfactory cells, while a human has only 5 to 10 million cells in his olfactory membranes. Man's scent system is small and simple, or microsomatic; the olfactory system of the canine is macrosomatic, or large and complex. Your dog is exceedingly aware of change in your vocal sounds, so a sharp reprimand or a word of praise are quickly recognized by him. So as not to confuse your dog all commands should be *simple*, single-syllable words whenever possible.

Dogs vary in intelligence, willingness and sensitivity, just as people do. Your training, therefore, must be fashioned to fit their character and temperament. A sensitive dog must be addressed with quiet firmness and handled with greater care than an aggressive Shepherd. The latter animal must be instructed with much greater firmness and sharper commands. Sometimes there is a physical reason why a dog will balk at a command. For instance, a Shepherd with undisclosed dysplasia may refuse to jump because, when he does, he experiences pain.

Always end a training period on a happy note of achievement with your pupil performing a lesson which he enjoys doing and does well. He will then approach the next instruction with eagerness. Both praise and punishment must be administered immediately after the dog has committed the act that deserves your attention. The animal's memory of any given act he has performed is extremely limited and in a short time he will have completely forgotten what he has done, and your praise or punishment will not be connected, in his mind, with the act.

What you have learned here is a basic approach to training. Other than this meager approach the equipment you will need is a nylon or chain choke collar, a soft leather leash and a six-foot-long leather or nylon mesh leash.

FIRST COMMANDS

"Come!", "No!", "Shame!" and "Good Boy!" are the initial commands your pup will learn. When you command the pup to "Come!" and he runs away from you instead of coming, do *not* pursue him. He has four legs and you have only two and you will never catch him. Instead turn and run in the opposite direction calling lightly, "Come!" prefaced by his name. He will hesitate momentarily, then come galloping to catch you. When he reaches you do not scold him for running away; praise him for coming to you.

Give him his own toys to gnaw on and he will leave your shoes and other household articles alone. A puppy's gums ache sorely when he is teething and he needs something to chew on to ease the pain. The word "Shame!" can be utilized during the process of housebreaking and also when demanding that the pup not chew valuables during teething time.

When training the pup to collar and leash do not pull or drag him to make him follow you; he will balk, pull back and fight the lead. Use short, sharp jerks on the leash, squat down facing the pup and urge him to "King, come!" In these early stages of training a tidbit can be used, something tasty as a reward when he obeys. During the Armed Forces Super Dog Program we used tidbits as a reward constantly, especially when working with plastic explosives, but not during the attack work. Do not allow your Shepherd to haunt the table, drooling and begging, while you are eating. Find a place for him to stay during your mealtime that is away from the table.

As soon as the pupil walks easily on the leash the initial training is finished. Through this early training he has learned fundamental manners. He is housebroken, he knows what "No!" and "Shame!" means, he is aware of what "Good boy!" means, he will come when called, and he can be taken out for a walk without snaring you too badly in the leash. Now it is time for you to learn a few important tricks of training when *"positive"* training methods fail to have the desired effect. These come under the heading of *"negative"* training, and the idea is to make your Shepherd think he is punishing himself because you will not, in his mind, be the instigator of his punishment.

Puppies and young dogs grow so quickly that they are constantly hungry and, given the opportunity, will steal food from the kitchen counter or the table. If your dog becomes a food thief, and no amount of scolding will cure him, you must trick him into quitting this disgraceful habit. Attach together with string empty tin cans, bells, and anything else that will make an ungodly racket. Tie a succulent piece of meat or anything else he craves to the other end of the string, and place the meat as bait near the edge of the table. Leave the room, and the pup will, as soon as you have gone, voraciously grab the meat—and pull the assortment of noise makers down around him. If he attempts to run with the meat the cacophony will follow him and he will be undone. Intense silence is the sneak thief's (canine and human) cover, and when that quiet is shattered he is left completely exposed. One or two courses of this treatment usually result in a complete cure.

Jumping on the furniture or the bed, or finding refuge under a table or desk and growling when you attempt to dislodge him, can be handled by another bit of trickery. Purchase a dozen mouse traps and set them (unbaited but set) on the couch or bed upon which your Shepherd likes to snooze, or under the table or desk from which he dislikes to be dislodged. Cover them over with newspaper or brown wrapping paper and leave the house. The dog will immediately jump up on his favorite piece of soft furniture or venture under the desk or table. The mouse traps will snap shut and continue to snap as he moves, startling the wits out of him, and he will leave bed, couch, desk or table in a great hurry, unhurt but quite frightened.

If your Shepherd has formed a habit of jumping up on people he can be cured by simply holding onto his front paws—and keep holding on to them as he struggles to get free—until he becomes frantic, then release him. While you are holding him in this unlikely position speak to him in a jolly tone as though it is all a fine game. One or two treatments and you will have worked a complete cure. If your pupil, while running free outdoors, has fallen into the habit of placing a good deal of distance between you and him and does not return to you when you call, simply hide. When he looks back and can't find you he will hesitate, become alarmed, and rush back to find you. A couple of repeats of this treatment and he will stay much closer to you when running free.

Use your imagination and improvise a bit, and I am sure you will find other ways to trick your dog into good deportment. Dog psychologists have been using negative approaches to training to condition the dog's reflexes for specific results for many years.

I once taught a nine-month-old Shepherd bitch to sit and lie down by using a negative approach. I stayed with this bitch without cessation, during every waking moment for three days, watching her constantly. When she indicated by her behavior that she was about to sit down I would say "Sit!". When she gave evidence that she was about to lie down I would say "Down!". Those were the only words I spoke to her except during the third day when she was beginning to sit and lie down when I told her to, then I added "Good girl!" to our communicative vocabulary. At the end of the three days she would sit and lie down whenever I commanded her to. She had been conditioned to do so. It was a tedious task but I had the satisfaction of proving a personal theory.

Remember you are only tricking the dog into a behavior pattern by this method, you are not training him. Such negative training is quite limited in scope. Electric goads are used by some trainers as negative training devices. In my opinion such individuals are not trainers and their methods are sadistic and inexcusable. If you have a problem dog, or if you just feel that you cannot train your animal, take him to a qualified dog trainer, or a training class that has an instructor with a good reputation who will teach you to train your dog.

There is one other bit of negative training that I must impart because it can possibly keep your dog from journeying to that big kennel in the sky. It is a device to control the car-chasing dog. Attach a strong cord to the front of the dog's collar under his neck, and to the other end of the cord hang a piece of broomstick about two feet long to hang horizontally just above his pasterns. When he begins his car-chasing maneuver the stick will strike his forelegs sharply and should convince him that cars should be ignored from then on.

To teach your dog to ride in your car with aplomb is merely a matter of repetition. Keep the first few rides very short and talk to him constantly. Gradually lengthen them until your Shepherd can ride all day. If you have real trouble with a dog who persistently vomits, have your veterinarian supply you with medication to settle his stomach and sedate him slightly. He will eventually become used to car travel.

POSITIVE TRAINING BEGINS

Your Shepherd should have absorbed all the basic training necessary by the time he is from four to six months of age. It is now time for serious, positive training, and we begin by teaching him to "Sit!". This is an important command because it is the beginning exercise in many of the training drills to come.

Always work your Shepherd from your left side; it is the proper training position. Training period is a serious business and your dog must understand this. Afterward there will be a time for play, but not now. Use his chain choke collar with the six-foot leash attached to it. Gather the leash carefully and comfortably in your right hand, with your thumb through the hand loop, and the leash hanging in a slight and easy curve down to the collar. Speak the dog's name and at the same time pull straight up from the collar on the leash, tightening it; as you say "Sit!" press down with your left hand, fingers toward the rear, on the animal's croup, using the flat of your palm. Push downward firmly until his hind end collapses into a sitting position. Repeat the maneuver several times, remembering to hold the leash upward and taut. Each time praise your dog after he sits. Very shortly you will not have to exert pressure to make him obey. The mere touch of your palm on his croup will garner results.

Now step forward and with a quick jerk on the lead in your right hand command him to "Heel!". Step away with your left leg to remove this support from the dog. Always preface any command with the dog's call name. Walk a few steps forward, controlling the dog by quick jerks on the leash, then give him the "Sit!" mandate again. Repeat the whole maneuver over and over again. It is permissible to repeat the commands until you are certain he knows what you want of him. After that, mouth the signal only once. If his sit is rather sloppy, you can correct it and make him sit squarely after he has repeated the exercise several times without a mistake.

Now you can concentrate on the "Heel!". Move your pupil along at a good pace, holding him in the correct place with short jerks of the leash, and repeating the "Heel!" command with every correction until he is walking freely and correctly at your side. Never drag your pupil by the leash for this purpose. Combine the "Sit!" and "Heel!" commands and soon he will sit automatically when you come to a halt. When you walk, do it briskly, and when you come to a stop, make it abrupt, so there is no question in the dog's mind as to your purpose. From the sit position, when you give the vocal "Heel!" command, lightly slap your left thigh with your left hand, and soon your Shepherd will heel to this signal without the oral demand.

Now you can begin to teach him some turns, to the right and left, and a full turn. Signal each turn with a jerk on the leash. Work your pupil in these exercises for several training sessions and until he performs without error. If you have trouble with the dog forging ahead of you while heeling, or missing turns by his eagerness to move forward, there is a negative *"trick"* that is useful under these circumstances. Using the slack of the six-foot leash in your right hand, begin to whirl it in a circle toward your left and directly in front of you. Call for your Shepherd to heel and move off. Now if he moves in front of you the whirling leash will hit his muzzle or nose and he will back up to avoid this punishment. Continue this until he has learned his lesson and heels at your knee without forging forward.

To teach your Shepherd to sit-stay, order him to the sit position at your side. Lower your left hand to a position directly in front of his nose, fingers pointing downward. Hold the leash slightly behind his head, taut, and about two feet from the collar. Now step in front of the dog on your right foot, allowing your left leg to remain next to his shoulder. Command him to "Stay!" as you pivot on your right foot and bring your left foot beside it. You are now facing the dog, holding the leash above him at arm's length as he sits. Now hold your left arm and index finger up repeating the dictate "Sit-Stay!". Move back to his side and praise him. Repeat the instruction several times, then vary the exercise by taking a step to the left and then to the right and finally by walking completely around him and to his side again.

Once he has the "Sit-Stay!" in his repertoire, exchange the leash for a light, thirty-foot nylon line. Now, after putting your pupil in the "Sit-Stay!", face him and take two steps backward, away from him. As your lessons progress, move further and further away from him, until you are far enough away to be at the end of the nylon line. Always return to him fairly quickly before he chooses to break and come to you. Now we will vary the drill. When you are at the end of the nylon line, facing him, call to him, "King, come!". Jerk the line toward you, pat your thigh and bring him to a sit in front of you. Then walk around him and take your familiar position at his side.

To teach your pupil to "Down!" return to the six-foot leash and begin with the "Sit!" position. Then move in front of your Shepherd, reach forward and grasp his front legs at the pasterns. Utter the command "Down!" and pull his legs forward so that he must lower the front of his body to the ground. Squat or kneel in front of the dog and he will probably stay down. The hand signal is to hold your hand over his head palm down and parallel with the ground.

If this procedure does not produce the desired results another method can be resorted to. When you step in front of your pupil, keep standing, tighten

194

up on the leash, give the command and hand signal, then step on the leash and bear down with your foot, pulling the animal's head down until his whole front follows and he is in the "Down!" position.

The "Down-Stay!" is an easy lesson for your Shepherd to learn because he is in a comfortable position in the down. Repeat the procedure you utilized in the "Sit-Stay!", using the command "Down-Stay!" Duplicate completely until your Shepherd executes the command perfectly.

Remember to always praise your Shepherd when he completes an exercise and, at the end of the total routine, bring the training to a close with a bit of congenial playtime.

OBEDIENCE TRIALS

Your dog has now learned the specifics of good manners, how to obey, and how to work willingly with you. There is no better way to enhance the close relationship that is dawning between you and your Shepherd than by engaging in the sport of the obedience trial. Trials are sponsored by local dog clubs with the blessing of the American Kennel Club, and with their guidance and under their rules. There are point trials and sanctioned matches, the latter for the novice to reach some familiarity with the exercises before engaging in more serious competition. I recommend that if you are seriously entering into the world of obedience trials, write to the A.K.C. for the pamphlet entitled "Obedience Regulations" for a complete coverage of rules and regulations.

The classes in obedience trials are Novice A and Novice B (a dog cannot be entered in both at any one trial). These classes are for dogs not less than six months of age and they cannot be handled if they have previously won a C.D. (Companion Dog) title. In Novice A the handler must be the owner or a member of the family. Dogs in Novice B may be handled by anyone. The exercises and scores are:

1. Heel on leash.................35 points
2. Stand for examination.........30 points
3. Heel free ....45 points
4. Recall.......................30 points
5. Long sit.....................30 points
6. Long down....................30 points
                        Total   200 points

The Companion Dog title (C.D.) is issued by the A.K.C. after a dog has been certified by three different judges to have received scores of more than 50 percent of the available points for each exercise and a final score of 170 or more points, provided that no fewer than six dogs competed in each of the three licensed obedience trials entered.

All of the exercises in the Novice Classes were discussed previously in the basic training section with the exception of the Stand For Examination. This procedure consists merely of training the dog to stand off the leash without moving as you stand about six feet in front of him and the judge goes over him as in the conformation ring, touching him here and there.

The Open A Class is for dogs that have won their C.D. title. They must be handled by the owner or a family member. Open B is fashioned for dogs that have won their C.D. or Companion Dog Excellent title (C.D.X.) and may be handled in competition by the owner or anyone else. No animal may be entered in both Open A and Open B classes at the same trial. The Open exercises and scores are:

1. Heel free . . . . 40 points
2. Drop on recall . . . . 30 points
3. Retrieve on flat . . . . 25 points
4. Retrieve over high jump . . . . 35 points
5. Broad jump . . . . 20 points
6. Long sit . . . . 25 points
7. Long down . . . . 25 points
                                    Total   200 points

Once again for the C.D.X. (Companion Dog Excellent) the dog must have been certified by three judges and have received more than 50 percent of the available points in each of the exercises and a final score of 170 or more points to qualify. No fewer than six dogs must have been entered in competition.

The Utility Class, if the show-giving club so desires, may be divided into U.D. A and U.D. B. If divided, dogs may compete in the classes if they have won the C.D.X. title. If not divided, dogs that have won the C.D.X. and a previous U.D. title may compete. Anyone may handle the dog. The exercises and scores are:

1. Scent discrimination . . . . 30 points
   Article 1
2. Scent discrimination . . . . 30 points
   Article 2
3. Directed retrieve . . . . 30 points
4. Signal exercise . . . . 35 points
5. Directed jumping . . . . 40 points
6. Group examination . . . . 35 points
                                    Total   200 points

The author working with his Shepherd on the Retrieve on Flat exercise *(right)*. The Shepherd *below* completes the Retrieve Over High Jump exercise with good form.

Obedience tracking.

The same number of judges must certify the dogs; scores and final score are the same as in the other classes. The one change is that three or more dogs must have competed.

For the Tracking Test the dogs must be at least six months of age and must be judged by two judges. The title Tracking Dog (T.D.) is awarded by the A.K.C. when the two judges have passed a dog in tests in which at least three dogs have participated (in each test). If you have a dog that has a U.D. and acquires a T.D., you may use the letters U.D.T. after his name, signifying that he is a Utility Dog Tracker.

On the Heel Free the exercise is the same as Heeling On Leash but without the leash, and you must heel your dog through a figure-eight. In the Recall and Drop On Recall, you leave your dog, giving him the command to "Sit-Stay!", then walk about 35 feet away and turn to face your Shepherd. On a signal from the judge you call your dog who must come straight in and sit in front of you. You then bring him to the heel position on the judge's bidding to "Finish!". On the Drop in the Open Class, while the dog is coming to you, he must drop immediately to a "Down!" position upon command, and remain until you call him in to "Finish!"

A good gray (sable) dog taking the bar jump.

In the "Long Sit" in the Novice Class, and the "Long Down," all the contestants are lined up in catalogue order. Armbands and leashes are left behind the dogs, then the handlers give their dogs the command to "Sit!" or "Down!" and walk to the other side of the ring. For the "Sit!" they remain away from the dog for one minute. For the "Down!" they return after three minutes.

In the Open Classes the "Long sit" and "Long down" are accomplished in the same manner except that the handlers leave the ring and are gone out of sight of their dogs. They are absent three minutes for the "Sit!", and five minutes for the "Down!".

For the "Retrieve On Flat" the handler stands with his dog at heel and throws a dumbbell straight ahead ordering his dog to "Stay!", followed by the request to fetch the dumbbell. The dog brings it back and sits in front of the handler who takes the dumbbell and orders the dog to heel. On the "Retrieve Over High Jump" the same routine is followed. The jump for a Shepherd would be about 36 inches high.

In the "Broad Jump" the handler takes a position midway between the first and last (fourth) jump, and the Shepherd must clear all hurdles in one jump. These jumps are about 72 inches long and 6 inches high. He then returns to sit in front of his handler as in the Recall. While his dog is effecting the jump, the handler performs a neat right angle turn and waits for his dog to return.

During the "Scent Discrimination" test, your Shepherd must select by scent one article among other articles that has been held by the handler. There are two sets of articles, comprised of five identical pieces, with one set made of metal and the other of leather. Each article is numbered, and a steward will place the articles (all but two, which the handler shall hold to implant his scent). About fifteen feet, with back to the articles, the handler shall stand, the dog at heel. The handler places the articles he has held in the judge's book; the judge then puts it among the other articles. The handler makes a right about turn, facing the articles, and sends his dog to them. The dog finds and retrieves the article permeated with the handler's scent (hopefully) and returns it to the handler, then assumes the heel position. The second scent exercise is accomplished in the same manner.

When engaged in the "Directed Retrieve," the handler must provide three white work-gloves, two of which will be placed at each corner of the ring and one in the middle. Only one glove will be retrieved at the judge's command, either the side gloves or the center one. Your Shepherd will be in the sit position at your side, and you will turn to the glove the judge has indicated is the one to be retrieved. The handler gives his Shepherd the order to retrieve and indicates with his left hand and arm which glove. The dog goes to and picks up the glove and brings it back to his handler, completing the exercise as in the "Retrieve on Flat."

For the "Signal Exercise" heeling is done in the same fashion as in the "Heel Free," but the handler uses only hand signals and never vocal instruction. At the judge's request the handler gestures the dog to perform a left turn, right turn, halt and normal, slow, and fast gaits. These commands are followed by a stand at the heel position and the directive by the judge to "Leave your dog," whereupon the handler signals the dog to "Stay!", walks to the far end of the ring, turns to face his pupil and cues the dog to drop, to sit, and to come and finish as in the recall.

The jumps in the "Directed Jumping" exercise are placed midway in the ring about eighteen feet apart, the high jump on one side and the bar jump on the other side. The dog is at heel-sit and is about twenty feet from the

Training Equipment

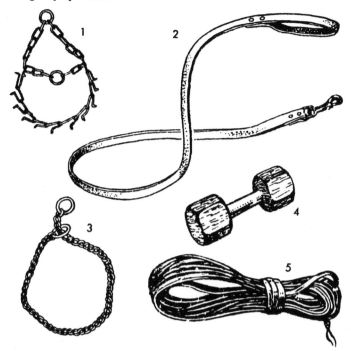

1—Torquatus, limited choke. 2—Six foot pliable leash. 3—Chain choke collar. 4—Dumbbell (wooden). 5—Longe, or long leash. Items 2 and 3 are sufficient for simple basic training.

jumps. The dog is sent out between and beyond the jumps where he turns and sits, watching his handler. At the judge's bidding the handler signals the dog which jump to take. The dog performs the exercise and returns to the handler. When he is in the heel-sit position the handler again sends him out. He turns, sits, waits. At the judge's dictate the handler again signals the choice of jumps, the dog obeys and returns and sits at heel at the handler's side. The heights of the jumps are equivalent to those in the Open Classes. The bar jump is painted in alternate black and white, and the dog should clear the jumps without touching them.

All the dogs go through the "Group Examination" together. The handlers and their dogs line up in catalogue order down the center of the ring. The handlers place their armbands and leashes behind their dogs. All the dogs are commanded to "Stand," and the handlers leave them and walk to the other side of the ring, then turn and face their dogs. The judge approaches the dogs and examines them individually. At the judge's bidding the handlers return to the animals, walk around them to the heel position and the exercise is finished.

"Tracking" is the test devised to assess the animal's olfactory prowess. The dog wears a harness to which is attached a twenty- to forty-foot light nylon line. The handler must follow at no less than twenty feet behind the dog. The length of the track must not be more than five hundred yards, or less than four hundred yards, the scent between one-half and two hours old. It has been laid by a stranger who will leave an object (wallet, glove, etc.) at the end of the track. This item must be found by the dog and picked up by the handler. Flags stake out the track and the handler must not, in any way, influence the direction of the dog while tracking.

TRAINING FOR THE SHOW RING

Show ring training is not a complicated affair. It is comprised of teaching your dog to stand without moving when you stack him in a show stance, not to cringe from or bite the judge, and to move properly on a loose leash without desperately pulling during the gaiting. If your Shepherd will work better with baiting, oven-baked liver, chicken, or dry-food tidbits can be used. Recognize your dog's faults and virtues and, when in the ring, attempt to disguise his faults and advertise his good points . . . not boldly, but with subtlety and finesse.

Points vary with the number of Shepherds entered (or shown) and the locale of the show. The classes above are all divided by sex. The Winners Class is divided by sex and is for all class winners of first prizes. From this class the

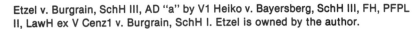

Etzel v. Burgrain, SchH III, AD "a" by V1 Heiko v. Bayersberg, SchH III, FH, PFPL II, LawH ex V Cenz1 v. Burgrain, SchH I. Etzel is owned by the author.

Dog-Show Class Chart

Puppy—6 months and under 9 months	Must be whelped in U.S. or Canada.	
Puppy—9 months and under 12 months	As above.	
Intermediate 12 to 18 months	Fairly new class to bridge gap between classes	
Novice	Dog or puppy which has not won Adult Class or higher award at point show.	After 3 first place novice wins, ineligible for Novice.
Bred By Exhibitor	Any dog or puppy other than Champion owned and bred by exhibitor.	Must be shown only by immediate family member.
American-bred	All animals except Champions whelped in U.S. or possessions.	Also from breeding that took place in U.S.
Open Dogs	All dogs, 6 months and over, including Champions & foreign breds.	American Champions shown in Specials.
Specials	Champions, American & foreign American Champions. Winners Dog and Winners Bitch Intersex competition here.	Compete for B.O.B. No points.

judge shall select Winners Dog and Winners Bitch. Then they are excused and the dog and bitch who came in second in the class from which the Winners Dog and Winners Bitch came is called into the ring and competes with the other class winners for Reserve Dog and Reserve Bitch (dogs and bitches are judged separately). In the classes from which these winning dogs came, only the first four dogs are placed and given ribbons. The Winners Dog and Winners Bitch are awarded the points. Whichever of these two dogs is named Best of Winners by the judge is allowed the greater number of points. For instance, if the male classes only offer two points and the female classes have three points, and the male is accorded Best of Winners by the judge over the winning bitch, the male will then be awarded the same number of points garnered by the bitch. In this example three points. I have gone through this before, but in this context it bears repeating.

The Winners Dog and Winners Bitch compete for Best of Breed against the Specials (Champions) and any dogs winning in non-regular classes. The Best of Breed is then judged following the Best of Winners judging. Immediately following these judgments the Best of Opposite Sex is awarded. No points are offered for Best of Breed. But if you are exhibiting in an All-Breed Show, the Best of Breed goes on to compete in the group (the German Shepherd dog will be in the herding group).

It is important that you train your Shepherd to perform perfectly in the conformation ring if you wish to win, and that of course is the entire reason for exhibiting. Remember that no matter how perfect a thing of beauty may be it can be marred by an indifferent approach to its presentation. A Kandinsky or a Cezanne, tacked frameless to a kitchen wall, are not lessened in artistic value, yet lose significance by their environment and lack of selective surroundings. So take time to train your Shepherd for competition.

To become a Champion your Shepherd must accumulate fifteen points under three different judges and must win at least two major shows offering at least three points at each show. The maximum number of points he can win at any show is five. No points are offered at match or sanctioned shows, but they are excellent vehicles to hone your Shepherd's attitude in the show ring and ready him for point competition.

At the National Specialty each year, sponsored by the parent club, The German Shepherd Dog Club of America, the titles of Grand Victor and Grand Victrix are awarded, and there you will find the finest dogs in the country competing for these prestigious awards.

Obedience work is a tremendously satisfying way to achieve concrete results with your Shepherd. Unlike the show ring, you depend upon mathematical certainty of performance to a greater degree, not upon the whims or varying interpretations of the breed standard by an adjudicator who may or may not be correct in his placings. Day by day you will have a closer rapport with your dog, until some tenuous thread of feeling joins you together, and there are no words that can describe this sensation. It is deep inside of you, a mixture of pride in your dog, a wonderful sense of closeness, and a warmth that can only be expressed by the words "This is *my* dog."

Should your thing be the show ring you will feel an intense pride in your Shepherd's winnings and satisfaction and fulfillment if he becomes a Champion. For it means that your Shepherd is above the herd, that he has been touched by greatness. If you have a really top Shepherd and you wish it to make its championship, and you can afford it, I suggest you put your dog in the hands of a professional handler to finish it for you.

Chapter 15

The Growing Schutzhund Movement in the U.S.

Throughout the country there has been a vast surge forward in the sport of Schutzhund training and competition. All over the country clubs are springing up, competitions are being held, and working German Shepherds are being imported from Germany to fill the needs of the people involved in this new sport. Puppies from these imports are being sold at high prices, and stud fees to imported dogs with good sources in Schutzhund III are quite high.

In conversation with Schutzhund enthusiasts I find that their zeal, besides enjoying Schutzhund as a sport, is derived from a sort of psychological rebellion against the—what they term—dilettante dogs being exhibited in the conformation rings, and what Schutzhund people consider the uselessness of the show-type animals; linked to this feeling is the belief that in a crime-ridden society the need for protection-trained dogs is a reality.

The American Kennel Club will not recognize the Schutzhund movement because of what they consider the stigma of the attack or protection training. As a result the Schutzhund people declare that they do not need the A.K.C. or the parent club, (G.S.D.C.A.) which is tied to A.K.C. rules. And, as it is always with a pristine sport or activity, there is controversy and rivalry among the three main groups in this country, NASA, Schutzhund U.S.A. (United Schutzhund Clubs of America) and the Deutscher Verband der Gebrauchshundsportvereine (DVG in America), which is the German Alliance of Utility Dog Sports Clubs. The three clubs should certainly find some mutual accommodation since they are basically striving toward a common goal, the strong establishment of Schutzhund in the United States. And the American Kennel Club will have to find a way to accept this important

205

sport. It has grown (and keeps on growing) too big not to be approved by the sole imperial canine club in the country.

Schutzhund, which is a German word meaning "Protection Dog," has existed in Europe as a sports form for many years, and in Germany it is practically a way of life for Shepherd dog owners. Conformation shows and Schutzhund training go hand-in-hand in Germany. Knowledge of this long association in Germany with the Schutzhund movement has prompted American Schutzhund enthusiasts to adopt the rules and training methods of the mother country, and to attempt to lure competent Schutzhund judges to adjudicate at Schutzhund trials here. One such German judge, Paul Theissen, a long time trainer, has settled near my home here in Florida. There are several more qualified Schutzhund judges in other sections of the country.

The president of the German Shepherd Dog Club of America, George (Bill) Collins, has attempted to change the attitude of the A.K.C. toward the Schutzhund sport, but at the time of this writing, without success. Since the S.V. in Germany is taking a vacillating attitude at the moment, yet recognizes only one club as representing the breed in the U.S., the German Shepherd Dog Club of America, and that club is under the jurisdiction of the A.K.C., Bill has been in the middle of a controversial situation with all the elements concerned. He has shown a great deal of interest in the work and problems of the Schutzhund clubs in the U.S. and is well regarded in Germany. I had the pleasure of working with Bill when I was a member of the board of the German Shepherd Dog Club of America, and feel that he is one of the most far-sighted and capable presidents that the board has ever had. He has formed the German Shepherd Dog Club of America—Working Dog Association, which will encourage local Schutzhund Club affiliation and will make it possible for a team from the U.S. to compete in the European trials of the World Union of German Shepherd Dog Clubs (WUSV). It is a promising beginning.

To complicate matters still further there has recently been a drastic turnover of influence in the German S.V., with Dr. Rummel being voted out and Hermann Martin made Chairman of the German club and Dr. Ernst Beck as his second in authority. How this will affect the various components concerned in the potpourri of events affecting the Schutzhund movement in the U.S., the S.V., the A.K.C. and the G.S.D.C.A. remains to be seen.

Both the Schutzhund U.S.A. and the D.V.G.-America publish interesting magazines. Other local clubs also print Schutzhund literature. In reference to the Shepherd dogs used by the Schutzhund people, the genetic qualities best liked are involved with animals that have received working titles (Bundessiegers) such as Racker vom Itztal, SchH III, and a "V" dog in conformation; "V" Enno v. Antrefftal, SchH III, FH, Int. (Bundessieger); Enno's son the Bundessieger "V" Drigon v. Fuhrmannshof, SchH III, FH, Int.; "VI" Heiko vom Bayersberg, SchH III, FH, PFPL II, LawH; the Kirschental combined herding and show breeding; Busecker Schloss;

Schutzhund tracking *(above)*. On-the-spot testing *(below)* by Captain Arthur J. Haggerty, Dog Trainer, New York, New York. This Shepherd is a graduate of Captain Haggerty's School for Dogs and is one of the working pupils assigned to protect a New York shoe store from vandals and thieves.

Bungalow and Stahlhammer breeding. Of the show dogs liked can be listed "VA" Quanto v.d. Wienerau, SchH III; "VA" Hero v. Lauerhof, SchH III; Sieger Marko v. Cellerland, SchH III, son of an HGH (herding) dog; Sieger Bodo and "VA" Bernd von Lierberg, brothers; and "VA" Frei v.d. Gugge, SchH III, FH, a black dog who sired the Bundessieger, Enno v. Antrefftal.

Occasionally one will find a Schutzhund dog who was started very early on the sleeve, who has a missing tooth which had been caught in the web of the sleeve and plucked out by an overzealous agitator. Mentality, willingness to work, character, and courage are all as much a part of the dog's genetic design as are the visible conformation traits and should be selected for if you want working potential and good performance in Schutzhund work.

Trial handling must be practiced religiously to keep both you and your Shepherd keen and in condition to participate. You will reach a plateau in your work with your dog when you will both become instinctively aware of each other and you will become one with your Shepherd, working in complete unison. Following is some pertinent general information.

A. DEGREES

The rules* are divided into:

Schutzhund A (SchH A)
Schutzhund I (SchH I)
Schutzhund II (SchH II)
Schutzhund III (SchH III)
Tracking Dog (FH)

B. ELIGIBILITY

Minimum trial entry ages

14 months
14 months
16 months
18 months
16 months

C. POINTS

		German Terms
0 to 109	Not acceptable	Ungenugend (U)
110 to 219	Unsatisfactory	Mangelhaft (M)
220 to 239	Satisfactory	Befriedigend (B)
240 to 269	Good	Gut (G)
270 to 285	Very good	Sehr Gut (SG)
286 to 300	Excellent	Vorzüglich (V)

*Note: Rule changes can take effect every three years.

When you enter and bring your Shepherd to an actual Schutzhund Trial, there are many details of which you, as a handler, should be aware. I will list some of these items below.

GENERAL OBSERVATIONS

1. Present yourself with your Shepherd to the judge as each division of the trial begins (Tracking, Obedience, Protection). The dog's pedigree and scorebook (if you have these items) must be presented to the trial chairman.

2. The dog's name must not be used in the obedience routine.

3. You may pet and praise your dog only between exercises.

4. Bodily signals by the handler are not permitted.

5. No leather or spike collars are allowed. The chain choke collar (dead ring) must be used.

6. Gun-shy dogs are disqualified.

7. The dog's attitude and the swiftness with which he works are important.

TRACKING

1. Inform the judge of the dog's preference to either pick up the article or simply indicate it.

2. The dog must move at a constant pace.

3. The wind direction can change the dog's tracking pattern, so wait for definite turn indication to be certain he is on the track.

4. When article is indicated by your Shepherd, retrieve it and show it to the judge.

5. Wait for the judge's whistle indicating you may leave the track.

OBEDIENCE

1. Do not attempt to initiate any extra sits, turns, etc.

2. Whenever you change pace you may repeat the heel command.

3. Do not look back at your dog when you leave him during moving exercises; it can cost you points.

4. Do not call your dog back to heel should he refuse to jump on retrieve. Simply repeat the command.

5. Should your dumbbell throw over the wall not be particularly good, ask the judge for another throw.

PROTECTION

1. When sending your dog on a "blind" search stay in the middle of the field and do not heel him between searches.

2. When your dog barks at the agitator in the blind, do not give him a "sit" or "down" command. If he does not obey, or stands up again, points will be deducted from his score.

3. When the agitator begins the courage test routine you may excite and encourage your dog by shouting at the agitator.

Allow me to inject here an observation that may aid in your dog's performance. Your Shepherd may become bored by the same training routine executed at each training session. To re-ignite his motivation and stimulate his desire to work with eagerness, effect a change in the overall procedure. Utilize a different work area, change the time of training, vary the articles for scent discrimination, use a family member to lay track, try night tracking, mix the attack work with obedience, have the agitator run behind a barrier as the dog attacks, etc. A bit of imagination can make a big difference in the style and eagerness of your dog's performance.

From a breeding standpoint, it is not really necessary to become too absorbed in an animal's scores. The trainer, the length of time spent in training, the consistency of training, and the handling of the animal in competition has much to do with the scores the dog achieves. If the Shepherd attains a passing score and indicates his physical and mental ability by completing all three phases of a Schutzhund trial, it is all that a breeder should be concerned about.

SCHUTZHUND A EXAMINATION

Total points 200

The Schutzhund A examination does not require tracking. It consists only of the exercises in Part B (Obedience) and Part C (Protection) of the Schutzhund I survey.

SCHUTZHUND I EXAMINATION
Part A. Tracking

Total points 100—Command, "Go Find"—German command, *("Such")*

On a track 300 to 400 paces long, laid at least 20 minutes before by the handler, the dog searches for and finds two articles. The tracking leash should be 32 feet 9 inches long. Track contains two ninety-degree turns. Handlers may handle dogs on long leash or free. On or off the leash the handler follows at distance of 10 meters (33 feet). Articles must be no larger than a wallet and of neutral color. The dog may either indicate the article or pick it up.

Part B. Obedience

Total points 100.—Command, "Heel"—German command, *"Fuss"*

1. Heeling On Lead—15 points

From the sit position the dog, on lead, heels at handler's side, walking straight ahead at least 40 paces and back. Exercise done at normal, slow and fast pace. One right turn, one left turn, and one about turn are executed at normal pace. The handler may use the command, *"Heel!"* at the beginning and with each change of pace. There must be a distance of at least twenty paces between each turn.

At judge's direction the handler walks his dog through a group of four or more people and stops at least once (dog sits) during the exercise. The group members move about freely.

2. Heeling Off Lead—(20 points)—Command, "Heel"—*("Fuss")*

From the "sit" on leash in the group, the handler moves with dog away from the group and turns to face them again, then finishes the on leash exercise in the basic position. Then, while walking he frees his dog and "sits" him. Again he walks through the group with at least one "sit," leaves the group and exercises a short "sit." The handler begins the same exercise as before. With the dog unleashed he walks at least 20 paces slowly and 20 paces quickly, one right turn, one left, and one about turn with a distance of at least 20 paces between each turn. Two shots are fired at a distance of 15 paces and at 10 second intervals during the exercise. The dog must be indifferent to the shots.

3. *Walking Sit*—(10 points)—Command, "Sit!"—*("Sitz")*

The handler moves his dog straight ahead at heel from sit position. After a minimum of 10 paces the dog sits alertly at "Sit!" order while handler moves ahead without breaking stride for 30 paces more. Handler then turns and faces dog. Judge directs handler to return to his Shepherd and take his position at the dog's right side.

4. *Walking Down With Recall*—*(10 points)*—Commands, *"Down!"*— *("Platz")*—"Come!"—*("Hier")*—"Heel!"—*("Fuss")*

Handler, giving his Shepherd the mandate to "Heel!", walks straight ahead ten paces, then commands the dog to "Down!", and the dog downs quickly as the handler continues ahead for another 30 paces, then turns and faces the dog. At the judge's request the handler calls his dog ("Come!"), who returns at a rapid gait and sits directly in front of handler until given the "Heel!" instruction, which he executes.

5. *Retrieve On Flat Ground*—(10 points)—Commands, "Fetch!"—*("Bring")*—"Heel!"—*("Fuss")*—"Give!"—*("Aus")*

Sitting off lead, at the handler's request to "Fetch!" the dog quickly retrieves an object thrown about 8 paces away, brings it back and sits in front of the handler. The handler takes the object with the demand "Give!". At the "Heel!" command the dog finishes. A wooden dumbbell may be used as the thrown object.'

6. *Retrieving Over A Hurdle*—(15 points)—Commands, "Over!"—*("Hopp")* "Fetch!"—*("Bring")*—"Give!"—*("Aus")*

Hurdle is 1 meter high (39 inches), and 1.5 meters wide (59 inches)

Handler, dog at side, throws dumbbell over hurdle. At the command "Over-Fetch!", the Shepherd jumps over the hurdle without touching it, retrieves object, jumps back and brings object to handler, sitting directly in front of him. Handler takes the object with directive "Give!" The dog then takes heel position upon demand.

7. *Go Out With Down*—(10 points)—Commands, "Go out!" *("Voraus")*—"Down!" *("Platz")*—"Sit!" *("Sitz")*

The judge directs the handler to walk forward with the dog at heel off lead. Handler stops, raises arm, and gives his Shepherd the command to "Go out!". The dog trots at least 25 paces in the designated direction, then drops to the ground at order "Down!". At the judge's bidding the handler than walks to his dog taking a position at his right side and directs him to "Sit!".

8. *Down Under Distraction*—(10 points)—Commands, "Down!" *("Platz")*—"Sit!"—*("Sitz")*

The handler sits his dog at the judge's request, removes the leash, "downs" the dog and, in the dog's sight, walks 40 paces away without looking behind him, and stands with his back to the dog. Meanwhile the judge has begun obedience examination of another dog, and the downed dog must remain in that position until the other animal has completed exercises 1 through 6. Finish as in exercise 7. If the dog moves from his place in the down position prematurely all 10 points are forfeited.

Part C. Protection

Total points 100. Commands, "Go on!" *("Voran")*—"Come" *("Hier")* *Points are no longer allocted for fighting instinct. Instead the following is used: 1. (Ausgeprägt)—Pronounced, 2. (Vorhanden)—Sufficient, 3. (Ausreichend)—Insuffient.*

Scoring

Hold and Bark..............................5 points (3 and 2 points)
Attack Upon Agitator.....................................35 points
Follow And Hold (courage test)............................60 points

At a distance from the dog of about 40 paces, the agitator hides behind the blind. At the instruction "Go on!" from the handler, the dog begins to search for the agitator. Upon reaching his quarry, the dog must bark strongly but not bite. On demand of the judge the handler goes to his dog and, on leash, they leave the area.

The agitator now hides in another blind, fully 50 paces from where dog and handler enter the area. At the judge's request the handler, with his dog on lead, walks about 25 paces toward the blind, unleashing his dog who heels off lead. The agitator springs out of the blind and attacks the handler. The Shepherd immediately bites the agitator, holding him strongly. The agitator strikes the dog on his hindquarters, ribcage or withers twice with the flexible wand. Vocal encouragement by the handler is allowed. The agitator, at the judge's order, quits the attack and the dog releases the sleeve at the "Out!" command.

The handler holds the dog by the collar as the agitator runs away indulging in threatening gestures. When the agitator is approximately 50 paces away, the handler sends the dog after him. When the dog is about 30 paces away the agitator turns and runs toward the dog, shouting and threatening. When the dog hits the sleeve the agitator quits his attitude and remains still. At the command "Out!" by the handler the the dog releases the agitator. The handler then approaches and disarms the agitator and escorts him to the judge, the dog at heel on leash. If the dog ignores the "out!" demand the handler, at the judge's instruction, removes the dog from the sleeve physically.

Aggressive behavior and hard biting are indicators of courage and fighting spirit, and only particularly aggressive animals will be allowed full credit in fighting instinct (ausgeprägt)—Pronounced.

SCHUTZHUND II EXAMINATION

In this examination for Schutzhund II there are some changes to make, the exercise being more difficult. These changes follow

Part A. Tracking

The track is 400 to 500 paces long and at least 30 minutes old.

Part B. Obedience

1. Heeling on lead garners 10 points for a full score. On lead the dog and handler move ahead 50 paces and back. *Heeling Off Lead* is essentially the same as in Schutzhund I. The *Walking Sit* is given only 5 points, otherwise it mirrors the Schutzhund I exercise. *Walking Down With Recall* is the same as in Schutzhund I. *Retrieving A 1 Kilogram Dumbbell On Flat Ground*—the only difference between this exercise and the Schutzhund I performance is the weight of the dumbbell, 2 pounds 3 ounces. *Retrieving A 650 Gram Dumbbell Over A Hurdle I Meter High (39 inches) And 1.5 Meters Wide (59 inches)*. The difference here is that only 15 points are allowed for the exercise instead of 20 in Schutzhund I, and the weight of the dumbbell is different.

This next exercise is new and does not appear in the Schutzhund I.

2. Climbing Jump Over A Scaling Wall And Retrieving An Object

The wall is to be 1.8 meters high (5 feet 11 inches) and 1.3 meters broad (51 inches).

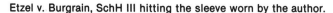

Etzel v. Burgrain, SchH III hitting the sleeve worn by the author.

(15 points) Commands, "Over!" *("Hopp")*—"Fetch!" *("Bring")*

The handler stands at a suitable distance from the scaling wall and the Shepherd sits off lead at his handler's side. Either a dumbbell or other object is thrown over the wall by the handler, who then directs his dog over the barrier with "Over-Fetch!". The dog climbs the wall, retrieves the object, climbs back and sits in front of his handler who receives the object at the "Give" order, and the dog takes the heel position on command.

3. Go Out With Down is the same as in Schutzhund I except that the dog must go out 30 paces instead of 25.

4. Down Under Distraction, is again the same as in Schutzhund I, but the dog is to remain down until the other dog the judge is examining has completed exercises 1 through 7.

Part C. Protection

1. Search—(5 points) Commands, "Go On!" *("Voran")*—"Come!" *("Hier")*

The agitator hides and the handler sends his Shepherd to search five or six blinds. The handler directs the dog vocally and with raised arm.

2. Hold And Bark—(5 and 5-10 points)

Dog barks at agitator without stopping. With directions from the judge, the handler walks to within four paces of the blind and calls the dog to him. Handler orders agitator out of blind and downs the dog three or four paces from the agitator. The handler searches agitator and then blind for any objects he may have thrown down.

3. Escape and Defense—(escape 10 points—defense 30 points)

While handler searches the blind and is out of sight, the agitator attempts to escape, and the dog intercepts him by biting solidly. When the agitator stands without movement the dog releases him. Suddenly the agitator attacks the dog, defending himself with the stick but not actually striking the dog. The Shepherd returns immediately to the attack, biting hard. If the dog bites solidly the agitator strikes him twice. The handler approaches the dog. The agitator does not give up his weapon but carries it so that the dog cannot see it.

*4. Escort—*5 points

The handler escorts the agitator for about 40 paces, following with his Shepherd about 5 paces behind agitator.

*5. Surprise Attack, Courage Test—*30 points

a. After the escort the agitator launches a surprise attack on the handler and the dog prevents it with a solid bite. The handler holds the dog by the collar as he releases the agitator. The agitator slouches away but after about 50 paces he threatens again, then runs. The dog is sent after him to prevent his escape, and when the Shepherd has covered half the distance between them, at the judge's instruction, the agitator turns and charges toward the dog, attacking him. The dog immediately bites the sleeve solidly and the agitator quits

Police dog engaged in attack work.

fighting. At the command "Out!" the dog must let go of the sleeve. If the dog does not let go at the "Out!" command the handler goes to his dog and disarms the agitator, then escorts him to the judge.

Fighting Instinct—Pronounced, sufficient, insufficient

b. Throughout the entire protection examination the judge must clearly observe the fighting instinct of the dog. Hard biting and aggressiveness toward the agitator are outward indications of fighting instinct. When the animal is hit with the stick, if he indicates sensitivity to this punishment and quits biting, he must return immediately to the attack with vigor and belligerence. Should the dog run back to the handler after the courage test or remain near the agitator without watching him closely, he will not receive a full score for fighting instinct. Only truly aggressive Shepherds will be given full points.

Note: Dogs that bite again after the "Out!", or release reluctantly in all exercises, may lose points. No passing score can be given to a dog that does not release upon command throughout the exercise.

SCHUTZHUND III EXAMINATION—Summary
Procedure and Scoring

The Schutzhund III performance must be accomplished with complete control and greater precision than Schutzhund I and II, and must be judged accordingly. I will merely list the basics since they generally follow the procedures of Schutzhund I and II, but with the changes noted in the text.

Tracking—(100 points)
From 800 to 1000 paces long, at least 50 minutes old and laid by a stranger. Three articles are used and there are four turns.

Obedience—(100 points total) (For details see Schutzhund I)

Heeling off leash . . . . 10 points
Sitting From Walk. . . . . 5 points
Running Down With Recall. . . . . 10 points
Walking Stand-Stay . . . . 5 points
Running Stand-Stay . . . . 10 points
Retrieve On Flat
   2 kilogram dumbbell (4 pounds 6 ounces). . . . . 10 points
Retrieve Over Hurdle (1 meter high—1.5 meters wide)
   (dumbbell 650 grams—1 pound 7 ounces). . . . . 15 points
Climbing Jump Over Scaling Wall (1.8 meters high—
   (5 feet 11 inches—1.3 meters wide)
   retrieve article or dumbbell . . . . 15 points
Go Out With Down. . . . . 10 points
Down With Distraction (handler out of sight). . . . . 10 points
Protection—(100 points total) (see Schutzhund II for details)
Search For Agitator. . . . . 5 points
Hold and Bark (5 points + 5 points). . . . . 10 points
Escape and Defense (escape 10, defense 25). . . . . 35 points
Escort . . . . 5 points
Attack and Courage Test (10 + 10 + 25). 45 points

There has been a growing interest in the use of the German Shepherd as a herding dog, which was the identical purpose of the breed. When the pastoral age in Germany dwindled, von Stephanitz, fearful that this would result in

Gottfried v. Kleinsteffin, C.D.X. (a son of Nox of Ruthland) and Asta v. Terryville, a German-bred dog, herding sheep ... the ancient heritage of the breed. These Shepherds are owned and were trained by Clifford Hendricks.

the gradual demise of the breed he loved, used his political influence to foster the German Shepherd as a police and army dog, and genetic selection was utilized to shape the Shepherd for these new roles. Yet, to this very day, a great many German Shepherds are used to herd the woolly flocks of the Fatherland.

Another interesting development in the breed is the growth in the United States of service dogs for the police and the armed forces. Service dogs are being trained to Schutzhund performance, but this training does not completely qualify, for Service Dog Trial rules differ to some extent from Schutzhund Trial rules. It is an area that should be explored by the Schutzhund enthusiasts, for it could prove to be fertile ground for a broadening of the Schutzhund concept.

As a vehicle for recreation Schutzhund competition has no equal. Surely this is as close to a meaningful relationship between man and dog that can be found. To own a properly trained Schutzhund Shepherd is a new adventure, a new thrill in dog ownership. Today with transgression so widely spread, with crime in the streets, evil in the night, and criminal activity everywhere growing stronger and more widespread every day, a Schutzhund dog is needed to stand between you and this abomination. There are no locks, no alarms, no chemical sprays that can keep you as safe in your home or on the streets as a Schutzhund-trained German Shepherd dog. This is not a dream or a grandiose flight of fancy; it is the simple truth. Ask the police! Ask the men of the armed forces! Ask yourself!

Some of the highest scoring man/dog teams at the First Annual Western Regional Police K-9 Trials.

The German Shepherd Dog has proved itself as a working breed, offering its services as guard dog (*above*) on an Air Force base and as sentinel dog (*facing page*) on an Army base. Guard dog Chinook is pictured with his master Technical Sergeant Donald Williams.

German Shepherd Dogs figured importantly during the 1974 Middle East crisis, as they accompanied a United Nations Emergency Task Force, in this case a Swedish Battalion, *(above and facing page)*. These Shepherds demonstrated their ability to sniff land mines during a mine training course organized by the Polish Logistic Team. Photos courtesy of the United Nations/Y. Nagata.

Chapter 16

How to Buy a German Shepherd

When you buy a German Shepherd you buy a dream—a dream that this dog will be the finest, the best behaved, the most intelligent and beautiful dog in all the world. Unhappily the dream soon fades, but as long as it doesn't turn into a nightmare you can be well satisfied. Actually, most people who own German Shepherds really do think that there isn't another dog on this planet that is quite as wonderful as their dog. And this is as it should be. Your Shepherd is an important part of your family; it guards your home, your children, your chattels and asks only for your love in return. The exchange is certainly all in your favor.

There are several things that you, as a prospective purchaser of a Shepherd, can do to help balance the scale in your favor. To begin you should study the standard and the interpretation of the standard found in this book. Read these two chapters over and over again and attempt to understand them and imprint them in your mind so that you have a clear idea of what they mean and how they delineate a living dog.

Next find out where and when dog shows (particularly Shepherd Specialties) are being held in your area, and sit at ringside and closely watch the judging and make an effort to understand why the judge selected the animal he or she did. This is not an easy chore because of the varied opinion of many judges and their interpretation of the standard. Also, attempting to select dogs from the outside of the ring precludes examination of teeth, tails, testicles, and a close comparison of the dogs entered.

But you will, hopefully, be able to find a correlation between the judge's selection and the standard you have studied. While at the show make a pest of yourself; ask questions and tuck the answers away in your memory. Observe, absorb, listen, and question. When you return home, tired but bursting with what you have learned, recall all the words that were spoken, pluck them out of your mind and parade them like a diminutive army, and examine them closely for small nuggets of truth.

Begin now to earnestly study the structure of the Shepherd. Study the drawings here in this book; first the parts of the Shepherd, then the skeletal illustration. This, the skeleton, is the basis of the physical dog. You need not remember the names of all the bones and cartilage that forms the skeleton. Just become familiar with the general structure and angulation of the various parts. Begin with the head; note that the teeth (42 in number when the dog matures) meet in a scissors bite, and check the depth of the jawbone from which the dog derives the many hundreds of pounds of pressure when it bites hard. Now examine the neck vertebrae. There are seven neck vertebrae, and all mammals have the same number, including the giraffe, mouse, pig, dog, and human being.

Study next the angulation of the shoulder bones, the flat scapula and the connecting humerus. All the bones of the Shepherd's body connect one to another in a chain of interconnected links; all except the shoulder bones. They are held in place by muscles and tendons and remain rigid except for their flexing when the dog moves. You will note the prosternum jutting ahead of the shoulders in profile. It is necessary that this be so because, though the skeleton of man and dog have many similarities, the dog lacks the scapula (collar bone) that man has, so the muscles and tendons of the front of the neck and the front of the chest connect with the prosternum. Primates, including man, possess a scapula, and so do a few other mammals that find it necessary to reach above their heads, like the Australian marsupial, the koala bear.

In the skeletal illustration see how the spine forms the withers, the back, the lumbar region and the croup, and note the slope of the pelvis that provides the shape of the croup. The sacral vertebrae, between the lumbar vertebrae and the coccygeal (bones of the tail), are fused. Now check the hindquarters, study the angulation of the bones, and note how they connect to the hip in a ball and socket joint. Here is where hip dysplasia occurs. This disease can be present only in a ball and socket joint and there is another ball and socket joint in the shoulder of the dog. Note the front legs, the pasterns and their slope, the foot bones and the hock bones behind. Rickets can affect the entire skeleton of the dog, but it is most easily seen in the front leg bones. Note how the rib cage is composed of both bone and cartilage. Now study the illustration of the musculature and visualize particularly the muscular power of the thighs from which the drive in gait originates.

It takes time to study all this and assimilate it, but when you buy a refrigerator or a car you shop around and you study the various makes. This Shepherd you are about to purchase will not be inexpensive, and it will probably last at least twelve to fifteen years, probably longer than the life of a refrigerator or a car, and it is a living creature to which you will give your love and affection and find these emotions returned to you manyfold. Therefore, you must learn as much as you can about the breed so that you narrow the margin of mistakes and find the right Shepherd to live with and love over the years.

SELECTING A PUPPY

If you are going to purchase a puppy, you must first shop around and find a reliable kennel or breeder whose integrity and reputation are impeccable, who has a depth of knowledge of the breed and consistently produces superior stock. You must decide in which direction your choice dictates; do you want a show dog, a pet, or a working dog to train for obedience or Schutzhund? Not infrequently the buyer of a puppy wants only a pet, but when the pup gets older he decides to show it or train it for Schutzhund. Only once in several thousand times does the pup bought as a pet become a show champion or a top Schutzhund competitor. It can happen, but usually only in the movies.

Show dogs and working dogs have different breeding behind them, and this genetic background dictates the role that they can best fill. But in picking a puppy you must select one that is closest to being anatomically similar to the standard of the breed. Do not be in a hurry to acquire the pup. The breeder may have a litter coming that he thinks will be exceptional and, if this is the case, wait for that litter to be born. Meanwhile, if possible, view the sire and dam of the litter from which you will select your puppy. They can give you a good idea of what faults and virtues to look for in the puppies they produce. Finally the litter has arrived, or you have found the litter from which you will select your pup, and they are old enough for you to select the one you want to take home.

How would you pick the best puppy out of the litter? You can't! You can only pick the best puppy on the day you buy him and take him home. The reason for this is puppies change from day to day, their growth pattern varying one from another. But I will tell you how to at least pick the puppy on the dramatic day when you choose it and bring it home.

First get a general impression of the pups in the litter. Are their coats glossy and healthy looking; is the skin pliable and does it stretch easily? Scrutinize the litter running and playing. Watch for the puppy that is quick and balanced and doesn't back away, and do not necessarily pick the biggest pup in the litter; many buyers have a tendency to do just that. Avoid the morose pup who doesn't engage in playtime and sits by himself. Mark the one who comes to you and frolics at your feet. You must remember that the puppies are in familiar surroundings in their own domain and in the midst of their siblings, and so show excellent temperament and confidence. Perhaps when you divorce an individual pup from the known habitat he may not act with such

A good three-month-old male Shepherd puppy.

aplomb. But, all you can do is judge his character as he exhibits it under these circumstances.

As they run and play, notice if any of the pups have a tendency to bunny hop behind when going away. Avoid that puppy; he will probably develop dysplasia. Also, if you place a puppy on its stomach in a lying down position and are able to pull its hind legs out in a "frog" position without discomfort to the pup, it is a good sign that the puppy's hip sockets are correlated correctly.

Watch for a good forward reach in front when the pup runs; it indicates sufficient shoulder angulation. By this time you have probably singled out one or two puppies that look good to you. Pick them up one by one and set them on a crate or box and stack each quietly and separately in a show stance. Look first at the pup's head. You want dark eyes, rather almond-shaped, not round, ears that are beginning to reach upward and a comparatively wide skull and strong muzzle which together form a blunt wedge. Examine the teeth. They should form a scissors bite; one cannot tell at this age whether or not there will be missing teeth when the second, mature set appears. Avoid the overshot or undershot puppy, particularly the latter, for an undershot jaw is a disqualification and you will spend the next several months opening its mouth daily and praying. Are the pup's withers high and is the back level or with a

A litter of puppies with their ears in all stages of erectness.

slight roach? Both are acceptable; the roach will settle down. Croups are difficult to gauge in young puppies. Simply make sure the croup is long enough and the tail-set is not too high. The croup will slope down and round out into the tail-set later—hopefully. A high tail-set usually signifies a short croup.

Examine the shoulders. Do they exhibit the proper ninety-degree angle? It will show in even so young a puppy. Move your hand down to the prosternum. It should jut out ahead of the shoulders. Now place your finger (index) at the top of the withers between the shoulder blades. Your finger, flat along the pup's back, will slip into a groove between both shoulder blades. It should fit rather snugly without much room on either side. Along the back examine the length of the withers, back and croup. The back should be comparatively short.

Check the position of the tail, whether it is held properly, and run your hand down it; it should be smooth with no knots or bumps. Look at the hindquarter angulation. Are the bones long and the angulation sufficient? Shoulder placement does not change to any great degree, but hind angulation does, so make certain there is plenty of angulation and a short hock. Puppies stacked in a show stance will generally sink down a bit, exhibiting more than normal angulation behind. Well angulated pups frequently exhibit cow-hocks

228

at this age. This condition usually disappears as the pup grows older.

Are the pup's feet compact, tight and high knuckled? His front legs should be heavily boned with an exaggerated knot at the bend of the pastern, and the pastern should slope forward. But the leg must be straight from the elbow to the ground.

Run your hand along the puppy's underbody; is it deep enough? It should be down to the elbow. Examine the ribbing. It must not be too wide and rounded or it will interfere with the movement of the elbow. Find the last rib with your fingers (the floating rib that is not connected to the bottom cartilage), and check from it to the front of the pup's hindquarters. This is the loin, and it should be short. Now pick the pup up and hold him in your arms with his back against your chest, close your eyes and with the fingers of one hand gently probe to find his testicles (if your choice is male). They will be the size of a pea at this age, and one may be in the scrotum and the other further up. But as long as you can locate them you are home free. Lastly free the tender underbody where the umbilical cord had emerged to be sure that there is no umbilical hernia present.

Look for a rich, red tan on the sections of the coat that are not black, and check for black toenails. A small amount of white on the chest will eventually vanish and, as the pup matures, much of the black that blankets its body will gradually disappear, leaving a black saddle and dark shadings where they should be. Of course there are black pups that remain black, and others that keep a larger amount of the black into maturity, but they are in the minority. If the puppy is a bitch, she will likely exhibit a good deal of grizzled gray over the withers and back upon maturity.

If you have found all the physical properties in place as recorded here and the temperament of the puppy to your liking, congratulations! You have found that wonder of wonders, the perfect puppy. Chances are that there will be parts of the pup that will not be absolutely as you want them. Pick the pup that comes closest to your ideal. They change as they grow and, at about seven to ten months of age, become awkward and ungainly and lead you to despair. But they recover eventually and hopefully become the Shepherd that has everything in the right places as it reaches toward maturity.

From the breeder you should receive an A.K.C. registration (or a form for the registration of the puppy) signed by the breeder; a pedigree of at least three generations; and a guarantee that the ears will come up, the testicles (if a male) will come down (if they are not already down) and that the pup will not develop hip dysplasia. This last guarantee is not a commitment that means a great deal, unless the dysplasia is severe and crippling in its effects, because by the time you can be certain through X-rays that the youngster does or does not have hip dysplasia, it is no longer a puppy and you have given it your heart and would not part with it for any reason. The breeder could, though, be inveigled into making some concession if the contract was valid.

Can. OT Ch. Lana v. Kreuzberg, UDT, Am. CD, TD and winner of the *Dog World* Award of Canine Distinction for completing all of her titles in less than six months at the age of 19½ months. This photoraph was taken when Lana just turned 6½. Pictured also is Sean McLea. Lana was trained and is owned by Liv McLea of Leeven Rob Kennels, Ontario, Canada.

Facing page: Highland Hills Victorius and Highland Hills Victory pictured at ten weeks. Owner, Elli Matlin of New York.

Remember this: no one can guarantee that an eight-week-old puppy will be a champion. All that the breeder or kennel owner can pledge is that the pup has four legs, two eyes, and is healthy—and will have no disqualifying faults.

PURCHASING A GROWN DOG

The buying of a grown dog is a much easier and safer procedure than purchasing a puppy. Again, check the breeder or kennel owner's credentials. Is he or she honest? What quality stock do they have? Have they been successful with this stock in the area in which you are interested, show or working? Check the parents of the dog you are interested in, if they are at the kennel. A grown dog is generally from sixteen months to three years of age, and everything that he is visible; there is nothing to hide, except his teeth, and these you can quickly examine. There should be 42 teeth, 20 upper and 22 in the lower jaw, and they should meet in a scissors bite. Anatomists use a simple formula to indicate the arrangement of the teeth. In the chart the horizontal line is the division between upper and lower jaw. Begin with the incisors in the front of the mouth

$$I \ \frac{3+3}{3+3} \ +C \ \frac{1+1}{1+1} \ +P \ \frac{4+4}{4+4} \ +M \ \frac{2+2}{3+3} \ 42 \ \text{TEETH}$$

The letter I designates the incisors, C indicates the canine teeth, the premolars are labelled P, and the molars M.

Run your hand down the tail to check for any unseen deformity. Watch the dog gait. Movement is important in a German Shepherd; it should be smooth with good reach in front and strong drive behind. Coming toward you the elbows should not be loose unless the dog is fairly young. Going away the hocks should be parallel to each other and firm. The back should be strong, without bounce or sway during gaiting.

Though the mature Shepherd should not wear his heart on his sleeve, he should be approachable and outgoing, and never shy or cringing, or overly aggressive. An older dog should be housebroken, trained to collar and leash and have at least some basic training. His coat should be glossy, his eyes bright, and his nose cold. He should present a picture of vigorous health.

The breeder should supply you with a registration certificate (A.K.C.), signed by the breeder so that you can transfer registry to your name, at least a three generation pedigree, and a guarantee that the animal is not dysplastic, is fertile, and has no anomalies or diseases of which he is aware. If the dog is over two years of age he should have an O.F.A. certificate relevant to the condition of his hips.

Often older dogs can be purchased from a show kennel that has kept the animal as a show prospect but, though still a handsome Shepherd, it has not fulfilled the promise of its puppyhood and could not take top honors and make its championship. You could supply a happy home and a lot of love to such a fine animal.

BUYING AN IMPORT

The German import is not as easily bought as an American-bred. You must have contacts in Germany, or know someone who does. If you have a link with any German breeders you must be able to trust in their honesty and integrity in accurately describing the animals they have for sale. You will, of course, not buy a puppy; the expense of shipping is prohibitive and you will have no way of knowing what the pup will be when mature, or if the hips will be correct or dysplastic. You will want to purchase a grown dog between the ages of about sixteen months and two and a half to three years of age. You should be aware of the fact that German dogs do not mature as early as American-breds, and it will take from three to three and a half years for them to reach full maturity.

You will want a copy of the pedigree of the dog and to be told the color of the papers (a pink pedigree indicates a qualified breeding). You should be advised by the seller as to the dog's hip condition; "a" normal is completely normal, "a" fast normal means near normal, and you must not accept any lesser classification, and preferably only the "a" normal category should be acceptable. The younger animal (about sixteen months or slightly older) should have a Schutzhund I degree and an AD (Ausdauerprufung-endurance test). An older dog should have Schutzhund II or Schutzhund III and should have a Körklasse I rating, and all these records should be sent to you with the dog.

You will want a couple of good photographs of the dog, or a film showing him standing, gaiting, and working. Be warned though: photos and films are not as accurate as viewing the animal in the flesh. But under the circumstances it is the best you can do. Any placings in shows should be sent to you, and ask for an accounting of any faults the dog may have, particularly in teeth, tail and temperament, which cannot be seen in a photo. Character, temperament, and intelligence are particularly important. If the dog is to be used in Schutzhund his score should be high "S.G's," just below a "V," or a "V," with a full count for courage and fighting instinct. Most all German dogs are fully house, car, kennel, and child trained.

If it is a bitch that you are importing two years old or over, find out if she has been bred before, how many whelps she had, and their quality. If she is coming in season shortly, have the owner keep her and breed her to a fine German stud dog before shipping her. If the breeding takes, as it likely will, and she whelps her litter here, her cost will almost be covered by the sale of

the puppies and you will be off to a flying start with an imported bitch that you obtained for practically nothing.

Any dog shipped from Germany must go through customs here, and it should be insured for the full price you paid for it. Attached to the crate you will find an envelope with all the dog's papers, including the pedigree, Kör report, Schutzhund booklet, AD report, and health booklet, which contains a complete medical history of the dog. When the dog arrives, remove the crate to an enclosed area in case the animal gets loose. Speak to the dog quietly and with a friendly lilt to your voice; then open the door just enough to get your hand inside and clip the leash to the dog's collar, open the door wide and take your new acquisition for a walk before you take it home. Remember, it has been in the crate a long time and needs to relieve itself. I have imported a host of German dogs into the United States for friends of mine, over the years, and I have yet to find one, even Schutzhund III dogs, who did not walk out of the crate like a lamb, without one bit of trouble.

After you arrive home with your new import do not attempt to work him immediately. He will not acknowledge you as his master, or your home as his. Pet him a lot, talk to him, feed him well and take him for long walks. After about two or three weeks he will suddenly alert and bark at someone coming to your door. That is the signal you have been waiting for; he has accepted your home as his and is protecting it. Now you can begin working him using German commands. He is your dog, he has accepted you as his master, and it is the beginning of a wonderful companionship.

I have always found that it is best to purchase a grown dog. You can see exactly what you are getting and do not have to go through the anxiety periods of housebreaking, teething, and basic training. Any training that is necessary is absorbed much more rapidly by the older dog. But it is your choice. I must admit that a puppy can pull at the heartstrings and make even a Scrooge smile and discover the devastating emotion of pure puppy love. Puppy, grown dog, or import—you are the master of your fate. Whichever you choose, let it be all you want it to be, all you wished for.

Assi v. Gropeln *(facing page, above)* by Olden v. Asterplatz, SchH II ex Landa v. Gropeln, SchH I. Photograph was taken at sixteen months. Assi is half sister to the 1972 Siegerin. Xandra v. Uesener Werk *(facing page, below)* by Res. Sieger Nick v. Dreimarkenstein, SchH III ex Yaffa v. Uesener Werk, SchH I. This lovely, fleet-gaited daughter of a famous show dog and sire is half sister to the 1971 Siegerin. Assi and Xandra were imported and are owned by the author.

Chapter 17

Feeding

Your German Shepherd's diet is correlated with the structure of his alimentary system. He has an uncomplicated stomach and a short intestine, and there is a high degree of reciprocation between the sense organs of the canine and its mode of feeding. Your Shepherd, due to its macrosomatic olfactory system, can smell separately every food element in the pan you place before it at feeding time. The olfactory nerve bundles (there are 608 nerve bundles) carry signals to the olfactory lobe which is situated in the canine's brain. There, in the brain, food and other odors are recognized and interpreted.

The domestic dog *(Canis familiaris)* is closely related to the wolf and jackal through a common ancestor, and it has an elongated jaw like them, bearing forty-two teeth. In front of the carnassials there are flattened molars, indicating that the canine is not completely carnivorous, and neither are his close relatives the wolf and jackal. Consider the feeding methods of those feral hunters of the family Canidae. They chase, run down and kill their prey, then lap the blood that pours from the wounds of their victim. They then rip open the belly and devour the contents of the stomach, which is partly digested vegetation; they consume the heart, kidneys, liver, lungs, spleen, and the intestines wrapped in fat. They chew the connective tissue, the fatty meat, crush and suck the marrow from the bones, and then devour the muscle meat. The predator licks his bloody muzzle, grunts in satisfaction, and trots away through the sun to a stream of cold, rushing, burbling water where he drinks his fill.

During the process of devouring his prey the wild canine has consumed proteins, carbohydrates, fats, minerals, vitamins, fatty acids, roughage, and, from the sun and the water he drank, he absorbed more vitamins and minerals.

My dictionary defines the word "nutrition" as: "The act or process of nourishing or being nourished. Food; nutriment." And nutriment is interpreted as "Any matter that, taken into a living organism, serves to sustain it in its existence, promoting growth, replacing loss, and providing energy."

So the wild canine has absorbed its nutriments and, in so doing, has ingested a well-rounded meal that "sustains it in its existence." Of course we cannot readily supply game for our Shepherds, but we do not have to. So retire your gun and your hunting cap and drive to the nearest supermarket, pet shop or feed store, and you can purchase there a wide variety of manufactured and cleverly blended dog foods that will supply all the nutrients necessary for your Shepherd's well-being and good health. Complete dietary elements for your dog are:

BASIC FOODS

Proteins are found in meat, dairy products, eggs, soybeans. *Fats* are incorporated in butter, cream, oils, fatty meat,milk, suet. *Carbohydrates* are in cereals, vegetables, confectionary syrups, honey. These three essentials form the basic nutritional needs of your Shepherd, and all three are necessary and complement each other. Proteins, composed of amino acids which differ with the various proteins, build flesh and body tissue. The protein in your Shepherd's diet is best derived from a combination of animal and vegetable protein. Fats produce energy through heat, which allows your animal to store that energy until it is needed. Approximately 95 percent of most ingested fats are digested by the dog. They supply taste appeal to foods and produce twice as much energy as an equal amount of proteins and carbohydrates do. Carbohydrates furnish fuel or growth and energy. The fatty acid contents of most cereals is highly unsaturated, so some cereals and grains are a fine source of fatty acids. The fibrous material stimulates intestinal action and helps maintain a healthy digestive tract. Carbohydrates provide an inexpensive source of calories.

The cell activity regulators of the life process are the vitamins and minerals that your dog must have. They fall into two broad categories; one group includes the water-soluble vitamins and the other the fat-soluble vitamins.

a. Vitamin A: found in greens, peas, beans, asparagus, eggs, milk.

b .Thiamine: in vegetables, legumes, grains, organ and muscle meats, milk, eggs, yeast.

c. Riboflavin: green leaves, milk, liver, egg yolk, yeast, beef, chicken, wheat germ, whole grains.

d. Niacin: incorporated in milk, lean meats, liver, yeast.

e. Vitamin D: fish that contains oil (salmon, sardine, herring, cod), fish liver oils, eggs, fortified milk.

f. Ascorbic Acid: tomatoes, citrus fruit, raw cabbage. Not necessary for dogs.

g. Iron, Calcium, Phosphorus: milk and milk products, vegetables, eggs, blood, liver, oatmeal, bone marrow, soybeans.

Zinc is now known to be a necessary part of your dog's diet. It guards against skin diseases and furnishes your dog with a luxuriant coat.

TYPES OF DOG FOOD

There is a great diversity of *dry dog foods* to be found today, practically all of them good and nourishing. Compare the labels and you will find that they vary very little in the percentages of nutritional food values. The difference in the brands is generally in the basic materials from which the proteins, fats, carbohydrates, vitamins and minerals have been derived. Try offering the various dry foods to your dog to see which of them he thrives on best.

In the realm of *canned foods* there is also an exceedingly wide choice, but from the standpoint of nourishment it would take a great deal more canned food per pound of dog to nourish him completely than it does through the use of dry dog foods. The label generally states that "Water sufficient for processing" is a part of the ingredients and, upon examining the water content we generally find "Moisture (Max) 78%." We also find "Crude Protein (Min) 8.00%, Crude Fat (Min) 1.50%, and Crude Fiber (Max) 1.50%."

Compare these ingredients with that of a dry dog food which usually promises Crude Protein, 27%; Fat, 10%; and Moisture only 12%. It does not take a genius to appreciate the advantage the dry food has in comparison to the canned food. It is a great deal cheaper to feed dry food and inexpensive water than to pay for 78% water in the canned food, and much less protein and fat. I would recommend the addition of 10% more fat to the diet than is processed in dry food. If a greater proportion of fat were projected into the dry food during manufacturing, it could produce rancidity. It is good for the coat. And it helps the dog retain his food longer, thereby giving more nourishment and creating heat that produces the energy for exercise, which your Shepherd needs to keep in excellent condition.

Canned Foods are fine to feed if you are traveling with your dog in a car or van, though biscuits, lean meat, and not much water is even better. Both diets produce much less general voiding because the residue from such a diet is negligible. Both are lacking in nutritional values and are not regimens one would pursue for more than a few days. Canned foods are often used to give taste to a dry food diet.

Biscuits do not have the nutritional ingredients that a complete dry dog food possesses, mainly because the vitamin and mineral content has been partially destroyed by baking. They also contain too much flour, a necessary agent to retain their shape. Biscuits are an excellent tidbit and also aid in keeping the teeth free of tartar and the gums healthy, but they should not be considered as an actual diet.

Once you have found a good dry food that produces all the nourishment and the food essentials that your Shepherd needs to keep him in good condition with a glowing coat, clear eyes, a good stool and *joie de vivre*, stay with it. Such foods are the result of generation tests in kennels where the larger dry dog food manufacturers scientifically examine the efficacy of their foods under controlled conditions.

It must be remembered, however, that in these controlled tests smaller breeds that are easy to keep and easy eaters are used. They are generally Beagles. A Beagle will reach his full size at six months of age, while a larger dog, such as our Shepherd, needs from fourteen months to over two years to reach full size and maturity. It is therefore generally necessary to supply supplements to the diet of a Shepherd. To accomplish this we can add meat and fat and vitamins.

FOOD SUPPLEMENTS

As previously mentioned, fat should be supplied in its pure form. Kidney fat is best for this purpose; it is white and crumbles easily to mix readily with the dry food. Also liquid fats from cooking can be supplied. Pure fat supplies the fat soluble vitamins E, K, A, and D, and lessens the amount of dry dog food necessary for each meal.

Ratio is important to your animal's diet. The food pan must not only contain all the nutritional essentials but it must also combine those essentials in the proper proportions to supply a *balanced diet*. This means you must not supply more supplements than good basic foodstuffs. Do not go on the assumption that if a little bit of supplement is good a lot will be that much better. This is a false philosophy and will do your Shepherd no good. Supply only what supplements are necessary. Consult with your veterinarian if you are in doubt.

Puppies certainly need more nutritional values, and so do pregnant bitches, than the ordinary house dog. There are special puppy foods that contain more calcium for bone growth and vitamins A, D and K. Pregnant bitches can be fed their regular food but with the cautious addition of calcium phosphate and the vitamins A, D, and K.

Again I must caution you to use discretion in adding supplements to the diet. For instance, cod liver oil, if given in excess, can cause bone malformation and toxicity. Toxic reactions can be caused by the addition of too much chemical calcium and phosphate. Milk is recommended in the diet to produce the calcium needed, and has other additional nutritive compensations. If excessive phosphorus is offered in the diet the result can be metabolic bone disease with a susceptibility, due to hyperphosphatemia, to fractures, bone brittleness, and a reduction of below-normal blood calcium. Wolves, jackals and coyotes in zoos, when fed only muscle-meat diets, exhibited excessive

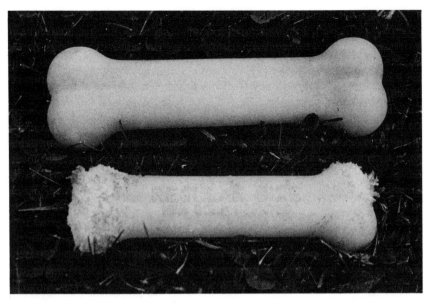

Nylabones® help remove tartar from your Shepherd's teeth and can be purchased in pet shops everywhere.

bone resorption. If you have a very heavy Shepherd puppy who is quite down in pasterns, half a teaspoonful of pure cod liver oil a day can prove beneficial. When the condition is relieved discontinue the treatment.

Soft rib bones can be fed to your grown Shepherd—not for their nutritive value but because they help to remove tartar when your dog's teeth pierce them, in the same way that biscuits keep the teeth clean. Do not feed any other kind of bones to your dog, and especially not chicken bones, which can splinter into sharp shards that can injure the gums, intestines, throat lining, and the anus. The safest "bones" are Nylabones® , bone-shaped nylon pieces that serve as toothbrushes for dogs.

WATER

Water should be supplied lavishly to your Shepherd. Your dog's body is composed of approximately 70 percent water distributed throughout the tissues and organs of the body, so the importance of this principal dietary necessity is easily grasped. Water acts as an inner body solvent, supplies vital minerals, flushes the system and aids in regulating the dog's temperature. Dehydration, a serious condition, will result if the dog is kept from water for an appreciable length of time. Water is the least expensive element in your dog's diet, so be a bit lavish with it.

240

THE RIGHT AMOUNT OF FOOD

The food requirements for your Shepherd can vary with its lifestyle. If it is a show dog and exercised to keep in perfect show shape, it will require more food than a house dog who indulges in very little activity. An old dog slows down considerably and does not need too much food or he will become obese. Dogs that are being trained in obedience, and especially Shepherds that are being instructed in the intricacies of Schutzhund work, need relatively plentiful meals. A dog kept in an outdoor kennel during a northern winter needs more caloric intake than an animal basking in Florida's sun and living indoors. A nervous, very active young dog needs more food to complement his frenetic mode of life than does a phlegmatic, underactive older dog. It is better to keep your Shepherd slighly underweight than overweight. He must appear, at all times, to be ready for work or play.

FEEDING THE PUPPY

Puppies should be weaned when they are about five weeks of age or less, the latter particularly if the litter is large or the pups are not doing well on the bitch, and she does not seem to have enough milk. If this occurs, the puppies should be given supplementary feedings, or weaned completely. You can generally begin to wean German Shepherd puppies when they are approximately four weeks of age and not encounter any nutritional problems. They should be weaned on evaporated milk with about one-third cow's milk, and with the addition of an egg yolk and albumin to make the mixture more comparable to bitch's milk. Goat's milk is also excellent, again with the egg yolk additive. Or your veterinarian can recommend any one of the effective dried milk products used as replacements for bitch's milk.

To any of these mixes, after several days, add finely ground meat and about five percent (of total feeding) fat and, after a few more days, add a good manufactured dry puppy food, which is far superior to Pablum or human cereals. Remember always, when comparing dog food to human food, that a human takes eighteen years to reach maturity and a dog takes only one year or a bit more, and human foods are geared to that ratio of growth. The texture of the mixture should be similar to a sloppy gruel. When weaning serve the mixture (the early milk blend) in a shallow pan and dip the pup's chin into it, being careful not to allow the mix to reach the puppy's nostrils. Once he is eating with gusto, add the meat, fat, and puppy food as advised. Feed a minimum of four times a day, and up to six times a day if the pup has been weaned early, and feed it *warm*.

If you are the breeder of the litter and the bitch dies or dries up almost immediately after whelping, use a puppy nurser or a doll's bottle and a soft nipple to feed the milk mixture. Or you can feed through a stomach tube. With the tube it takes a lot less time to feed a litter. Use a number 8 to 10 French catheter, measure it from mouth to stomach (on the outside of the pup) and mark it. Moisten the catheter and pass it over the puppy's tongue and slowly into the throat and the pup will begin to swallow it. When you reach the mark you made, allow it to go no further down. Attach a syringe (without needle) filled with the milk mix, and squirt it down the tube. When the full amount is gone, remove the catheter. Feed about 10 to 12 cc. By judging the size of the fed puppy's stomach you will know how much to feed. After feeding massage the puppy gently under the tail and on the stomach with a piece of wet cotton to stimulate defecation and urination.

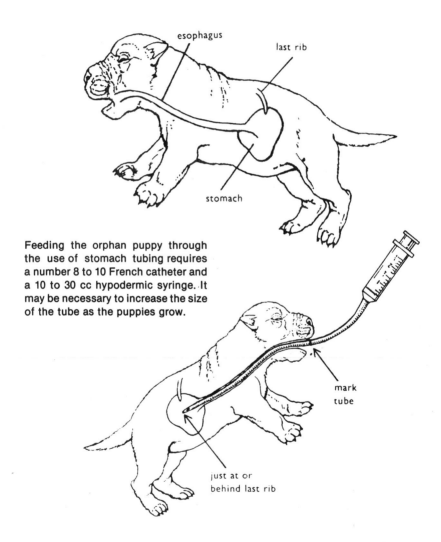

esophagus

last rib

stomach

Feeding the orphan puppy through the use of stomach tubing requires a number 8 to 10 French catheter and a 10 to 30 cc hypodermic syringe. It may be necessary to increase the size of the tube as the puppies grow.

mark tube

just at or behind last rib

Rickets may develop in a Shepherd pup suffering from a dietary deficiency, particularly from a lack of vitamin D and calcium, and phosphorus.

E.H.H.

When a litter is from two-and-a-half to three months old the mother will frequently regurgitate her stomach contents of partially digested food for her puppies to eat. She is beginning the process of weaning the litter and it is, for her, an instinctive and very natural performance. If you have begun supplementary feeding of the litter, the weaning attempt by the bitch will seldom occur. Do not add lime water, glucose, or dextrose to the weaning formula, or you will be modifying it in the wrong direction. A puppy is not a child. You must modify the food to simulate bitch's milk, not cow's or human milk. A bitch's milk is comparatively acidic; it is rich in ash and protein and contains far more fat and less sugar and water than cow or human milk. Lime water neutralizes stomach acidity, a condition which is necessary for the puppy so it can assimilate fat, and 70 percent of the pup's energy is derived from fat.

While you are feeding and handling the puppies check their navels every day. Sometimes the scraping of their soft little bellies on a rough surface can cause infection. This can be avoided by supplying them with layers of soft cloth or hay in the nest box. The eyes of the pups will open in about ten days, and their nails should be trimmed so that they cannot cause damage to their littermates' eyes when playing. If the pups are born with dewclaws on the hind legs, cut them off with a pair of manicure scissors when the pups are two days old. These need not be bandaged; the bitch will lick and heal them. When the pups are three to three and a half weeks old have your veterinarian check their stool for worms and, if they are infested, worm them immediately.

The pause that refreshes. Katie Pastorius and her Shepherd pal, Macho. Water should be made available at all times, especially when travelling on a hot, humid day, for it helps your Shepherd regulate its body temperature.

As the puppy grows, the food should become thicker and less watery. Allow the pups to nurse on the bitch as much as possible until it is time to dry her completely. The number of feedings can be increased as the pups feed less and less on the bitch. At six weeks the pups should be completely weaned and fed five times daily. These feedings should continue until the youngsters are three months of age. Then begin four feedings a day, up to five months, and switch from complete puppy meal to half puppy meal and half dry, high protein grown dog food. Keep using the milk and add some extra calcium and vitamin A and D.

From five months to eight months, three feedings are enough with a possible bonus of a dog biscuit in the morning. From eight to eighteen months, two meals a day are sufficient and the dog can be switched entirely to the mature dog's high protein dog food. Keep using the fresh or canned meat, ⅓ of a can mixed into the total feed (about three scoops of dry food), milk or water, fat and calcium with vitamin D.

FEEDING THE GROWN DOG

For the fully grown dog a good high protein dry dog food should be the basis of the meal. Add a complete vitamin supplement made for dogs and including vitamins A, D, and B-complex. Add about 10 percent extra fat and increase to 15 percent in winter if the dog lives in the snow belt, and particularly if he is kenneled outside. Do not give him more than 20 percent fat or it may cause nausea. To this mixture add about ⅓ of a can of meat or the equivalent in fresh meat. Serve at body temperature, mixed well, and supply one feeding a day. If your Shepherd does better on two smaller meals a day, by all means cater to his whim. Perhaps a dog biscuit and a little warm milk for breakfast, and the full dinner later on in the·day will better satisfy him.

Do not rule out table scraps. Most writers of books on the care of dogs advise never to feed table scraps. I think they add flavor and variety to the feeding hour. Just be certain you do not base the entire meal on table scraps; they scarcely make for a balanced diet.

I realize that most breeders and owners feed their dogs a diet that has done well for them and that they prefer. The diets delineated here are suggestions that I know dogs thrive on, but they must not be considered an adamant dictum. If you feed a diet that suits you and your dogs, stick with it.

We, the human animal, have made a fetish and a ritual of our food ingestion. We don't eat, we "dine," and many of us "dine" so well that we become obese and eventually suffer for our habit. We suffer metabolic disorders, digestive upsets, high cholesterol, and proudly name ourselves "gourmets." We also have the distinctive habit of projecting our methods of eating to our pets, and quite frequently those pets also suffer from the effects of overeating. Please do not foist this food philosophy upon your helpless pet. Feed your Shepherd enough to keep him healthy and in excellent condition, and no more or less.

Next to breeding correctly, feeding correctly takes precedence over any other concern relative to your dog. Your Shepherd's breeding may be superlative, a monument to the breeder's art, knowledge of genetics and selection within a strain's sphere. But he will never attain the promise of his heritage without full and correct nourishment, especially through the adolescent stage of his growth.

Chapter 18

General Husbandry

Your German Shepherd is a typical predacious mammal. It is a warm-blooded, four-footed vertebrate, wearing a hairy and comparatively thick skin, and though far removed physically from such other mammals as whales and elephants, your Shepherd has in common with them two distinguishing attributes of all mammals—body hair and milk-secreting glands.

The only mammal we are really interested in is the German Shepherd dog, and we must cater to its predator's appetite, care for its mammalian hair, give mental exercise to its well-developed mammalian brain, and provide the proper care for its mammalian young, once they have been weaned from their mother's mammalian milk.

We who own dogs have acquired dependents, for they are without freedom to forage, to drink from streams, to sleep in caves or under trees. Our dogs are, in fact, prisoners of our society, just as you and I are prisoners of our environment. We must care for our Shepherds, feed and water them, house them, and keep them clean and groomed, and not allow them to roam, for their own protection. Actually where could they forage, these predators of ours? Where could they find wild food? If they could find game, it would probably be poisoned. The stream they would drink from, were they free, would undoubtedly be polluted, and instead of a damp cave we supply them with a dry and cozy place to sleep. We keep them close, so they will not be maimed or killed by the frenetic traffic that flings noisy, metallic swarms along our highways.

So we create this bargain between ourselves and our dogs: we will care for you and tend you, and what will you give in return? The dog wags its tail and looks up at us, and in its eyes is all the love, the idolatry that can pour out of one living creature to another. Not a bad bargain, is it?

If you have a kennel of several or many dogs, good husbandry will pay off in dollars and cents. When the dogs and the kennels are clean and free from parasites, the health of the dogs will improve and your veterinarian bills and nursing time will be substantially reduced. Good feeding practices and proper exercise will keep your animals in top shape and better able to resist disease.

Cleanliness applies to the dog's environment as well as to the dog itself. Feeding utensils used in the process of feeding and watering must be kept clean. Plastic becomes soiled and cracks, and porcelain chips. Aluminum or stainless steel are the best materials for your feeding and watering utensils, and are washed easily. Feed your dog in the same place and at the same time, and in a quiet atmosphere, and never coax him to eat. Leave the food pan down no more than half an hour and, if he hasn't eaten by then, retrieve the pan and do not attempt to feed him again until the next meal time. If his appetite continues to be poor and you cannot put weight on his frame, consult your veterinarian. Never, but never, force feed your dog. This is a practice to be used with boa constrictors, not dogs. It is better to starve your Shepherd until he begins to eat than to force feed him. If he is a healthy, intelligent animal he will soon realize that if he wants to indulge his appetite he had best eat when you put down his food pan.

If you are feeding a kennel of dogs, furnish the filled food pans as you go down the line of kennels. By the time you are finished you can go back to the first run and begin picking up the empty pans, clean them and then stack them, ready for the next meal. If you have more than one dog to a run, keep watching them as you feed to make sure that one of the dogs is not driving the other from its food pan and gulping down most of the other dog's meal also.

Alway supply lots of fresh, clean water for your charges, and especially in hot weather. Rinse out the water pails frequently. Most water leaves a mineral residue in the pail and this should be removed. Always be sure to provide water within an hour after feeding.

Generally speaking, dogs kept in outdoor kennels are thriftier than house dogs. The outdoor dog will have regular shedding periods, living in a more natural environment, and its new coat comes in hard and strong. The house dog lives in circumstances that are falsely modified, with air-conditioning or fans in the summer and artificial heat in the winter. Because of this habitation pampering he is much more susceptible to changes in temperature and never quite obtains a hard, non-shedding coat. Don't baby your Shepherd. He is a tough working dog; don't make him into a canine hypochondriac.

GROOMING YOUR SHEPHERD

You should groom your Shepherd every day, if it is only to run a brush through his coat to remove dust and dandruff. Actually, grooming can become a delightful time of communication between you. Have him stand in an easy show pose and first comb him with a dog grooming comb. Be careful not to irritate the skin or pull out hair that has not come loose. You can use a wire grooming glove after the combing and finish off with a brush. During the height of the shedding season you might use a coarse-toothed hacksaw blade to remove the wealth of dead, loose hair that is constantly present.

Good grooming eliminates dead hair, dust, and skin scales and eliminates the necessity of frequent bathing, which may dry the coat. You may wish to spray onto his coat any of the dry skin products that can be bought from your veterinarian or pet shop. A good vitamin supplement, provided orally every day, that incorporates a generous amount of unsaturated fatty acids is very beneficial for the dog's coat. It is a good time also to spray on and brush in a flea spray, followed by the use of a flea comb.

You should inspect your dog for incipient skin disease during the grooming and perhaps catch any such pests in their early stages. Also investigate your dog's ears, teeth, and toenails. You could find many annoyances that could grow into health hazards.

BATHING YOUR SHEPHERD

Any time your Shepherd becomes dirty and you think it necessary to bathe him, feel free to do so—as long as you do not feel free to do so too often. Make certain you rinse him well and dry him off thoroughly afterwards. The skin of your dog differs from yours, so the soaps and shampoos you use should not be used for your dog. There are germicidal soaps, and liquid soaps designed for use on dogs available at pet shops that can be used.

Be sure to work the soap deeply into the coat to get through the undercoat to the skin. Occasionally it is good practice to give your dog a medicinal dip after his bath, but be sure to rinse the dip off thoroughly. You may use an emollient shampoo, or a tar-based cleansing agent and deodorant shampoo. If your Shepherd's skin is inclined to be dry use a canine shampoo made especially for this condition. Ask your local pet shop owner for assistance.

Be careful, when you are lathering your Shepherd, not to get soap in his eyes, and after he is dried walk him in the sun. You can also find canine soap that requires no rinsing, canned prepared lathers, and dry shampoos, all available at pet shops. If you have entered your Shepherd in a show, remember it will take a few days after bathing for the natural oils to return to his coat and skin, and until they do his coat will lack "body."

If you do not wish to give your dog a full bath but feel that he needs cleaning, swish some mild dishwashing detergent in a pail of warm water, dip a towel in it until it is soaking wet, then drape the towel like a horse blanket over your dog. Rub the moisture into your dog's coat from behind his ears to his hindquarters and tail and down his legs. Rinse the towel in fresh water and repeat the process, wiping away the first liquid application. It may be necessary to repeat this last procedure several times to rinse out all the soapy water. Dry the dog thoroughly, groom him and then walk him in the sun. If the weather is warm, or you live in a tropical or semi-tropical climate, you might consider utilizing an airline crate as a drying cage.

If your Shepherd has trod in tar that you find ordinary soap and water will not remove, try kerosene. But it must be removed quickly with soap and water or it might irritate the skin. Turpentine must also be removed with alacrity, but is recommended for the removal of oil-based paints. Check the labels of any paints, varnishes, enamels, and such preparations to determine what the thinning agent may be, for this is generally what must be used to remove them from your Shepherd's coat.

Should your dog come in contact with a skunk, pour several cans of tomato juice over his coat, rub it in well, then wash it out. If tomato juice is not readily available, use hot water and soap. Whichever you use, the trick is to walk him in the sun afterwards, for hot sun will help to dissipate the odor.

FLIES ON EARS

Several species of flies and small gnats chew on the upright ears of your Shepherd during the summer months, causing your dog much discomfort. Their bites cause scabs to form, sometimes baldness in the area, and even infection. One of the many insecticides used to eliminate flies or flying insects should be rubbed or sprayed on the dog's ears. Be certain not to spray the insecticide in the animal's eyes.

TOENAILS

You must keep your Shepherd's nails cut short or you risk lameness from foot ailments, spread toes, and hare feet. Some dogs can automatically keep their toenails short by walking on cement, but most of our dogs need nail care. Use a guillotine nail cutter, or any cutter designed to trim a large dog's nails.

It is necessary to cut off the dead, horny end of the nail. Be careful that you do not nick the vein that runs through the part of the nail that is alive. To avoid this, hold a flashlight under the nail and you will be able to discern the vein. If you do clip the vein keep the dog quiet; some dogs bleed profusely for quite some time. Use a styptic pencil (aluminum sulphate, used to stop bleeding after shaving) to stop the flow of blood.

After you have cut the nails use a file, one made specifically for dogs, or a coarse file that can be procured in any hardware store, and smooth the nails off, filing downward to round them. Do not attempt to file a nail that has bled for twenty-four hours. If you find it impossible to clip your dog's nails, take him to your veterinarian and have him sedate your Shepherd and cut the nails well back. Thereafter you may be able to cut them yourself without being afraid of cutting into the vein.

BEDDING

You can purchase attractive dog beds, 36 inches in diameter, that are pillow soft. The outer casing can be zipped off and washed; the inside bag is filled with shredded poly foam or a piece of carpet of the right size. Both are excellent for the Shepherd that sleeps in the house.

For the outdoors dog, shredded red cedar makes an excellent bedding material and will control fleas. Alfalfa, oat, rye, wheat straw, or pine shavings are all good bedding material for a dog house. In winter supply enough of this material for the dog to burrow into and keep warm. Before you put it into the house, sprinkle some flea powder on the floor of the house. Each time the bedding is changed use flea powder.

Change outdoor bedding about once a month, except in muddy, rainy, or snowy weather when it must be changed more frequently. Old bedding must be burned or it may become a breeding place for parasites.

CARE OF TEETH

Tartar can form on your dog's teeth just as it can on yours. Examine your Shepherd's teeth once a month and check for broken teeth, infected gums and tartar buildup. It will take only a few minutes for this observation and can save your dog a great deal of mouth trouble. When your dog's mouth is well cared for his breath will be sweeter. You may purchase a dental tool that will scrape the tartar from your dog's teeth or you can allow your veterinarian to do this. A hard biscuit in the morning and an occasional soft rib bone will help to keep tartar from forming. Nylabones, recommended by many as the best all-around therapeutic chewing devices made for dogs, are available at all well stocked petstores. They are long-lasting and very effective. A mouth examination is particularly important when your Shepherd has passed his prime. Abscessed teeth and gum disease can affect the general health of your dog.

EAR AND EYE CARE

Inspect your Shepherd's ears every two weeks, and examine them immediately if you observe him shaking his head, holding his head to one side with his ears held unevenly, or scratching at his ears. All these symptoms signify some kind of ear infection or infestation from ear mites, ticks, or ear canker, and he should be taken to your veterinarian for diagnosis and treatment.

When you inspect his ears, clean them gently with baby oil or vegetable oil on a cotton swab to dissolve dirt and wax. Smell his ears if he has been fussing at them. Ear mites and canker have a distinctly odious smell that you will be able to recognize. Your veterinarian can recommend a product for the removal of necrotic tissue and debris from the dog's ears. If you should suspect by the appearance of the ears, or your dog's actions, that something is wrong, call the vet immediately.

You will seldom need to give your Shepherd's eyes any special care. When you groom him wipe any matter away with cotton moistened in warm water. If your dog has developed a definite eye problem he should be seen by your veterinarian.

A RUN FOR YOUR DOG

Every dog should have a run of his own to keep him outdoors and protect him from disturbance by other animals and children. When he is in his run he is also safe from traffic and he cannot stray or be stolen. If possible, build your run around a tree for shade from the hot summer sun; a piece of canvas or plywood over a portion of the top of the run can serve the same purpose.

Within reason your run can be as large as possible; twenty feet or more long for one or two dogs. If you are building one or several runs, remember that the length is much more important than the width. The surface of your run is limited only in texture to the amount of money you care to spend, and the extent of the labor you wish to expend in doing it. You can use a gravel, dirt, grass, rock, or a packed-down fine cinder run, the latter much in favor in German kennels. German breeders claim this type of surface provides good drainage and is excellent for the animal's feet, keeping them compact and high-knuckled. Undoubtedly, if kept on a soft surface that turns to mud when it rains, your dog's feet will have a tendency to spread. But the tightness of a dog's feet is generally governed by its genetic heritage, not by the composition of the surface of its run.

All the surfaces mentioned make admirable breeding surfaces for parasites—worms, lice, fleas and ticks—and are almost impossible to thoroughly clean except with a blowtorch. Cement is a better surface, but even cement is porous enough to harbor parasitic eggs, and can be kept clean only through daily disinfectant scrubbing and periodic scorching of the surface.

Besides parasitic infestation, gravel, grass, and rock make the removal of stools a problem. Cement can be hosed down, but none of these surfaces are the ultimate answer. There *is* a surface that gives you better control over parasites. It is a cement run with about four inches of builder's sand packed on top of the cement. Your dog generally defecates in a rather confined area in his run, and his stools can be scooped up and carried away and new sand shoveled into the places where the sand and stool have been removed. Do not rake the stools together or you will spread worm eggs, if they are present, over a larger area. Remove the stools one by one, deposit them in a container and empty the container in a previously prepared hole away from the run. Immediately cover this over with dirt. A liquid disinfectant can be applied to the run surfaces about every 10 days, and periodically all the sand can be removed, the cement scorched, and a new sand covering applied.

I have for years used a pebbled run. First all grass is removed, leaving just the basic ground cover; then about six inches of pebbles or small rocks are

CEDAR POST RUN CORNER

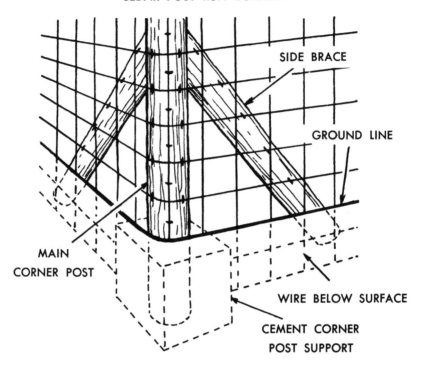

SIDE BRACE

GROUND LINE

MAIN
CORNER POST

WIRE BELOW SURFACE

CEMENT CORNER
POST SUPPORT

Posts set in cement offer good support when constructing a run for your Shepherd. Side braces help keep the fence material taut.

scattered evenly over the surface. Stools disappear as they are hosed down through the pebbles with a strong stream of water. Once a month rock salt is scattered over the whole surface and hosed down. And every ten days the whole surface is sprayed with a strong solution of liquid Sevin. Where I live in Florida we have a constant battle with fleas, and every few years with ticks. To win that battle, or even to win an occasional skirmish, I must keep the dog and his environment constantly defleaed and clean or hang out the white flag of surrender. His environment also includes our home, where he drops flea eggs that hatch and inevitably bite my wife. She seems to have an affinity for fleas.

There is a soil-cement run that you can lay down yourself. It is frequently used for runways at small, executive airports that do not allow heavy carriers to land. It is an inexpensive surface that can serve you well. Remove all the sod in the run area, then loosen and pulverize the soil to a depth of about four inches. On this surface of dirt spread dry cement, three-quarters of a sack to a square yard of surface, and mix it in well with the soil. Water the surface with a hose adjusted to a mist-spray. Now rake it down deeply to assure uniform moisture and level it with the rake. Immediately even it down with a tamper and then a garden roller. This must be done within half an hour or the surface will begin to harden. Mist-spray again, then cover with damp sawdust. In a week you can sweep off the sawdust and your run surface will be ready to use. Make sure you slope it slightly for rain runoff.

Heavy chain-link with metal supporting posts set in cement is the finest of fencing but such fencing is quite expensive, and you can substitute with hog wire, fox wire, fourteen gauge, or two-inch mesh heavy poultry wire and wooden posts. A mature Shepherd can easily scale a fence that is less than six feet high, though I must confess that I have never experienced any trouble training my dogs (in about two days) not to attempt to jump over a four-foot high fenced-in enclosure.

Stretch a string from one corner post to the other to keep the sides straight and the run corners square, and dig post holes deep enough to hold the posts securely. Leave approximately six feet between post holes, and paint with creosote each portion of the posts that will be in the ground. Plant the posts and pour cement and small rocks into the post hole and around the base of the posts to secure the base. Use side braces on the posts and rent wire stretchers to pull taut the fencing from post to post. Set double posts around the door section and frame it across the top. Use strong hinges and two slide bolts, one at the top and the other at the bottom of the door.

YOUR SHEPHERD'S DOG HOUSE

Your Shepherd's outdoor house need not be an elaborate structure. It should be substantial and fit his needs as well as yours. It should be built so that it will be easy to clean and change the bedding. The sleeping quarters should be three feet by five feet, and it should be about three feet high at the highest point. It should have a front porch two feet deep and the width of the house, with a roof over it to cast shade, while the porch itself allows your dog an outside place to lie.

Build the house very close to where you plan to put it, because it will be quite heavy when it is finished. Build the two side pieces first. The skeleton framework throughout should be of two by threes. Remember to allow six inches on the uprights for floor elevation. The porch size should be incorporated in the two side pieces. Build the other sections, framing them with two by threes, and cover them with tongue and groove siding or one half to five eighths exterior plywood. Allow the framework to show on the outside and you will have a smooth inside. Frame inside with two by threes on which to place the floor of the house. Frame the door section between the porch and the sleeping quarters, making it eighteen inches wide and two feet high, leav-

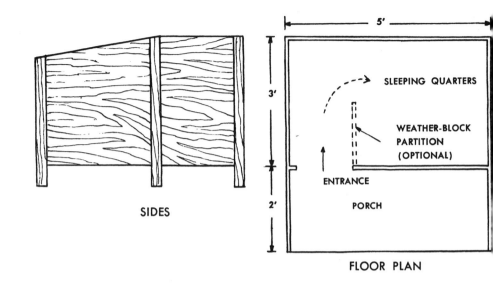

SIDES

FLOOR PLAN

- 5'
- 3'
- 2'

SLEEPING QUARTERS

WEATHER-BLOCK PARTITION (OPTIONAL)

ENTRANCE

PORCH

FINISHED HOUSE

A well-constructed dog house should be large enough for your Shepherd to lie down in, sturdily built, and easy to clean. The front porch allows your Shepherd to lie outside in the fresh air and in indirect sunlight.

ing space at the bottom of the door for a bottom lip about five inches high to keep the bedding inside from spilling out. For the roof of the sleeping quarters (which will be cut and built separately from the porch roof) leave an overlay of four inches on the back and two sides. Hinge this section on a cross two by three so that it can swing upward from the back for easy inside cleaning. Cover the entire roof with heavy tar paper. Paint the house; when it dries, nail a length of inner tube along and covering the edge where the hinged sleeping-quarters roof meets the porch roof to prevent leakage of water into the sleeping quarters

If you live where inclement weather brings blustering winter cold you can make the sleeping quarters of this house cozy through the installation of insulating board all around, and building a double floor with insulating paper between the floors; then erect the suggested weather-block partition. Hang a piece of carpet over the door to completely cover it, which will fall back in place as the dog goes in or out. Supply plenty of bedding for him to burrow in and his own body heat will keep his sleeping quarters warm and snug.

Situate the house at the narrow end of the run close to the door, so when you approach to tend to him he will not have to track through his excreta. Attempt to situate the house with its back to the west and side to the north. This will supply protection from the coldest point in winter and bring shade to the porch in summer. The size of house advocated here will be large enough for two Shepherds, particularly if the weather-block partition is eliminated.

THE LAW AND YOUR SHEPHERD

I think it is in the realm of good husbandry to protect your Shepherd as best you can should any overt act, engaged in by your dog, result in a court case. The United States is in the grip of a security hysteria, nurtured by sky-rocketing crime statistics and the need of the populace to protect themselves, their homes and chattels, from criminal assault.

When your home is broken into and valuable property is stolen there is, besides the monetary worth of the stolen goods, a sense of violation, a deeply ingrained feeling that you have been touched by something unwholesome and shocking. I know! My daughter's home was so invaded, even though she owns a Shepherd that is an excellent watchdog. But because he was shedding she had left him in his run while she went shopping. Whoever were the perpetrators of this crime were evidently watching the house closely and saw her put the dog in the run and drive away. As soon as she had departed the premises they drove in, broke the glass on the front door, unlocked and quickly removed all the stereo equipment, radios, television sets and jewelry and drove away while the dog undoubtedly barked like mad but, the neighborhood being sparsely settled, no one heard his protestations. The thought of an unknown someone watching, lurking, waiting for the right time to invade your home gives one the creeps.

We need to educate the public about our breed: the Shepherd that is trained in protection dog work, like Bora v. Athonhof, SchH I, Mex. TD, TT shown working with J. McKinney, can be the perfect companion dog and gentle with children. Bora is owned by Christine Schulz and Jackie Athon and was trained by C. Schulz and Ron Athon.

The fear of becoming the victim of thugs or morally defective psychos has inspired many people to buy large dogs, such as German Shepherds and Dobes. There are also many organizations and training kennels that specialize in supplying businesses with trained canine protectors and also "fence dogs," which are generally psychological deterrents but can become physical hindrances to criminal activity if the circumstances demand it.

What is your position and that of your dog in reference to the law under certain pertinent circumstances? At one time the common law divided animals into two distinct categories: domestic and wild. The dog came under the heading of a domestic animal, and its owner was not liable for damages unless those damages resulted from willful carelessness or negligence on the part of the owner. This is no longer necessarily true, as the trend has been to modify the common law through the enactment of regulations that make the dog owner strictly liable to anyone injured as a result of actions performed by the owner's dog.

Under the common law a plaintiff generally had to prove that the owner committed an act of negligence and had to establish that the dog was inclined to attack, that its owner was aware of this propensity and that despite the owner's knowledge of this propensity he did nothing to properly restrain his animal.

Even under the common law dogs kept as watchdogs or trained in Schutzhund work can, in many jurisdictions, no longer be considered domestic animals. Therefore many courts admit evidence of a dog's training to determine whether it can be considered dangerous. Under these circumstances, should you exhibit a sign reading "Bad Dog," "Watch Dog," or "Protection-trained Dog" you are undeniably admitting that the dog is dangerous.

A frequently cited case is *Carlisle verus Cassassa,* decided quite some time ago (1931), but a popular and oft-cited verdict to this day. Both judges and lawyers accept it as authoritative, which is an example of the crass imbecility of the conveyers of the law. The concept in this case concerned the fact that German Shepherd dogs should be considered wild animals and not domestic animals. The stupidity of the whole edifice of this landmark case can be interpreted by the court record which states that the dog in question was: "What is known as a police dog . . . a cross between a collie and a wolf." The judge, in sentencing, stated: "It is a matter of common knowledge that police dogs are, by nature, vicious, inheriting the wild and untamed characteristics of their wolf ancestors." For that moronic statement the judge should have been given psychological counsel.

The same case was cited any number of times. I know that in 1962 a verdict was handed down against a dog owner based on the 1931 decision, and again in 1972 *Carlisle versus Cassassa* reared its ugly head in a courtroom in New York, in the case of *Kelly versus Hitzig.* Again and again court cases have resulted in the same idiotic judgments against owners of so-called "German police dogs," because ill-informed judges render judgments based upon ridiculous misinformation. What is needed is expert testimony in such cases, to reverse the prejudices and half truths that hamper judges, and that produces their blatant lack of canine knowledge in general, and of German Shepherd dogs in particular.

As owners of German Shepherds we must take every opportunity to display the inherent good behavior of our Shepherds and their fitness to be a part of the community. We must also be certain our Shepherds are always under control and, by good example, attempt to illustrate how ridiculous are the statements and concepts of some of our judicial peers.

The law is subject to change from time to time and from place to place, so to be on the safe side of things you should check out the legalities involved in the situation.

Chapter 19

Care of the Stud Dog and Brood Bitch

The womb is where all life begins. It is the commencement, the ultimate, the portal from which the journey on earth originates; and it is the female of the species who bears the womb. Why, then, do we lavish so much attention upon the male of the species, in this case the stud German Shepherd dog? We study with intensity the male lines of descent and pay costly (and sometimes overpriced) stud fees for the male of our choice. Why is the male so important?

I have mentioned this in a previous chapter, but it bears repeating. The answer to why the male is so important is based on simple mathematics. The bitch comes in season twice a year and, if you breed her at every season (which you shouldn't), she will produce approximately ten to twelve puppies a year, or perhaps a few more. Let's say she produces twenty pups a year. In the same length of time a popular stud dog can be bred from sixty to one hundred times a year; the latter figure assumes that the dog is used twice a week, which is not exorbitant for a top champion in excellent health. The stud therefore has the opportunity of producing from six hundred to over a thousand puppies a year. Compare this yearly output with that of the bitch and you can easily grasp why the stud is much more important to the breed as a whole. The influence he wields over the gene pool of the breed is profound and almost incalculable in comparison to the influence of the bitch.

Rittmeister von Stephanitz, realizing even in that early time the importance of a knowledge of genetics, wrote in 1930: "Modern breeding research has taught us that it is not so much the appearance of an animal that indicates its breeding values, but rather the hereditary picture, which means the sum total of the qualities and characteristics that it has inherited from its ancestors." His evident grasp of essentials relative to the breed he loved was never more apparent than in this statement.

THE STUD DOG

Stud dogs can be used frequently, the number of times over a given period varying, like other aptitudes, with the individual dog. I can cite the fabulous stud records of many breeds of dogs like the great Cocker Spaniel Red Brucie, who at age thirteen was bred to seven bitches in one week. It is probably only coincidence that he died at the end of the week . . . smiling. All the bitches produced fine litters. In Shepherds, Grim v.d. Farmuhle was siring large litters at thirteen years of age and Pfeffer v. Bern was kept constantly busy at stud. Certainly a healthy and vigorous stud dog who takes his work seriously and performs quickly can be bred two or three times a week without harm to himself . . . or his owner's bank account, considering the stud fees asked.

Unfortunately it is a fact that sometimes the great champion is overshadowed in the breeding pen by his lesser known sibling who has fewer opportunities with top bitches than his illustrious brother. The reason for this is that the champion, an above average animal, sires many puppies that are average, because all extremes tend to breed toward the norm whether those extremes are good or bad. With few exceptions, if you were to check the number of excellent young produced by the top champion from excellent bitches against the total number of the puppies he has sired during any given period of time, you would find the really excellent youngsters to be very few. The brother of the champion could presumably be a better producer because he has inherited, but does not exhibit them visibly, the happy combination of genetic traits, dominant and recessive, that made his brother a famous champion, and passes them on to his get.

The care of a stud dog follows the same pattern outlined in the chapters on feeding and general husbandry. He needs a balanced diet, clean quarters, plenty of exercise, and a lot of affection. He must, because of his impact on the breed, be genetically as sound as possible and must be free of congenital diseases such as hip dysplasia, cataracts, retinal atrophy, and hypothyroidism. If three of four bitches that have been bred to him have failed to conceive, your veterinarian should make a sperm count. The stud should also be tested for *Brucella canis* twice yearly.

The stud dog should be outgoing and a bold and "macho" individual, but he must not be at all vicious. He should have been exposed to much socialization with both humans and dogs and should not have been removed from his dam and littermates until eight weeks of age. This way he can learn canine social behavior, which is so vital to normal reproduction later.

The stud dog should accept the owner's manipulation of his sexual organs during the act of copulation, for it is necessary if the bitch is too small, too large, or too reluctant, to sometimes aid the male in this endeavor. I advocate using the young male at twelve to fifteen months of age once with an older,

Nick v. Dreimarkenstein, SchH III *(above)* by Lido v. d. Wienerau, SchH III ex Dixie v. d. Wienerau, SchH II. By a famous sire, Nick himself is a proven stud. Ora v. Uesener Werk, SchH I *(below)* by Quanto v. d. Wienerau, SchH III ex Yana v. Uesener Werk, SchH I. A very typey bitch of great breeding potential.

wise and quiet bitch in full season who has been bred several times before, so that he can accomplish the act of copulation easily and without complications. After this breeding allow him to practice celibacy until he reaches maturity. It is not particularly wise to breed him until he is two years old and has been given a clean bill of health on his hips by the O.F.A. It is said that male dogs indicate maturity by the lifting of their leg when they urinate.

Before he is bred, feed the stud dog only a very light meal, for the excitement of breeding may cause him to vomit, a procedure not generally relished by the bitch. If the bitch seems reluctant to breed and snaps at the male, she should be muzzled and held securely for the mount. An experienced stud dog will often know if the bitch is ready to be bred or not ready and will not attempt to breed her if she is too early, too late, or has gone past estrus. If the bitch is a virgin and the stud has difficulty breeding her, she should be examined by a veterinarian to establish if there is some physical reason why the mating cannot be consummated.

If the libido of the stud is low, have him examined (a blood profile) for thyroid function. If, for any other reason, he seems unable to breed he should be examined by your veterinarian. The scrotum should be scrutinized, the penis protruded and checked, and the prostate gland manipulated. A count of his sperm should be made and examined for motility, foreign material, color, volume, number of sperm, and morphology.

Be sure to keep a complete record of all stud services; the bitch bred, her owners, the time of breeding, and the results of the breeding. A pedigree of the bitch should also be included so you can assess which bloodlines he produces with best.

Most carnivorous animals share the same organs and means of reproduction. The testicles of the German Shepherd produce spermatozoa and a small amount of semen fluid. The rest of the ejaculation's fluid is provided by the prostate gland. Besides the production of spermatozoa, the testes also secrete testosterone, the male hormone which controls secondary sexual characteristics and stimulates sexual drive. Spermatogenesis, occurring in the testes, results in cell division. The most important division is the formation of the secondary spermatocyte when the number of chromosomes (78) is reduced to half (39). When this reduced number unites with the female egg (also carrying half the chromatic number, 39), the embryo inherits a full count of 78 chromosomes, half from the sire and half from the dam.

The stud's penis consists of two muscles and the urethra. When the muscles become congested with blood they cause an erection. The *os penis* is a bone at the base of the penis that is combined with the *glans penis,* the large erectile tissue that forms the bulb that locks the animals in the "tie" position during copulation. The prostate gland is positioned at the beginning of the urethra and surrounds the neck of the bladder. When there is a dysfunction of the prostate urination becomes difficult.

The use of frozen canine semen has finally been smiled upon by the American Kennel Club. Frozen semen has been utilized by cattle breeders since 1950. Over twenty million calves in the United States are the result of pregnancy through the use of frozen semen. It is the only way that the breeding potential of valuable studs can be extended, semen transported easily, and better testing of progeny can be accomplished. Canine semen has been frozen and stored for as long as twelve years with no lowering of the sperm motility. The effect of frozen semen usage on the control of the genetic qualities of our dogs can be enormous.

Never forget that the genetic qualities of your stud dog are more important than his physical type. He is the container, the vessel of his heritage, and his fecundity can leave a lasting impression on the breed.

THE BROOD BITCH

If the stud dog is important because of the great number of get he can stamp with his phenotype, the bitch is even of greater importance to the breeder because of the precious few puppies she produces each year. Every breeding is extremely significant, and great deliberation must be brought to bear upon the selection of the best stud dog for her coming litter. She is the mother, the vehicle of life, and because of this she is precious beyond measure.

Like the male, the bitch's reproductive machinery is the same as that of the majority of mammals. She possesses two ovaries, two oviducts, two uterine horns that merge together, a cervix that separates the vagina from the uterus, a vagina, clitoris, and vulva. Two important functions are performed by the ovaries; they produce, mature, and release the eggs, and they fabricate hormones. They also manufacture, under the influence of follicle-stimulating hormones (FSH), and the luteinizing hormone (LH), the hormones estrogen and progesterone. LH directs progesterone to be produced by the ovary and to cause ovulation. When the LH peaks, the beginning of the standing heat period begins, and the bitch ovulates about three days following this peak, or the acceptance of the stud dog.

When your bitch is approaching her period of heat, and before the breeding takes place, deliver a sample of her stool to your veterinarian and have it examined for worms. These intestinal parasites must be eliminated, for worm larvae carried by the bitch can cross the placenta and infest the puppies. This can result in sickly puppies that will never fulfill their heritage.

The swelling and softness of the vulva indicates that she will accept the stud in about a week. You can remove a good deal of guesswork from your breeding plans by allowing your veterinarian to take a vaginal smear and examine it under a microscope. He can tell approximately what stage of the cycle the bitch is in and when she will ovulate. If she has previously had small litters he can also administer drugs that will aid in producing more ova.

Normal Bitch Mating Cycle

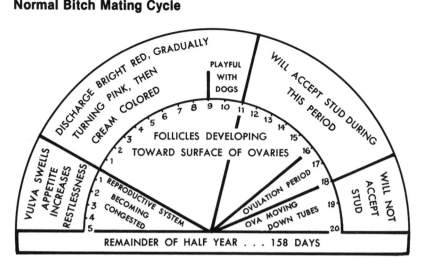

The bitch should be bred the first day that she will stand for the male, which should be about the tenth to twelfth day after she began to evidence a bloody discharge. She should be bred every other day for a total of three breedings. The vulva will be less swollen and her discharge will have changed from red to a pale straw color when she is ready to breed. She will lift her tail and arch her back. This period of acceptance lasts from five to nine days, after which she will no longer accept the stud. She should whelp approximately sixty days after the first mating.

Do not allow any male near her until you are absolutely certain the mating cycle is over and her time of acceptance past. I have known of one or more bitches who were bred to selected males at great expense (shipping and fees) before the bitch ovulated, and the stud's sperm remained viable within her. Then, somehow or other, a second male got to her and bred her and the sperm of both males mixed and a split litter was birthed, sired by the two males. It could happen that one of the males was not of the same breed. It is small, humorous incidents of this kind that cause earnest and dedicated breeders to commit hari-kari!

Metestrus follows estrus and is approximately two months in length. If the bitch is pregnant there will be activity in the uterus that will appear on the thirtieth day; but if she is not pregnant she will probably go through a false pregnancy that will continue into the thirty-sixth to fortieth day, or until the time of parturition (when she would normally whelp.).When the bitch has been pregnant for twenty-five to twenty-eight days after the first breeding, she can be palpated abdominally to ascertain if the breeding took and she is carrying a litter.

Fertilization

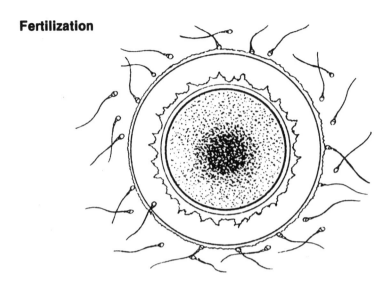

An egg, a special giant cell which the female ovaries produce, is being assaulted by sperm which are attempting to pierce the outer layer of the cell. The dark nucleus is the seat of the chromosomes, of which only half the required number are present. The first sperm to enter and reach the nucleus will bring with it the other necessary chromosomes for a normal cell number.

The bitch should be fed well and exercised daily while she is carrying a litter. During the last five weeks of pregnancy her maintenance ration should be increased twenty-five to thirty percent, and she should be fed three times a day. Her rectal temperature will drop to below 100° about twenty-four hours before parturition. You know then that she is about to whelp.

WHELPING

A few days before she is due to whelp your bitch should be introduced to the whelping box, and the long hair around her nipples should be cut. On the day she is due you should have ready towels, scissors (to cut the umbilical cord and dewclaws of the pups), an antiseptic and a bitch's milk substitute. On the day she is due to whelp she will begin with uterine contractions and soon will begin to whelp her litter. Incidentally, this will probably occur in the middle of the night. Never, but never, have I had a bitch whelp at a reasonable hour.

It is not necessary to attempt to be sterile; the pups are born surrounded by bacteria, some benign and others not, but they are born equipped to cope.

The bitch during the time of whelping must be kept quiet and protected against any disturbance. The puppies, one by one, will move down the birth

Perpetual Whelping Chart

	1	2	3	4	5	6	7	8	9	10	11	12	13	14	15	16	17	18	19	20	21	22	23	24	25	26	27	28	29	30	31
Bred—Jan.	1	2	3	4	5	6	7	8	9	10	11	12	13	14	15	16	17	18	19	20	21	22	23	24	25	26	27	28	29	30	31
Due—March	5	6	7	8	9	10	11	12	13	14	15	16	17	18	19	20	21	22	23	24	25	26	27	28	29	30	31	Apr 1	Apr 2	Apr 3	Apr 4
Bred—Feb.	1	2	3	4	5	6	7	8	9	10	11	12	13	14	15	16	17	18	19	20	21	22	23	24	25	26	27	28			
Due—April	5	6	7	8	9	10	11	12	13	14	15	16	17	18	19	20	21	22	23	24	25	26	27	28	29	30	May 1	May 2			
Bred—Mar.	1	2	3	4	5	6	7	8	9	10	11	12	13	14	15	16	17	18	19	20	21	22	23	24	25	26	27	28	29	30	31
Due—May	3	4	5	6	7	8	9	10	11	12	13	14	15	16	17	18	19	20	21	22	23	24	25	26	27	28	29	30	31	Jun 1	Jun 2
Bred—Apr.	1	2	3	4	5	6	7	8	9	10	11	12	13	14	15	16	17	18	19	20	21	22	23	24	25	26	27	28	29	30	
Due—June	3	4	5	6	7	8	9	10	11	12	13	14	15	16	17	18	19	20	21	22	23	24	25	26	27	28	29	30	Jul 1	Jul 2	
Bred—May	1	2	3	4	5	6	7	8	9	10	11	12	13	14	15	16	17	18	19	20	21	22	23	24	25	26	27	28	29	30	31
Due—July	3	4	5	6	7	8	9	10	11	12	13	14	15	16	17	18	19	20	21	22	23	24	25	26	27	28	29	30	31	Aug 1	Aug 2
Bred—June	1	2	3	4	5	6	7	8	9	10	11	12	13	14	15	16	17	18	19	20	21	22	23	24	25	26	27	28	29	30	
Due—August	3	4	5	6	7	8	9	10	11	12	13	14	15	16	17	18	19	20	21	22	23	24	25	26	27	28	29	30	31	Sep 1	
Bred—July	1	2	3	4	5	6	7	8	9	10	11	12	13	14	15	16	17	18	19	20	21	22	23	24	25	26	27	28	29	30	31
Due—September	2	3	4	5	6	7	8	9	10	11	12	13	14	15	16	17	18	19	20	21	22	23	24	25	26	27	28	29	30	Oct 1	Oct 2
Bred—Aug.	1	2	3	4	5	6	7	8	9	10	11	12	13	14	15	16	17	18	19	20	21	22	23	24	25	26	27	28	29	30	31
Due—October	3	4	5	6	7	8	9	10	11	12	13	14	15	16	17	18	19	20	21	22	23	24	25	26	27	28	29	30	31	Nov 1	Nov 2
Bred—Sept.	1	2	3	4	5	6	7	8	9	10	11	12	13	14	15	16	17	18	19	20	21	22	23	24	25	26	27	28	29	30	
Due—November	3	4	5	6	7	8	9	10	11	12	13	14	15	16	17	18	19	20	21	22	23	24	25	26	27	28	29	30	Dec 1	Dec 2	
Bred—Oct.	1	2	3	4	5	6	7	8	9	10	11	12	13	14	15	16	17	18	19	20	21	22	23	24	25	26	27	28	29	30	31
Due—December	3	4	5	6	7	8	9	10	11	12	13	14	15	16	17	18	19	20	21	22	23	24	25	26	27	28	29	30	31	Jan 1	Jan 2
Bred—Nov.	1	2	3	4	5	6	7	8	9	10	11	12	13	14	15	16	17	18	19	20	21	22	23	24	25	26	27	28	29	30	
Due—January	3	4	5	6	7	8	9	10	11	12	13	14	15	16	17	18	19	20	21	22	23	24	25	26	27	28	29	30	31	Feb 1	
Bred—Dec.	1	2	3	4	5	6	7	8	9	10	11	12	13	14	15	16	17	18	19	20	21	22	23	24	25	26	27	28	29	30	31
Due—February	2	3	4	5	6	7	8	9	10	11	12	13	14	15	16	17	18	19	20	21	22	23	24	25	26	27	28	Mar 1	Mar 2	Mar 3	Mar 4

canal, one-half to one hour between births, and will present themselves in an embryonic sac (unless the sac is torn during birth). If the bitch chews open the sac and cleans the puppy as soon as it is born, do not interfere. The placenta (afterbirth) should be left attached to the pup until its blood has drained into the baby and the bitch bites the cord off. You can remove the placenta or allow the bitch to eat it. I prefer to remove it and keep it in a pail until the litter has been completely whelped. I can then count the placentas to be certain that none have been retained within the bitch. About forty percent of the pups will have breeched (feet first) births.

If the bitch ignores the puppies as each is born you will have to peel off the sac, clean the pup's head, face and mouth and, holding it in a towel, rub its body briskly to start respiration and dry it at the same time. If the umbilical cord breaks and the placenta is retained within the bitch, it will probably be pushed out with the birth of the next puppy; if it isn't, the bitch should be given an injection of oxytocin. There is no way to definitely tell when the bitch has quit whelping, but any straining over a prolonged period indicates that she has not completed uterine evacuation.

As each puppy is born, cleaned and dried and is mewling and moving, put it on the mother's teats and see that it begins suckling. Make certain it is warm in the nest and all the pups are nursing during the first twenty-four hours after whelping. If the pups are reasonably quiet, nursing and sleeping, they are well and filled with milk. If they cry a good deal and are restless, they are not doing well and are probably not being fed enough and you will have to begin supplementary feeding. If it is at all possible try to find a foster mother for half the litter. German Shepherds generally have large litters, and a foster mother can be worth her weight in gold.

The whelps should open their eyes a slit ten days after the normal date of birth. By the next day the eyes should be almost completely open. Bitches past their prime generally have a shorter breeding cycle, and must therefore be bred sooner than young bitches.

And so the miracle of birth has happened. After all the days of waiting it has come to pass, and in the whelping box the little bull-necked, mostly black whelps suckle and grunt, cry a bit and crawl blindly to reach for their dam's mammary glands to fill their bellies with protective and life-giving milk. What will they be like when they mature? That is up to you, to the sum of breed and genetic knowledge you have brought to the breeding and to the nourishment you will provide for their growth as they open their eyes, as they are weaned and as they toddle on sturdy legs to the food pan. It is time now to arrange with your veterinarian for the vaccines they must have to fight disease and keep them healthy and strong; and hey . . . lots of luck!

Chapter 20

Diseases and First Aid

This will necessarily be a rather long chapter, but I hope not a tedious one. It is a chapter for reference, to find out what is wrong when your Shepherd becomes ill and what to do about it. The subject, as I am sure you are aware, would need at least one or two volumes for complete coverage, but all I have is a chapter in which to cram all that I possibly can about canine medicine and disease, and particularly that which affects our German Shepherd dogs. I am not a veterinarian, so it was necessary for me to find guidance and aid in the elements pertinent to this chapter. This help was supplied to me by my son, Allan H. Hart, B.V.Sc., and for the knowledge he lent me . . . "Thanks, Doc."

VACCINATIONS AND IMMUNITY

The skin of your Shepherd is its initial barrier against disease entering its body. Yet it is rather a strange paradox that your veterinarian must pierce your dog's skin with injections to protect him against the most pernicious diseases.

But before injections to protect himself against illness, your Shepherd produces antibodies which are anti-disease units that protect his body against antigens, foreign proteins that cause a variety of physical ailments. Cells are also capable of creating immunity by blocking antigens from entering the Shepherd's body. The amount of immunity your dog can develop from antigen invasion depends upon its hereditary ability and the capacity of the antigens to contest immunity. You must remember this: *immunity of any kind does not, ever, last a lifetime.*

Your puppy is born with some immunities, but he must be shielded before these immunities fade and leave him unprotected. It is at this time that your veterinarian dramatically steps in and vaccinates your Shepherd against these destructive diseases: distemper, hepatitis, parvo, leptospirosis, and rabies. Combined injections for some of these dread diseases may be given by your veterinarian. Only live virus vaccines are available for distemper inoculations. Potency in all available vaccines is excellent, and the stable cell line used by most pharmaceutical companies allows for better vaccine control.

Distemper (Carre's Disease) is the most important ailment from which your dog needs protection. It still destroys and cripples more than fifty percent of all puppies (all breeds and mixed breeds, not just Shepherds). The virus is spread by a dozen different means and the disease affects all areas of the dog including the brain. Diarrhea, vomiting, pus discharge from the nose and eyes, muscle tremors, convulsions, collapse of the hindquarters are all symptoms, and death is not far behind.

Hepatitis (Rubarth's Disease) closely mimics distemper in its effects. The virus attacks the liver cells and causes mucous membrane congestion, corneal opacity, swelling around the head, and jaundice.

Hepatitis vaccines are live. There are two types: an older vaccine that has been in production for over twenty years, and the Adenovirus type 2. The advantage of using the Adenovirus vaccine is that it produces less reaction and protects against a variety of respiratory viruses that may interact in kennel cough.

Leptospirosis (Weill's or Stuttgart's Disease). There are two kinds of leptospirosis that affect dogs, *Leptospirosis canicola* and *Leptospirosis icterohermorrhagiae,* and the mode of transference is through urine. Rats are the prevalent carriers of this bacterial disease. The spirochete attacks the kidneys and liver, but the disease is also present in the intestinal tract, pleura and peritoneum. The dog exhibits depression, the coat is dry, the temperature elevated, the gums and mucous membranes may become jaundiced, and vomiting is common.

Both types of leptospirosis are controlled by the vaccine, but the protection may be limited. Depending upon the animal's ability to utilize the vaccine the protection may last from six months to a year. It is the least dependable of the vaccines and sometimes causes allergic reaction. For this reason, if an area is relatively free of the disease, some veterinarians have dropped it from their program. Leptospirosis can leave permanent kidney damage that can be instrumental in shortening your dog's lifespan.

Rabies (also called hydrophobia) is a viral disease that affects the brain of all mammals including man. Death, in a dreadful form, is the end result once the symptoms of the illness have begun. To control the disease vaccination is absolutely essential. The virus is present in the afflicted animal's saliva and enters the body of the victim through any wound, then travels through the nerves to the brain. Bats are a reservoir of infection, but the virus can be carried by any mammal.

The affected mammal exhibits a change in its behavior patterns; there is an excess of saliva and the victim quits eating and drinking and seeks quiet, dark places to rest. There is increased urination and, after a few days, the animal enters either the paralytic or furious phase. In the paralytic form the head muscles become paralyzed, the jaw hangs open, and paralysis continues to increase leading to death. In the furious form the animal becomes a "mad dog," is aggressive and attacks moving objects, exhibiting absolutely no fear of anything. Incoordination and convulsions lead to the extinction of life.

Rabies inoculation is usually given after your Shepherd is six months of age. The live vaccines protect for greater lengths of time than do the killed vaccines. Protecting your dog also protects you and your neighbors from this dread disease.

Parvovirus. At this time the vaccine and the methods of use are still in a suspended state and could very well change by the time this book is published. Most authorities agree that the modified live canine parvo vaccine is the most protective and allows the highest immunity for the longest period of time. There is some evidence that early vaccination, if given with distemper vaccine, may lower the puppy's ability to build full distemper antibodies at *that* time. It is therefore recommended that the initial vaccine be given at a separate site or on a different day. Subsequent combined vaccines are recommended.

Canine parvovirus is an extremely contagious disease that is thought to have developed from a mutant strain of feline distemper. It attacks mainly the intestinal tract and results in a high fever, loss of appetite, lethargic appearance, bloody diarrhea, and vomiting. It strikes with great rapidity and young puppies, most vulnerable to this dread virus, can be lively and seemingly well, and dead two hours later.

One part of chlorine bleach to twenty-five parts of water is effective in eliminating the virus in runs, on shoes, etc. A friend of mine in Germany, Josef Wassermann (recently deceased) of the famous Zollgrenzschutz-Haus Kennels, lost fifteen valuable dogs and puppies in one week to parvo. It was at the beginning of the spread of this virus and in Germany they had no medicine and were helpless to prevent the malady from sweeping through kennels like a devastating storm.

Parainfluenza. The purpose of the vaccination for this disease is to make negative a virus which is the most virulent in the disease complex—"kennel cough." The vaccine will reduce the effects of the clinical disease but does not completely eliminate it. Veterinarians consider the vaccine clinically unsuccessful because it has changed the whole clinical picture. Vaccinated animals exhibit a much milder malady, are more easily treated, and are more responsive to treatment.

Bordetella Bronchiseptica vaccine is a bacterial vaccine utilized to fight against another of the bacteria that is involved in the kennel cough syndrome. It can cause reactions both local and general, and is therefore not generally used. It can be utilized as an intranasal application for puppies three to four weeks of age that are housed in kennels having an indemic problem.

Measles Vaccine is derived from human measles virus and works on the cross-immunity principle. Measles virus and distemper virus are "look-alikes," and the antibodies give cross-protection. It is best used on young pups when natural antibodies might block the effectiveness of distemper vaccine. Since the puppies' dam has no maternal antibodies against measles, this vaccine is not affected. It is used before the pups are eight weeks old so that the bitch puppies will not build permanent antibodies that would affect the measles vaccine used in the next generation. It is said that "Antibody memory is poor before eight weeks of age." The immunity produced is not quite as strong or protective as normal distemper vaccine, and its use should be limited to the five-to-seven-week-old puppy. It should not be depended upon to aid the puppy past nine weeks of age.

Vaccine failures are due to:

1. Spoilage—due to improper storage, heat, and the use of out-of-date vaccine.

2. The dog is infected with disease before vaccination.

3. Passive antibody interference from either serum or the dam renders the vaccine ineffective.

4. The use of chemicals to sterilize the syringe or the site of vaccination on the skin can kill live vaccines. Only disposable or heat sterilized syringes to be used.

5. Inability of the patient (the dog) inherently to utilize vaccine immunity.

In general vaccine principles remain unchanged. Puppies become susceptible to disease as soon as maternal antibodies disappear. The time varies with each litter. If the premises are free of disease it is best to begin with a measles vaccine and parvo at five weeks of age. Vaccines can then be continued as often as every two weeks to four weeks, until sixteen weeks of age, when all maternal antibodies cease.

A typical program using the following symbols—Measles (M), Hepatitis (H), Parainfluenza (P), Distemper (D), Parvo (at a second site at five weeks) would be:

D.H.M.P.—Parvo	....	5 weeks
D.H.L.P. —Parvo	....	8 weeks
D.H.P.　—Parvo	....	12 weeks
D.H.L.P. —Parvo	....	16 weeks

Depending upon the disease currently prevalent in the area, the agenda may be increased to extra vaccines of all or any part of the program. Veterinarians in different areas will build a program to suit the circumstances.

INTERNAL PARASITES

Over the years there have been numerous medications developed to rid your dog of worms. The old methods are no longer viable and a completely new area of medications has come into use. Worms infect dogs in many ways: by ingestion, through an insect bite, by penetrating the skin, or through prenatal infection. Infection can be direct or through the use of an intermediate host. In its life cycle every parasite may utilize one or more of these methods for its continued existence.

Dogs who are afflicted with internal parasites indicate unthriftiness, poor hair coats, vomiting, diarrhea, anemia, and underdevelopment. When you visit your veterinarian to ascertain whether or not your dog has worms, bring a small sample of your Shepherd's stool. Your veterinarian will examine the stool through a microscope or use the flotation method (which is more accurate). No one drug can kill all internal parasites, so from his diagnosis your veterinarian will select the necessary drug to eradicate the kind of worms your dog displays. It will be up to you, the owner, to break the link of infection; this will be your role in the prevention and control of parasitic invasion.

To accomplish this task you must eliminate infestation in the environment and prevent your Shepherd from coming in contact with infected areas. You must control fleas and lice by applying spray treatment to your dog. You will have to use sodium borate, ten pounds per one hundred feet of surface on your runs to kill larvae, check brood bitches for parasites, disinfect whelping boxes, clean up fecal matter every day, and in general keep your dog's environment clean and uncontaminated. Also do not use old-fashioned worming medicines that are not in use anymore. New and much better remedies are available today. Just ask your veterinarian about them.

Some of the various internal parasites which can infect your dog are: roundworms *(left)*, tapeworms *(middle)*, and whipworms *(right)*.

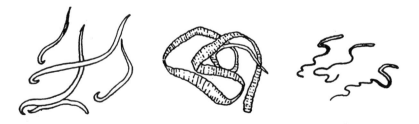

Roundworms (Toxocaro canis and Toxascaris leonina). Both these species of roundworms can infest the small intestine of your Shepherd. Aside from the basic life cycle there are intermediate hosts that can bring the larvae to your dog. Roundworms are most dangerous to puppies and seldom affect dogs over a year of age. Puppies can accrue lung damage, unthriftiness, diarrhea, and interference in the intestines to the extent of a complete blockage.

Piperazine compounds are very effective, are mild and require no period of starvation. Repeat treatments are required, possibly several times at ten to fourteen day intervals. Treated dogs usually acquire immunity to the helminths at about six months of age.

Hookworms (Ancylostoma caninum) are hair-like, thin and infest the intestines as do roundworms, but are much more dangerous. Diarrhea and anemia, the latter caused by the blood-sucking propensity of these tiny worms, can cause havoc, circulatory collapse, and death.

Treatment consists of the use of Canacur tablets according to weight, D.N.P. injections, which are very effective and least toxic, and Task or Telimintic drugs. Your veterinarian will select the appropriate drug and give your dog the correct treatment.

Whipworms (Trichuris vulpis). This worm is found in the upper part of the large intestine and in the caecum. Like hookworms, they are not easy to find unless the stool is strained. Constant rechecking is necessary because this helminth's eggs take longer to develop. Examination will also ascertain if the infection occurred after treatment. The sick dog may exhibit bloody diarrhea, secondary anemia, and be unthrifty in appearance. If treatment is not undertaken when blood is found in the fecal matter, death can follow.

The treatment consists of Task-Telimintic or Styquin injection. Reexamination and retreatments are generally necessary.

Tapeworm. There are a variety of tapeworms that can affect your Shepherd that range from one inch in length to sixteen feet in length. *Dipylidium caninum* and the *Taenia* species are the most prevalent and common. These helminths require an intermediate host to complete their life cycle. *Dipylidium caninum* utilizes the flea or louse as a host and therefore is found most frequently in dogs. The *Taenia* species commonly use cattle, rabbits, sheep and rodents as hosts. If your dog catches and eats a rabbit he can become infected.

The drugs Yomesan and Drocarbil are commonly used to expel these worms but are harsh and require starvation. A more modern treatment is Droncit, injectable or oral.

Hookworms, whipworms, and roundworms can also be treated with Panacur, and some of the large animal (horse) worming products are indicating great promise with fewer side reactions than some of the established worm medication. But these drugs are not approved at this time.

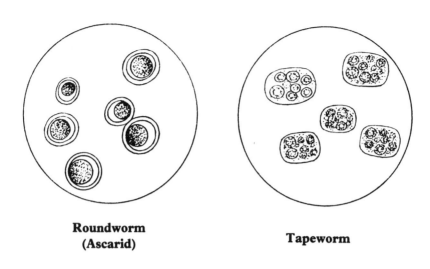

**Roundworm
(Ascarid)**

Tapeworm

Hookworm

Whipworm

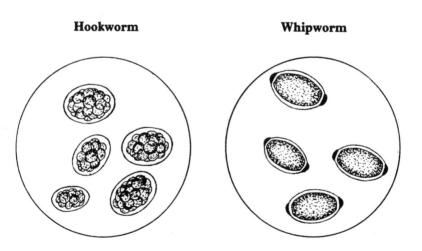

The eggs of certain parasites commonly seen in dogs.

Your dog must be wormed more than one time, and each worming must reflect the life cycle of the particular helminth. Roundworms and hookworms appear in a three-week life cycle, while the cycle of whipworms can be up to three months. Tapeworms need a secondary host so require only one worming.

Heartworms (Diroflaria immitis) can, when adult, reach a length of a foot and inhabit the large veins, the right side of the heart, and the pulmonary arteries of the lungs. The intermediate heartworm host is the mosquito, where the worm develops into infective larvae. The mosquito then infects the dog. These worms are extremely dangerous. The clinical picture discloses a dog that tires easily, coughs, and has difficulty breathing, particularly after exercise. The animal can even exhibit symptoms of congestive heart failure.

Treatment can be surgical or through the arsenical drugs and antimony. It is much better to prevent heartworm through medication than to attempt to cure it once it has become established. Decacide tablets (Diethylcarbamazine citrate), one 400 mg. tablet a day for a fully grown German Shepherd will prevent heartworms. Decacide treatment should not be given to dogs harboring adult heartworms.

A new drug is being tested at this moment that can be given only once monthly, or even over a longer period of time. It is not yet marketable by the pharmaceutical firms. There is also a new test being sent through the mails to breeders to use to detect heartworms. It is highly inaccurate and should not be used.

Coccidiosis is a protozoan that infects the intestinal tract. Dogs can be affected by four species of coccidia, which is manifest mainly in puppies, affecting the entire litter. The symptoms are blood-stained diarrhea, often containing mucus, loss of appetite and, in extreme cases, nasal and ocular discharge and coughing. The puppies die in convulsions, and clinically the disease is not unlike distemper. Many "cured" animals become carriers of the disease.

Treatment consists of the use of several drugs; sulphonamides, wide-range antibiotics, and nitrofurazone, the latter favored.

There are many less common internal parasites which need not be mentioned here because of the infrequency of their appearance. Those that I have mentioned are the most prevalent of the internal parasites that can affect our Shepherds.

EXTERNAL PARASITES

The dog is usually infested by two species of fleas, *Ctenocephalides canis* and *Ctenocephalides felis*. Fleas are not host specific, are wingless, and the female is larger than the male. The flea can carry tapeworm to your dog or act as an intermediate host for heartworm. A canine allergy to flea saliva is not uncommon and can be the cause of much canine skin trouble.

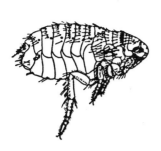

The common flea that affects canines *(left).* The sticktight flea *(right).* Illustrations courtesy of the United States Department of Agriculture.

Not only is the dog infested but so are his run, his dog house, and any place he has been. One female flea during her lifetime of two hundred days can lay five hundred eggs which hatch in larval form in two to ten days. Control of fleas is squarely on the shoulders of the dog owner, a job that must be diligently accomplished on a year 'round basis and includes your house, the dog's run and house, as well as the dog itself.

There are a host of new sprays, dips and powders, as well as constantly changing insecticides and new flea collars. It is quite possible that these wretched little parasites become immune to many of the products used, so it is best to change occasionally whatever it is you are using. Rely on your veterinarian for help with this problem. Some oral medications do not prevent fleas and lice from congregating on your dog, but they do allow a build-up of the product in the skin of your dog so that when the parasite bites the dog it is poisoned and dies.

A fairly new product is Spot-On. It is painted on the dog's back, generally by a veterinarian, and evidently discourages fleas from using your dog as a host. The product is very toxic and is not approved in all states because of this.

SKIN DISEASES

Skin diseases of any kind can be as irritating to the owner as they are to the dog. To see your Shepherd's coat fall out in handfuls, to see the constant scratching and his skin becoming dry and scaly, and to see that beautiful full tail becoming no thicker than a Pointer's is heartbreaking. There are many causes of skin disease; they are difficult to diagnose and often take months to cure. I will cite and we will examine the most important of the skin diseases your dog will be most prone to get.

Mange is caused by an external parasite mite, and there are two main forms, *Sarcoptic* and *Demodectic.* Skin scrapings can divulge the culprits even though lesions, secondary trauma, and infection aids the parasites to elude identifica-

The sarcoptic mange mite, viewed here from the underside, tunnels under the skin where it causes large lesions to form. Skin scrapings aid in diagnosis. Illustration courtesy of the United States Department of Agriculture.

tion. The dog scratches constantly, and the sarcoptic mange lesions are usually found, in the early stages, on the head and legs. Treatment involves the use of insecticides contained in a soothing skin-lotion base, medicated baths, and adjunctive therapy.

Demodectic, or *Red Mange* was, some years ago when I was young, considered incurable and the victim destroyed. It evidences itself through small, dry areas which are traumatized by scratching until they are red and raw. Medication containing insecticides should be vigorously applied, and medicated baths are indicated. Your veterinarian should be contacted immediately and advised as to the animal's condition and treatment left in his capable hands.

Eczema or *Summer Dermatitis* is most prevalent in hot weather. It is probably a syndrome rather than a single affliction. It begins with wet, raw spots that the dog licks, and it spreads rapidly. The areas become inflamed and your Shepherd scratches and traumatizes the afflicted region; bacterial infection follows, and you have a fine mixture of skin infections. Zinc in the diet can help prevent infection.

Treatment is directed in three directions: 1. Find and treat the underlying cause. 2. Stop the scratching. 3. Treat the affected areas. Identification of the underlying cause may not be easily accomplished. When it is found, specific treatment can be applied. Corticosteroids can be used to reduce the itch; also topical ointments and local anesthesia can be utilized. Medicated baths, lotions and ointments can be utilized to treat and heal the affected areas, and flea control is an absolute necessity.

Ringworm is an infection caused by a fungus and usually appears as a round spot on the face of your dog. It is quite contagious to humans. It can be controlled by the application of iodine-glycerine (50 percent of each ingredient), or girseofulvin, a potent fungicide.

General Skin Ailments. Actually there is no such thing as a general skin ailment. But if your dog exhibits a skin malady you might try Thiomar, a cleansing and deodorant tar shampoo, or for dry skin, Derma-Oil Shampoo, one teaspoonful to a gallon of water. Betaspan Aqueous Solution by injection can alleviate the constant scratching and H/B 101, a hydrocortisone liquid, applied to the sores can help. If there is some infection between the hind legs, 250 mg. Oxacillin, a broad spectrum antibiotic, can be given orally, two capsules three times a day for a German Shepherd. Ask your veterinarian to do a skin scrape, and a blood profile should also be done. Much of this kind of work is being done by the Animal Health Diagnostic Laboratory in Lansing, Michigan, by Dr. R. F. Nachreiner. I advise this because too often in our modern dogs the test analysis will indicate that the basic cause of the drastic skin trouble and loss of hair is due to thyroid difficulty. T L-Thiroxine must be administered to effect a cure. Recent research has also indicated that specific white blood cells (Lymphocytes) are not responsive and an individual dog's immunity to skin disease is lowered. Research into this phenomenon is still being done.

Seborrhea is a dermatosis caused by the increased activity of the sebaceous glands throughout the dog's body. The base of the tail, the shoulders, neck, face, and behind the ears are the areas generally affected. A thinning coat and scaly, greasy crusts are evident. The dog does not scratch too severely, but is extremely odorous, emitting a permeating "doggy" smell that is most offensive.

Treatment consists of bathing with cold tar soaps (Thiomar) and medicated shampoos containing sulphur, tar and hexachlorophene. The feeding of unsaturated fatty acids and Vitamins A, B-complex, and D and the supportive use of Corticosteroids and estrogen can be of help.

HIP DYSPLASIA

Hip Dysplasia is an inheritable disease that affects practically all breeds except, I am told, racing Greyhounds. German Shepherd fanciers are constantly made aware of this hip anomaly, even though there are other breeds where the incidence of the disease is higher. Perhaps because the German Shepherd

Hip Dysplasia in its various stages.

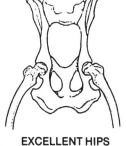 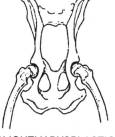 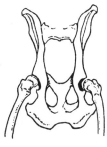

EXCELLENT HIPS   SLIGHTLY DYSPLASTIC   BADLY DYSPLASTIC

often toils at being a working dog (not a herding dog as the A.K.C. has seen fit to group assign it) that we are more conscious of the deleterious effect hip dysplasia can have upon our breed. I must make this observation; hip dysplasia and the extent of the joint damage can only be ascertained by X-ray.

Mild cases of dysplasia will be treated by your veterinarian with anti-inflammatory drugs such as aspirin and steroids, to keep the incidence of arthritis under control. Surgical cutting of the pectineus muscle, which is connected at the pelvis and attaches to the distal end of the femur, will reduce pain in moderate to mild cases. The pectineus seems to lose elasticity, shrinks, and exerts a pull on the femur head. Two theories exist at the moment: 1. That the surgery relieves pressure on the joint. 2. Since the muscle evidences pathological changes, removal (or cutting to release the pull) of the muscle relieves pain. It is controversial whether the development of the disease is delayed, but clinically most dogs are improved.

Hip excision is the removal of the ball (head) of the femur and the formation of a muscle joint. This surgery relieves pain and surgically bypasses the disease; without the joint there is no joint disease. This process returns from 80 to 90 percent normal action to the animal.

Of course dogs that have hip dysplasia should never be used for breeding for it is an inheritable malady. It would seem from what is known up to now, scientifically, that it is neither a definite recessive nor a dominant genetic trait but is determined by polygenic inheritance and evidences varied penetrance. Also muscle mass as opposed to bone weight may be a possible factor. Plastic hips are also an alternative, but expensive.

SPONDYLITIS

Spinal Cord Degeneration (Spondylitis) is not to be confused or identified as hip dysplasia, though it sometimes is. This paralyzing disease is prevalent mainly in German Shepherd Dogs. It is a demyelination of the spinal cord. The condition manifests itself by an unsteady gait beginning at any time after the animal has reached five to six years of age. As the spinal cord degenerates your Shepherd will become paraplegic and finally paralyzed, regressing rather rapidly. In most cases the infirmity stabilizes and the Shepherd again has mobility within reason. There is, at the moment, no known cure or treatment. There is definitely a breed (German Shepherd) incidence, but no genetic pattern has as yet been found.

BLOAT

The incidence of bloat is high in all large, deep-bodied breeds, which includes our German Shepherds. It occurs quickly and can be lethal if untreated for more than two or three hours. There are two kinds of bloat, simple and torsion. 1. Simple bloat (acute gastric dilation) is a kinking of either end of the stomach (entrance or exit). Passing a stomach tube down the stomach relieves the symptoms, and this is followed by sedatives and antacids. 2. Torsion bloat (gastric torsion) consists of a turning of the stomach on its own axis and/or a displacement of the spleen. Either situation serves to reduce or cut off circulation of blood to the stomach. Treatment is surgical and involves various methods of attaching the stomach wall to the abdominal wall to prevent further torsion. Torsion is a surgery emergency and an expensive procedure but, if accomplished in time, can be highly successful.

Most dog owners recognize the signs of bloat: the abdomen swells noticeably, breathing becomes labored because lung capacity is diminished by stomach distention, the animal appears listless and unable to vomit. The enlarging stomach causes increased pressure on the abdomen and lungs, which leads to severe shock and the necessity for veterinary intervention immediately.

There are many theories about the cause of bloat and a great deal of research is progressing to find an answer, but the origin is as yet unknown. Many years ago our only recourse when faced with a case of bloat was to jam a hollow needle below and past the last rib (the floating rib) to relieve the gas, then ply the dog with black coffee. Only the strong survived, but it was the only answer we had to the dilemma.

Brucellosis has become a cause celebre for the Shepherd fancy, as one can see from the stud advertisements in the *German Shepherd Dog Review*. It is a venereal disease that causes vaginal discharge in bitches and testicular disturbance in males. It is important to test for brucellosis if such indications appear in your kennel. Most veterinarians, though, consider it a greatly overstated disease and have seldom come in contact with a true case of brucellosis.

If a screen test is positive it is best to recheck, as an immune animal can create a false positive reading. The disease can be transferred to humans but is mainly passed from dog to dog. Infected dogs should be eliminated from the kennel.

EAR, EYE AND TOOTH AILMENTS

All of these subjects were partially covered in another chapter, the section on general husbandry. But I will elaborate a bit more here. Keep your dog's ears clean at all times. Mineral oil is excellent for this chore; a few drops are inserted in the ear and gently massaged, then any debris is removed with a cotton swab. When bathing your Shepherd be sure that no water flows into his ears. Never use ether, alcohol or any other irritating solvents as ear cleansing agents.

Bacterial ear infection. Infected ears are painful. Shaking of the head, scratching at the ears, bad odor (in the ear) and purulent discharge are all signs of infection. Shepherds have fewer ear problems than other breeds because of their erect ear carriage.

If bacterial ear infection has progressed for a lengthy period the dog may have to be sedated or anesthetized by your veterinarian in order to cleanse and treat the ears properly, and treatment can be prolonged. Surgical opening of the ear may be necessary for drainage.

Cleansing of the ears can be done with baby oil (mentioned before), hydrogen peroxide or surgical soap; a wax dissolving agent can also be utilized if needed. External ear infections are commonly treated with an antibiotic, which should be applied to the cleaned ear canal twice daily. Improvement should be evident in two to three days. But continue to medicate the ears, for a severe infection is not easily cleared up. An antibiotic injection is generally necessary and the ears must be treated for at least three weeks.

Fungal infection. A common cause of external otitis, secondary fungal infection, occurs frequently when antibiotics are utilized in the treatment of concurrent ear infection. The ears are fully inflamed and painful. Characteristic is a rancid odor emanating from the ears. Treatment is similar to that of bacterial infections.

Ear Mites (Otodectic cynotis). Puppies and young dogs are commonly afflicted with these mites. Itching, scratching and violent head shaking are symptomatic. The discharge is either black or reddish in color and waxy in consistency.

Treatment consists of thoroughly cleaning the ears, then medicating with a miticide twice weekly for at least three weeks. If you stop medicating too soon a new crop of mites will hatch and reinfest your Shepherd. Use an insecticide dip for bathing, and spray or powder your dog with flea repellents. If there is

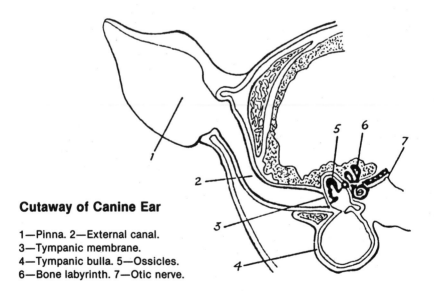

Cutaway of Canine Ear

1—Pinna. 2—External canal.
3—Tympanic membrane.
4—Tympanic bulla. 5—Ossicles.
6—Bone labyrinth. 7—Otic nerve.

Dog ticks greatly magnified. Illustrations courtesy of the United States Department of Agriculture.

a complicating bacterial involvement an antibiotic should be utilized. At this time there are no preparations available containing both an antibiotic and a miticide with a steroid to reduce itching.

Ticks In Ears. These pests adhere to the skin of the ear. Spray the tick or ticks with an insecticide or apply fingernail polish remover directly to the tick with a cotton swab. In a few minutes it will die and can then be removed. The use of tweezers for removal is recommended. Make certain, however, that you pluck the *entire* tick; be careful not to leave the tick's head embedded in the skin where it can cause infection.

Ear Allergies are accompanied by itching and redness. Steroids are recommended treatment (1 percent Hydrocortisone cream). Scratching is intense and can cause a secondary bacterial infection.

Hematoma. This disease is identified by a large blood pocket in the ear flap. There is a rupture of small blood vessels caused by trauma and a fluctuated swelling in the ear flap. It is usually a secondary complication to canker and ear mites, and it is due to the pawing at and vigorous shaking of the ear. Surgery by your veterinarian is necessary.

Eye Problems. Entropion is an eyelid inversion that results in ulcers and infection. It manifests itelf when the puppy is several months old.

Your dog can develop cataracts in his eyes. You will recognize this anomaly by the white and opaque appearance of the pupil. It most often affects older dogs, but sometimes cataracts can affect young animals and their surgical removal can result in the return of normal sight.

Tooth Problems. Periodontal disease in dogs is quite common. Plaque from bacteria forms on the teeth and can lead to kidney, heart and internal disease. Periodic scaling by your veterinarian is necessary, as is weekly brushing by you with a small toothbrush and toothpaste made specifically for canines. The object is to remove soft plaque before it becomes hard calculus. Biscuits and rib bones help remove plaque.

Visible Parts of the Canine Eye

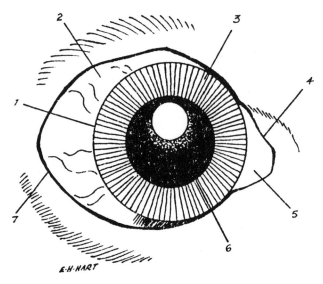

1—Limbus. 2—Sclera. 3—Iris. 4—Medial canthus. 5—Membrane nicitans. 6—Pupil. 7—Lateral canthus.

UROGENITAL DISEASES

These are generally ailments of dogs that are over middle age. The kidneys are primarily affected, and their function is to filter approximately 25 percent of the blood, removing toxic products, particularly urea, and to extract all useful material. Infection can enter through the bloodstream or the bladder.

Nephritis is a kidney disease that is manifested when chronic or progressive infection occurs due to past disease and geriatric changes. The dog may exhibit depression, increased thirst, advanced temperature, vomiting, kidney-area pain, and the BUN (Blood, Urea, Nitrogen) is elevated. Urination is depressed to the point where the dog becomes dehydrated. The ailment can be caused by leptospirosis or other bacterial infections.

The water, electrolyte balance, and regurgitation must be controlled. Intravenous drips of electrolytic fluids and sugar are necessary, with added vitamin B-complex and antibiotics utilized for infection. High quality protein must be fed, and the dog should be given an abundance of fluids.

Cystitis is an infection of the bladder in which stones (calculi) predispose the animal to secondary infections. The dog indulges in frequent urination, the urine is often bloody and alkaline, and the animal indicates distress. The temperature may go up and the bladder is painful.

Treatment is accomplished through the use of antibiotics and occasionally with protolytic enzymes. Provide the patient with an abundant supply of water. If calculi or tumors are present, surgery is indicated.

Tonsillitis. The tonsils commonly become inflamed as an indication of a systemic disease like hepatitis, or a direct infection of the tonsils. Acute infections are bacterial and generally involve streptococcus bacteria. Coughing, swelling of the neck area, vomiting and bad breath are all symptomatic. The tonsils are, of course, inflamed and enlarged. Tonsillitis responds quite well to the application of the antibiotics.

Pneumonia is an infection of the lungs. *Interstitial pneumonia* involves the entire lung tissue and is viral in nature. Treatment is as for distemper since most cases are the pneumonic part of distemper. *Lobar pneumonia* involves a lobe of the lung and is usually bacterial and secondary to viral pneumonia. Blood, mucus, and pus are found in the lung.

There is *aspiration pneumonia* and *verminous pneumonia,* the latter caused by parasitic invasion. We also have *hypostatic pneumonia,* common only in old dogs, and *mycotic pneumonia,* a fungal pneumonia. General symptoms in all types of pneumonia are difficulty in breathing and shortness of breath.

Antibiotics, general nursing and eliminating the underlying cause (distemper, parasites, etc.) is the treatment of choice. The fungal type of pneumonia can be cured through the use of fungicides.

THE STOMACH

Acute Gastritis has many causes. Bloat we have formerly covered. Gastritis is characterized by persistent abdominal pain and vomiting and is caused by the licking of medications, bacterial infection, parasitic infestation and general disease.

Diet should be liquid and bland with solids added slowly over a period of time. Antiemetics and antibiotics, such as erythromycin and neomycin, are recommended.

Intestinal Upsets (enteritis). Diarrhea and regurgitation are common with enteritis, and full diagnosis is difficult to achieve. Fortunately the majority of intestinal illnesses are simple inflammations that necessitate only generalized treatment. Parasites are one of the several causes of intestinal upsets. Fecal examination and treatment to eradicate the specific helminths is all that is necessary. Bacteria and their toxins are another, and the most common, cause of enteritis. Stools are often bloody and the dog exhibits a fever. Antidiarrheal preparations are employed to tighten loose stools, then general antibiotic therapy may be used, if necessary.

Coccidiosis has been discussed previously. Other protozoans can be found through fecal smears, and anti-protozoal drugs are employed. Food allergies are always a possibility. Shellfish, eggs and horse meat are the usual offenders.

Life Cycle of Toxocara Canis (Roundworms)

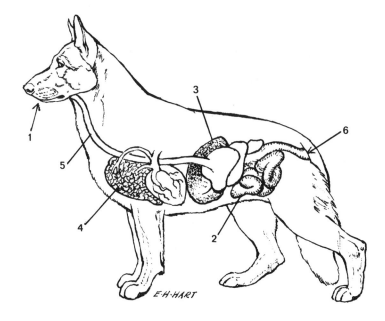

1—Worms are ingested by dog through food contaminated on ground, by nursing pups from dam's teats, or by larval invasion through placenta (prenatal infestation). Each egg contains embryo released by bursting of shell in the 2—intestine and then becomes larvae, which pierce intestinal wall, enter bloodstream, and carried by way of 3—the liver to the 4—lungs. From the lungs the worms crawl or are coughed up into the 5—esophagus and then swallowed again and reach the intestines. There they lay eggs which are 6—voided in the dog's stool. Microscopic eggs embryonate in two to three weeks and can remain viable for years.

Diarrhea is usually a symptom, not a disease, so diagnosis is imperative and treatment should be left to your veterinarian.

Constipation can be caused by the feeding of bones (a no-no) or dry, bulky foods without enough water. Prostatic enlargement, blocking tumors and anal gland infection are also possible causes. Mineral oil and parafin can be used to good effect, but an enema is more often needed. Sometimes surgery is necessary to remove the fecal mass.

Anal Glands. Near the anal opening of the dog are two glands, one on each side, that have little use to the dog as far as I can see. They are evidently vestigial glands that at one time, when the mammals were emerging into species demarcation, were used to mark territory. They discharge an odious scent during fright or excitement and they can become impacted and infected, or rupture, or even become neoplastic, and then should be emptied by your veterinarian. For infection, antibiotics can be resorted to; when ruptured, the glands should be removed. If they become neoplastic malignancy can follow and surgery is necessary.

HEART AND BLOOD SICKNESSES

Congestive heart failure is a common condition of dogs over six years of age. There are a dozen causes for canine heart conditions including growths on the valves, congenital defects, heart muscle disease, heartworms and tumors. Chest fluids and kidney stress eventually occur, and treatment is directed at both the heart and the side effects of the disease.

Digoxin, diuretics, bronchial dilators, antihistamines and cough repressants are utilized. The diet is adjusted to relieve liver strain, and salt intake is lowered. While the condition is being brought under control rest is important.

Hemorrhaging can be due to infection (leptospirosis and hepatitis), allergies affecting the permeability of the blood vessels, direct injury to the vessels, and hemophilia. Vitamin K deficiency, abnormalities in the blood, dicumoral poisoning or the breakdown of clots (fibrinolysis) are other causes of hemorrhaging.

To treat this ailment the cause must be diagnosed and removed or the defect corrected and the blood replaced via transfusion. For long term therapy the application of Vitamin B12 and iron is recommended. Coagulating drugs can also be used. Accident cases that are accompanied by shock and hemorrhage will necessitate transfusion.

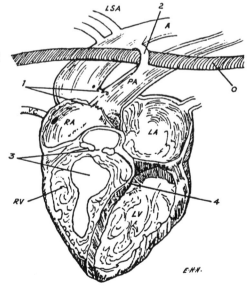

Cutaway of Canine Heart

A composite drawing of various congenital malformations which can occur in the puppy. 1—Patent ductus arteriosus. 2—Persistent tight aortic arch. 3—Stenosis. 4—Interventricular septal defect. A is the Aorta. PA is the Pulmonary artery. O is the Oesophagus. VC is the Vena Cava. RA is the right auricle. LA is the left auricle. RV is the right ventricle. LV is the left ventricle. LSA is the left subclavicle artery.

Hemophilia is a recessive, genetic, blood clotting deficiency disease carried by the female of the species but only exhibited by the male. It is incurable and any animal displaying the proclivity must be eliminated from any breeding program.

DISEASES OF THE NERVOUS SYSTEM

Functional disorders of the brain include epilepsy, hysteria and nervousness. The brain has a specific capacity to respond to stimuli, and when this capacity is exceeded a functional disorder may take place. This does not always happen but the capacity, lowered by disease or factors of heredity, can allow such occurrences.

Encephalitis results in convulsions, blindness, paralysis and chorea (muscle spasms) and is basically an inflammation of the brain. Distemper, rabies and other viruses can be the cause of encephalitis. Protozoan encroachment, bacterial infection and fungus (Cryptococcis) are likely invaders. Whatever the cause it must be diagnosed and treated separately.

Motion sickness is a common canine problem. It has been mentioned before but now it will be given specific attention because it can be a real problem. Irritating impulses are received by the middle ear of your dog and relayed to the cerebellum and the result is motion sickness. Drooling, regurgitation, restlessness and even occasional diarrhea characterize this malady.

Do not feed the dog for about six hours before traveling. Stop every two hours or so when you are on the road and let him have a romp and walk before continuing. Phenobarbital and tranquilizers help, but they are depressants and therefore counterproductive, especially if you are motoring to a show in which your Shepherd is entered. Some antihistamines have side reactions that alleviate motion sickness without depressing the animal.

Epilepsy is one of the oldest brain illnesses known to man and is becoming more prevalent in our dogs. In England the disease is more common than in the U.S. I have often judged in Trinidad and Barbados where, due to stringent quarantine laws, German Shepherds (or Alsatians as they had been called) were imported from Great Britain. Over the years I have seen incidents of epilepsy in several of the English imports.

Clinical signs include convulsive movement, unconsciousness, apprehension, howling or barking, urination and defecation and profuse salivation. Epilepsy in older dogs can be caused by tumors in the brain; young dogs can exhibit encephalitic seizures and evidence can be found of systemic disease. Toxic and metabolic maladies can cause seizures, as can a severe head blow and all physical causes that are from an outside source that can bring injury to the brain.

Treatment consists in controlling the seizures with anticonvulsant drugs, avoiding sedation. Drugs that should *not* be used in canine epilepsy are phenothiazine, tranquilizers, amphetamines and analeptics.

ENDOCRINE GLAND DISEASES

There are ductless glands that add hormones to the bloodstream, and the true endocrine glands are the thyroid, the pituitary, the parathyroid and the adrenal glands. Most of the glandular diseases affect other breeds, but thyroid disease and diabetes do effect German Shepherd dogs, and so we must know something about them.

Thyroid disease is recognized as affecting canines in general, but in the last few years I have heard, through the veterinarians, that quite a few German Shepherds have developed thyroid trouble. Thyroxin, the hormone secreted, is concerned with regulating the dog's metabolism. In the afflicted animal there is a low range of thyroxine and triodothysonine (hypo- function) which causes a drastic change in the dog's metabolism. It appears to be a skin disease, but there is a general character change: frenetic behavior and a ravenous appetite. Sores appear all over the body, hair begins to fall out drastically, there is a great deal of scaling of the skin and the dog appears very unthrifty in its appearance. To diagnose, it is necessary to have a blood profile done.

Treatment consists of oral medication of 0.3 mg. L-Thyroxine sodium tablets, two tablets twice a day for a German Shepherd. Skin and coat will begin to recover almost immediately, as will character modifications. To aid in more rapid recovery of the skin and coat, use bland shampoos (Allergroom, Derma-Oil), H/B 101 (Hydrocortisone) applications to the skin sores, Alpha-Keri oil and Humylac for dry skin (flaking and dandruff) and keep your Shepherd free of fleas.

Diabetes Mellitus (sugar diabetes) is a malady that affects the islets of Langerhans in the pancreas which secret insulin that regulates the utilization of carbohydrate/sugar. The disease is, in many cases, undetected, so that a much larger canine population is affected than is treated.

Symptoms of the illness are increased thirst and loss of weight accompanied by greater food consumption. High urine and blood sugar levels will be obvious in laboratory tests, ketone bodies will develop in the urine because of disruption of fat metabolism and the dog will develop acidosis. If untreated the end result is diabetes coma and death.

To treat the disease dietary adjustments must be made and daily injections of insulin are necessary. Canine diabetes is parallel in treatment to human diabetes and the cause is also the same. Your veterinarian will advise you how to treat your dog at home with very little trouble.

BONE AILMENTS

Arthritis is a joint inflammation. As an end result all diseases that afflict the joints invite arthritis. An increase of joint fluids that distends the joint is the simplest form of arthritis. The fluids become fibrinous or purulent, and the

Skeleton of a German Shepherd Dog

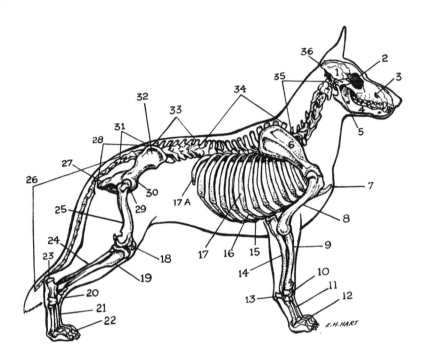

1. Cranium (skull). 2. Orbital cavity. 3. Nasal bone. 4. Mandible (jaw bone). 5. Condyle. 6. Scapula (shoulder blade, including spine and acromion process of scapula). 7. Prosternum. 8. Humerus (upper arm). 9. Radius (front forearm bone—see Ulna). 10. Carpus (pastern joint. Comprising seven bones). 11. Metacarpus (pastern. Comprising five bones). 12. Phalanges (digits or toes). 13. Pisiform (accessory carpal bone). 14. Ulna. 15. Sternum. 16. Costal cartilage (lower, cartilaginous section of ribs). 17. Rib bones. 17a. Floating rib (not connected by costal cartilage to sternum). 18. Patella (knee joint). 19. Tibia (with fibula comprises shank bone). 20 Tarsus (comprising seven bones). 21. Metatarsus (comprising five bones). 22. Phalanges (toes or digits of hind foot). 23. Os calcis (point of hock). 24. Fibula. 25. Femur (thigh bone). 26. Coccygeal vertebra (bones of tail . Number varies—18 to 23 normal). 27. Pubis. 28. Pelvic bone entire (pubis, ilium, ischium). 29. Head of femur. 30. Ischium. 31. Sacral vertebra (comprising five fused vertebra). 32. Ilium. 33. Lumbar vertebra. 34. Thoracic vertebra (dorsal, with spinal process or withers). 35. Cervical vertebra (bones of the neck). 36. Occiput.

Musculature of the German Shepherd Dog

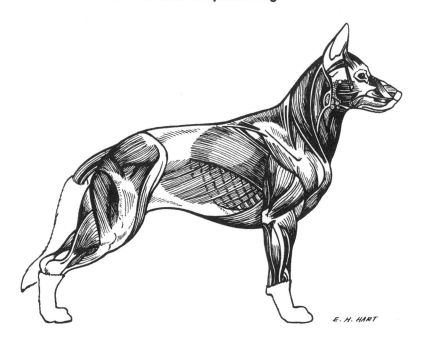

E. H. HART

Muscles, tendons, and ligaments work together with the skeletal system to enable your Shepherd to move.

result is an erosion of cartilage in the joint and joint pain. The condition becomes chronic unless the original cause can be treated.

The illness causes proliferation of the soft tissue lining the joint, and small pieces of cartilage become detached, ulceration occurs and sometimes infection develops. Movement in the area involved becomes restricted and quite painful. In extreme cases there occurs new bony tissue build-up, causing bone fusion (ankylosis).

Antibiotic treatment of infections should be instituted. Corticosteroids can be utilized to reduce inflammation and an oral administration of aspirin-type drugs can help to alleviate pain in the joint. Reduction of the animal's weight, rest and immobilization are recommended. Ultrasonic therapy (deep muscle massage and sound waves) is also advised.

Hip dysplasia fosters arthritis. It has been covered previously, but I must add that the basic trouble can be caused by one or a combination of three factors: 1. A shallow acetabulum. 2. Flattening of the femur head. 3. A defect in the teres ligament.

289

There is a similar dysplastic condition that can occur in the dog's elbow (also a ball and socket joint). Pain can be controlled to a limited extent by corticosteroid compounds.

Legg's Perthes Disease must not be confused with congenital hip dysplasia, though the end result is similar. It is due to the aseptic death of the femur head which causes wearing. If the condition progresses for any length of time it is difficult to diagnose whether it is Legg's Perthes disease or hip dysplasia. It is a congenital disease and the treatment, the control of side effects, is the same as for hip dysplasia.

Spondylitis is another illness that has already been mentioned. Once the condition settles down the dog can usually perform all normal functions without pain. Corticosteroids are generally used to treat the infirmity.

FIRST AID

In an emergency you may have to care for your dog until the veterinarian is available, and often emergency aid by the owner can prevent death or the chance of permanent injury. Because the animal is badly injured and in the grip of intolerable pain, he may not recognize you and may indiscriminately attempt to bite. Either muzzle your dog or use a strip of bandage or cloth to form a muzzle, looping it around the dog's muzzle, crossing it under the jaws, and bringing the two ends around behind the dog's head to tie. To prevent him from blindly running away or hiding, snap the leash on his collar immediately.

If you have to carry him or lift him, get a large handful of skin directly behind his head at the back of his neck. Lift him up until you can support him with your other arm and carry him, but hold onto his neck skin until he can be put down.

Every owner of a dog should have a first aid kit. In it you should stock surgical scissors, a thermometer, one-inch adhesive tape, three-inch and six-inch bandage, petroleum jelly, enema equipment, surgical cotton, a ten c.c. hypodermic syringe, hydrogen peroxide, an antiseptic powder, an ear remedy, mineral oil, aspirin, a styptic stick, tranquilizers and your veterinarian's phone number.

To give a dog a pill or pills, hold his head up, open his mouth with one hand and, with the other, place the medicine as far back on his tongue as possible. Close his mouth quickly but not too tightly. When his tongue emerges from the front of his mouth he has swallowed the pill.

To dispense liquid medicine, hold your dog's head upward and pull out the corner of his lip until it forms a pocket. Into this pocket slowly pour the liquid medicine. Powders are best given in food.

A few extra thoughts in reference to general medication. Eliminate milk and milk products while diarrhea is active, and urge the diarrhetic dog to drink a great deal of liquids to avoid dehydration. Never attempt to open or lance a boil, abscess or infection; allow your veterinarian to accomplish this task. Never apply a bandage over iodine. Do not use hydrogen peroxide on an abscess. Never give a greater dose of medicine than the prescription or label indicates. And do not use any ointment that is over one year old unless it bears a clearly marked expiration date.

Following are two charts, one for general first aid and the other a chart of poisons and antidotes. They are only for an emergency to aid you to help your dog until you can reach your veterinarian.

FIRST AID CHART

Emergency	Treatment	Remarks
Accidents	Automobile, treat for shock. White gums indicate internal injury. Wrap bandage around body tightly. Call vet.	Get veterinarian help quickly.
Bites	Tooth wounds; shave area, antiseptic flow into puncture. If badly ripped take to veterinarian.	If infected call veterinarian.
Bee stings	Aspirin, antihistamine. If in shock treat same.	Call veterinarian.
Broken bones	If limb, put in splints. Keep immobile. If other parts involved, keep dog from moving.	Call veterinarian immediately.
Burns	Apply ice compress. Then petroleum jelly.	Call veterinarian.
Choking	If foreign object can be seen at back of throat, remove with fingers. Otherwise rush to vet.	Get to veterinarian immediately.
Dislocations	Keep dog quiet and take to vet.	
Cuts	Allow dog to lick minor cuts If not in reach of dog, cleanse with hydrogen peroxide. For severe cuts, use pressure bandage and get to veterinarian.	If infected or needs suturing, take to veterinarian.
Electric shock	Artificial respiration. Treat for shock.	Call veterinarian.
Drowning	Artificial respiration. Lay dog on its side, push on ribs with hand every two seconds. Treat for shock.	

Heatstroke	Immerse dog in cold water or give him a cold water enema or lay him flat and pour cold water over him.	
Porcupine quills	Leash dog, hold between knees. Pull quills out with pliers. Check tongue and inside of mouth.	Veterinarian can remove quills deeply imbedded.·
Shock	Cover with blanket. Soothe. Do not administer liquids.	Bring to veterinarian.
Poisonous snake bite	Apply tourniquet toward heart if possible. Cut deep X over fang marks. Drop potassium permanganate into cut.	Use first aid only if veterinarian is not available.
Wasp stings	Dab vinegar on area. Treat for shock if necessary.	

TREATMENT FOR POISON

Poison	Household Antidote
Acids	Bicarbonate of soda
Alkalies (cleansing agents)	Vinegar or lemon juice
Arsenic	Epsom salts
Hydrocyanic acid (wild cherry; laurel leaves)	Dextrose or corn syrup
Lead (paint pigments)	Epsom salts
Phosphorus (rat poison)	Hydrogen peroxide
Mercury	Eggs and milk
Theobromine (cooking chocolate)	Phenobarbital
Thallium (insecticide)	Table salt in water
Food poisoning (garbage, etc.)	Hydrogen peroxide, followed by enema
Strychnine	Sedatives, phenobarbital, nembutal
DDT	Peroxide and enema

Good nursing is important for the sick dog. Keep him warm and eating flavorful but bland foods. Rest and quiet are also necessary. *Check label of poison, if possible, for antidote.*

Chapter 21

Geriatrics and the Death of a Friend

Gerontology is a science that is dedicated to the aging process, and the study of aging is concerned with tissue, cell, mental and physiological changes in the older animal. Influences brought to bear upon your dog that change its lifestyle are: organ damage from disease, change in environment, lack of nutritional value over the years and genetic proclivity to disease and rapid aging.

Senility overtakes all creatures on earth, and man and his canines are no exception. Mentally as well as physically, old age eventually becomes a major factor in the lives of our dogs. But due to a better understanding of the body functions of older dogs and increasing knowledge and use of new methods of diagnosing and controlling diseases and disorders, the longevity of your Shepherd has been increased.

When your Shepherd becomes aged and the signs can no longer be ignored, I think it is possible that we, the owners, are confronted with our own mortality and often the shock of this discovery is severe. But the wearing away of our physical and mental abilities must be faced if we are to come to terms with reality and find peace in our twilight years.

Your veterinarian will help your aging dog by constructing a new analysis of its mental and physiological norms. His examination will include kidney and liver function tests, blood chemistries, possibly an electrocardiogram, bone marrow tests and X-rays. What he learns from his examination can make your dog comfortable as a senior citizen and allow him a longer and more peaceful life.

Older dogs have generally a greater immunity to fatal, fast-acting diseases such as cancer. Their metabolism has slowed to such an extent that even such diseases do not wreak the havoc that they could if the dog were younger. But arthritis, muscular atrophy, depletion of muscle bulk and general mobility is, even as with you and me, a part of the aging process.

Parasitic control is an important part of the care of the senior citizen canine. Alpha-Keri oil should be sprayed on his coat, for his hair will become brittle and less abundant. Skin tumors and hormonal conditions can be kept to a minimum through veterinary care and the use of medicated shampoos, moisturizers and fatty acids. Anemia, toxicity and other illnesses must be recognized and treated. Bad breath will indicate the necessity of tooth and gum care. Bad teeth should be removed, and a blood cell check should be made to assess the condition of the bone marrow.

Food should be more bland and a blood profile should be done by your veterinarian. Nephritis is possible, and heart and organ changes must be checked. Also the dog's ability to defecate can alter. Canine senior citizens are more susceptible to stress, so the diet should not be suddenly and radically changed and he should not be exposed to extremes of temperature. He will want to laze about and sleep more, so provide him with a warm, dry bed in a quiet, peaceful place. If you have children do not allow them to pester the older dog and continually want him to play.

The old fellow's hearing, vision and sense of smell are all afflicted, and his reaction to stimuli is considerably slowed. Diabetes, kidney and liver disorders are all, sadly, part of the portrait of an older dog. He must have some exercise every day, but do not overdo it. Exercise allows him to stretch his muscles and tendons and move his bones to keep his body mobile. It is also something that he can look forward to that relieves the boredom of his declining years.

There are a number of other medical tests that can be made to diagnose your elderly dog's condition. Vitamins with digestive enzymes can be supplied, and special diets for specific anomalies can be employed. Every six months bring your old friend to the veterinarian for a complete check-up. Do all you can to allow your Shepherd to quietly achieve old age with dignity and the love he deserves.

Old bitches should be spayed to protect them from ovarian cysts, cancer of the reproductive organs and infections of the uterus. Female dogs, unlike their human counterparts, do not achieve menopause but continue to ovulate every six to eight months throughout their lives. Surgical risk is minimal and diseases of the reproductive organs, usually caused by sex hormone imbalance and estrogen-induced cysts and mammary tumors, can be avoided by spaying, and this often adds years to the senior bitch's life.

When the end finally comes, as it surely will, you must not overly grieve. Remember all the wonderful days you and your friend have spent together; celebrate his life, not his death. When life began on earth a pact was formed—that life must walk with the shadow of death beside it, for where there is a beginning there must also be an ending; it is the law of nature.

I remember so well a friend stricken with an incurable disease. He lay in a hospital bed and neither of us spoke. Finally he turned his head and there was peace in his eyes and he said, "I've spent my whole life avoiding death. Now I am faced with the knowledge that what I have avoided was inevitable."

No words that I can pen will ease the pain and the feeling of hopelessness that is the unavoidable companion to the death of a friend. And yet he hasn't gone away forever, for he will always live in your thoughts and your mind and be one of the best parts of the past.

To fill that void left by the death of your canine friend, let me suggest that you find another Shepherd to bring into your home. No, do not consider the new dog an interloper or that by welcoming him you are being disloyal to the dog that has gone. This new Shepherd is not a substitute, so make no comparisons; he is a completely new individual who will help you to remember your old friend. The old dog claimed your heart and the new one will too, in time, but in a different way.

The love and care we give to our dogs is a shining light in the blackness of the crime, political graft and useless killings that smear our newspapers and television screens with the bloody news of the day. When there are caring people like you it is a sign that humanity still touches us, and affection and devotion yet exists in the heart that cries at the death of a friend.

Chapter 22

The Future of the Breed

The future is a wonderful time. We have not yet reached it so we can, only in a vague but exhilarating way, imagine all the fabulous and magical things it will bring. What does that future of today, tomorrow and all the other tomorrows hold for our breed the German Shepherd dog? It holds many wonders that we have only a glimpse of now. There is the freezing and storage of canine semen, already an accomplishment, sparking the opening of cryobanks where complete services are offered, including documentation necessary for registering of frozen semen litters with the American Kennel Club. It is the modern method of perpetuating bloodlines and pursuing goals of breeding that were beyond our reach before.

Cryotherapy, the freezing of tissues by agents such as liquid nitrogen and freon via a probe, is being used successfully by many veterinarians. Laser beam surgery is not uncommon in the treatment of animal diseases. There are CAT scans, a form of X-ray that scans soft tissue. And prosthesis, to replace dysplastic hips. In fact there are many other methods available to your veterinarian to correct or find the seat of your dog's troubles whatever they may be.

Yes, the future will be a time to treasure, and we can scarcely wait until it becomes today. There will be computer pedigree diagnosis to determine hereditary factors and advise on breedings. Fed the proper information the computer will give you a complete print-out on your Shepherd's genetic formula. But it will not be a completely mechanical world in the future. You will have to supply the necessary input to receive information of any value from the computer, so the breeding of fine Shepherds will still be a bit of an art as well as a science.

With the advent of further research of recombinant genes in the future and knowledge gained from closer study of DNA (the material that sculpts genes

Nenzy v. Uesener Werk by VI Panther v. Eschenzweig, SchH III, FH ex Xenia v. Uesener Werk, SchH I. Nenzy did well in Youth Classes in Germany and is continuing her winning ways in U.S. shows. This lovely bitch was imported by the author and is co-owned by the author and his wife and Mr. and Mrs. D. Watson.

and chromosomes), an amazing shower of now unknown factors will be presented to aid us in our breeding ventures. Research into genetics should offer us a fantastic variety of facts and a newer understanding of the very core of life on this planet. New theories will dispute old ideas and be proven valid, and you and I, if we are still here, will stand spellbound, bathed in the white light of this proliferation of new knowledge.

I am not a soothsayer or a medium to see into the future, so I will make no more prophesies. Just remember that the future becomes the now, but there is always the future left from now until eternity.

Use the future well, because it is yours and always will be, for it is part of time and of the cosmos, and is the heritage of man.

Appendices

G.S.D.C.A. AMERICAN GRAND VICTORS AND VICTRIXES

Grand Victors

1918 Ch. Komet v. Hoheluft
1919 Ch. Apollo v. Hunenstein, PH, Sgr, Aus, Fr, Belg.
1920 Ch. Rex Buckel
1921 Int. Ch. Grimm v. d. Mainkur, PH
1922 Int. Ch. Erich v. Grafenwerth, PH, German Sieger
1923 Int. Ch. Dolf v. Dusternbrook, PH, German Sieger
1924 Int. Ch. Cito Gergerslust, SchH, German Sieger
1925 Int. Ch. Cito Gergerslust, SchH, German Sieger
1926 Ch. Donar v. Overstolzen, SchH, German Sieger
1927 Int. Ch. Arko v. Sadowaberg of Jessford, CD, SchH, German Sieger
1928 Int. Ch. Arko v. Sadowaberg of Jessford, CD, SchH, German Sieger
1929 Int. Ch. Arko v. Sadowaberg of Jessford, CD, SchH, German Sieger
1930 Ch. Bimbo v. Stolzenfels
1931 Int. Ch. Arko v. Sadowaberg of Jessford, CD, SchH, German Sieger
1932 Not awarded
1933 Ch. Golf v. Hooptal, ZPr
1934 Ch. Erikind of Shereston
1935 Ch. Nox of Glenmar, CD
1936 Not awarded
1937 Int. Ch. Pfeffer v. Bern, ZPr, MH, German Sieger, ROM
1938 Int. Ch. Pfeffer v. Bern, ZPr, MH, German Sieger, ROM
1939 Ch. Hugo of Cosalta, CD

1940 Ch. Cotswold of Cosalta, CD
1941 Am. and Can. Ch. Nox of Ruthland, ROM
1942 Ch. Noble of Ruthland
1943 Can. Ch. Major of Northmere, Am. and Can. Grand Victor
1944 Am. and Can. Ch. Nox of Ruthland, ROM
1945 Ch. Adam of Veralda, CD
1946 Ch. Dex of Talladega, CD
1947 Am. and Can. Ch. Dorian v. Beckgold, Am. and Can. Grand Victor
1948 Ch. Valiant of Draham, CD, Am. and Can. Grand Victor, ROM
1949 Ch. Kirk of San Miguel
1950 Ch. Kirk of San Miguel
1951 Ch. Jory of Edgetowne, CDX, ROM
1952 Ch. Ingo Wunschelrute, ROM
1953 Ch. Alert of Mi-Noah's, CD, ROM
1954 Ch. Brando v. Aichtel, SchH I
1955 Ch. Rasant v. Holzheimer Eichwald, SchH II
1956 Am. and Can. Ch. Bill v. Kleistweg, SchH I, ROM
1957 Int. Ch. Troll v. Richterbach, SchH III, FH, ROM, Holland Sieger
1958 Ch. Yasko v. Zenntel, SchH III
1959 Ch. Red Rock's Gino, CD, ROM
1960 Ch. Axel v. Foldihaus, ROM
1961 Ch. Lido v. Meller Land, SchH III, FH
1962 Ch. Yorkdom's Pak, ROM
1963 Ch. Condor v. Stoerstrudel, SchH I, AD, ROM
1964 Not awarded
1965 Ch. Brix v. d. Grafenkrone, SchH III
1966 Ch. Yoncalla's Mike, ROM
1967 Am. and Can. Ch. Lance of Fran-Jo, Am. and Can. Grand Victor, ROM
1968 Ch. Yoncalla's Mike, ROM
1969 Ch. Arno v. d. Kurpfalzhalle
1970 Ch. Hollamor's Judd
1971 Ch. Mannix of Fran-Jo
1972 Ch. Lakeside's Harrigan, ROM
1973 Ch. Scorpio of Shiloh Gardens, ROM
1974 Ch. Tellaheide's Gallo
1975 Ch. Caesar on Carahaus
1976 Ch. Padechma's Persuasion
1977 Ch. Langenau's Watson
1978 Ch. Baobab's Chaz
1979 Ch. Schokrest On Parade
1980 Ch. Aspen of Fran-Jo
1981 Ch. Sabra Dennis of Gan Edan, Am. and Can. Grand Victor
1982 Ch. Kismet's Impulse v. Bismarck

Ch. Amigo v. Land der Berge, SchH II by V Jack v Furstenberg, SchH III ex Dunja v. Schippkapass, SchH I. At the German Shepherd Dog Club of Greater Miami the author awarded this strong male Best of Breed from the Open Class.

Facing page: Select Ch. Bel-Vista's Joey Baby *(above)* by Bel-Vista's Loredo ex Diedra v. Knaffl-Hof. A beautiful well-balanced animal, winning a Specialty Show award from the author. Terry Hower handling. V Gaus Di Fondovilla, SchH II, Kkl 1/a *(below)* by Held v. Flosserhaus, SchH III ex Gitta Di Casa Gatto. This excellent son of Held was whelped in Italy. His dam shows the genetic qualities of the great German breeding behind her, being linebred on Dido v. Richterbach and carrying also the bloodlines of Ajax v. Haus Dexel and Veit v. Busecker Schloss. He was imported into the U.S. by the author from Josef Wassermann in Germany. Handled by Richard Mc Mullen and owned by Richard Mc Mullen and Carmelo Pino.

photo by Ashbey

Grand Victrixes

1918 Ch. Lotte v. Edelweiss
1919 Ch. VanHall's Herta
1920 Ch. Boda v. d. Furstenberg
1921 Ch. Dora v. Rheinwald
1922 Ch. Debora v. Weimar
1923 Ch. Boda v. d. Furstenberg
1924 Ch. Irma v. Doernerhof, SchH
1925 Ch. Irma v. Doernerhof, SchH
1926 Int. Ch. Asta v. Kaltenweide, Siegerin
1927 Ch. Inky of Willowgate
1928 Ch. Erich's Mercede of Shereston
1929 Ch. Christel v. Stimmberg, PH
1930 Int. Ch. Katja v. Blasienberg, HGH, ZPr, Siegerin
1931 Ch. Gisa v. Koenigsbruch
1932 Not awarded
1933 Ch. Dora of Shereston
1934 Ch. Dora of Shereston
1935 Ch. Nanka v. Schwyn
1936 Ch. Frigga v. Kannenbackerland
1937 Ch. Perchta v. Bern
1938 Ch. Giralda's Geisha, CD
1939 Ch. Thora v. Bern of Giralda
1940 Ch. Lady of Ruthland, ROM
1941 Ch. Hexe of Rotundain
1942 Ch. Bella v. Haus Hagen
1943 Ch. Bella v. Haus Hagen
1944 Am. and Can. Ch. Frigga v. Hoheluft, ROM
1945 Ch. Olga of Ruthland
1946 Am. and Can. Ch. Leda v. Liebestraum, ROM
1947 Am. and Can. Ch. Jola v. Liebestraum, ROM, Am. and Can. Grand
      Victor
1948 Ch. Duchess of Browvale
1949 Ch. Doris v. Vogtlandshof
1950 Ch. Yola of Long-Worth
1951 Ch. Tawnee v. Liebestraum
1952 Ch. Afra v. Heilholtkamp, ROM
1953 Ch. Ulla of San Miguel
1954 Ch. Jem of Penllyn
1955 Ch. Solo Nina of Rushagen, CD, ROM
1956 Ch. Kobeil's Barda
1957 Ch. Jeff-Lynn's Bella
1958 Ch. Tan-Zar Desiree

1959 Ch. Alice v. d. Guten Fee
1960 Am. and Can. Ch. Robin of Kingscroft, Am. and Can. Grand Victor
1961 Ch. Nanhall's Donna, CD
1962 Ch. Bonnie Bergere of Ken-Rose, UDT, ROM
1963 Ch. Hessian's Vogue, ROM
1964 Not awarded
1965 Ch. Mar-Sa's Velvet of Malabar
1966 Ch. Hanarob's Touche
1967 Ch. Hanarob's Touche
1968 Ch. Valtara's Image
1969 Ch. De Cloudt's Heidi
1970 Ch. Bel Vista's Solid Sender
1971 Ch. Aloha v. Bid-Scono
1972 Ch. Cathwar's Lisa v. Rob, ROM
1973 Ch. Ro San's First Love
1974 Ch. Lor-Locke's Lotta of Fran-Jo
1975 Ch. Langenau's Tango
1976 Ch. Covy's Rosemary of Tucker Hill
1977 Ch. Charo of Shiloh Gardens
1978 Ch. Jo-San's Charisma
1979 Am. and Can. Ch. Anton's Jesse
1980 Ch. Lacy Britches of Billo
1981 Ch. Anton's Jenne, Am. and Can. Grand Victor
1982 Ch. Merkel's Vendetta

G.S.D.C.A. OBEDIENCE VICTORS AND VICTRIXES
1968 Heide v. Zook, UD
1969 Not awarded
1970 Schillenkamp Duke of Orleans, UD
1971 Bihari's Uncle Sam, UD
1972 Ruglor's Reboza v. Zook, UD
1973 Brunhild of Ravenna, UDT, SchH I
1974 Kenilworth Lady Jessica, UDT
1975 Penny a. d. Heide, UDT
1976 Natasha v. Hammhausen, UD
1977 Herta v. Hammhausen, UD
1978 Indra v. Hoheneichen, UD
1979 OT Ch. Johnsondale's Kool Kaper, UD
1980 OT Ch. Von Jenin's Link, UD
1981 Not awarded
1982 Martin's Kassel v. Lohberg, UD

1960 Grand Victor and Ch. Axel v. Poldihaus (*above*) owned by the Waldeslust Kennels and handled by Axel's co-owner. The judge is the redoubtable Lloyd Brackett, widely known in Shepherd circles and master of the famous Longworth Kennels. Allyn H. Weigel (*facing page, above*) with his lovely young German bitch imported for him by the author. Whiskey v. Uesener Werk (*facing page, below*) by Argo v. Benjorito Hof, SchH III, FH ex Xenia v. Uesener Werk, SchH I. A well bred, powerful young male from the Uesener Werk Kennels of Helmut Kurk. Whiskey was imported to the U.S. by the author and is owned by Mr. and Mrs. Watson.

GERMAN SIEGERS AND SIEGERINS
Siegers

1899	Joerg v. d. Krone
1900 and 1901	Hector v. Schwaben
1902	Peter v. Pritschen
1903	Roland v. Park
1904	Aribert v. Grafrath
1905	Beowulf v. Nahegau
1906 and 1907	Roland v. Starkenburg
1908	Luchs v. Kalsmunt Wetzlar
1909	Hettel Uckermark
1910	Tell v. d. Kriminalpolizei
1911 and 1912	Norbert v. Kohlwald
1913	Arno v. d. Eichenburg
1919	Dolf v. Duesternbrook
1920	Erich v. Grafenwerth
1921	Harras v. d. Juech
1922 and 1923	Cito Bergerslust
1924	Donar v. Overstolzen
1925	Klodo v. Boxberg
1926	Erich v. Glockenbrink
1927	Arko v. Sadowaberg
1928	Erich v. Glockenbrink
1929	Utz v. Haus Schutting
1930 and 1931	Herold a. d. Niederlausitz
1932	Hassan v. Haus Schütting
1933	Odin v. Stolzenfels
1934	Cunno v. Georgentor
1935	Jalk v. Pagensgrüb
1936	Arras a. d. Stadt Velbert
1937	Pfeffer v. Bern
1955	Alf v. Nordfelsen
1956	Hardt v. Stuveschacht
1957	Arno v. Haus Gersie
1958	Condor v. Hohenstamm
1959	Volker v. Zollgrenzschutz-Haus
1960	Volker v. Zollgrenzschutz-Haus
1961	Veus v. d. Starrenburg
1962	Mutz a. d. Kuckstrasse
1963	Ajax v. Haus Dexel
1964	Zibu v. Haus Schütting
1965	Hanko v. Hetschmuhle
1966	Basko v. d. Kahler Heide

1967	Bodo v. Lierberg
1968	Dido Werther-Koenigsallee
1969	Heiko v. Oranien Nassau
1970	Heiko v. Oranien Nassau
1971	Arras v. Haus Helma
1972	Marko v. Cellerland
1973	Dick v. Adeloga
1974	Dick v. Adeloga
1975	Canto Arminius
1976	Eros v. Hambachtal
1977	Herzog v. Adeloga
1978	Canto Arminius
1979	Eros v. Malvenburg
1980	Axel v. d. Hainsterbach
1981	Natan v. d. Pelztierfarm
1982	Natan v. d. Pelztierfarm

Siegerins

1899	Lisie v. Schwenningen
1900	Canna
1901	Elsa v. Schwaben
1902 and 1903	Hella v. Memmingen
1904	Regina v. Schwaben
1905	Vefi v. Niedersachsen
1906	Gretel Uckermark
1907	Hulda v. Siegestor
1908	Flora v. d. Warthe
1909	Ella v. Erlenbrennen
1910	Flora v. d. Kriminalpolizei
1911 and 1912	Hella v. d. Kriminalpolizei
1913	Frigga v. Scharenstetten
1919 and 1920	Anni v. Humboldtpark
1921	Nanthild v. Riedekenburg
1922 and 1923	Asta v. d. Kaltenweide
1924	Asta v. d. Kaltenweide
1925	Seffe v. Blasienberg
1926	Arna a. d. Ehrenzelle
1927	Elli v. Fuerstensteg
1928 and 1929	Katja v. Blasienberg
1930	Bella v. Klosterbrunn
1931	Illa v. Helmholtz
1932	Birke v. Blasienberg
1933	Jamba v. Haus Schütting

1934	Grete v. d. Raumannskaule
1935 and 1936	Stella v. Haus Schütting
1937	Traute v. Bern
1955	Muschka v. Tempelblick
1956	Lore v. Tempelblick
1957	Wilma v. Richterbach
1958	Mascha v. Stuhri-Gau
1959	Assja v. Geigerklaus
1960	Mascha v. Stuhri-Gau
1961	Assie v. Hexenkolk
1962	Rike v. Colonia Agrippina
1963	Maja v. Stolperland
1964	Blanka v. Kisskamp
1965	Landa v. d. Wienerau
1966	Cita v. Gruchental
1967	Betty v. Glockenland
1968	Rommy v. Driland
1969	Connie v. Klosterbogen
1970	Diane v. d. Firnskuppe
1971	Kathia v. d. Wienerau
1972	Katinka v. d. Netten Ecke
1973	Erka v. Fiemereck
1974	Anja v. Bertenbrunnen
1975	Mosca Val del Tiepido
1976	Nanni v. Kirshental
1977	Diana v. Patersweg
1978	Ute v. Trienzbachtal
1980	Dixi v. Natoplatz
1981	Anusch v. Trienzbachtal
1982	Perle v. Wildsteiger Land

GERMAN SHEPHERD DOG CHAMPIONS IN AMERICA
FROM 1913 TO 1916

Ch. Herta v. Ehrengrund (lst certified Ch.)
Ch. Luchs
Ch. Gero v. Rinklingen
Ch. Friggo
Ch. Southbay Anni v. Lerchrain
Ch. Minka v. Affolter
Ch. Apollo v. Hunenstein (Grand Victor, 1919)
Ch. Lux v. Leonberg
Ch. Carin v. Toyon
Ch. Bodo v. Weissenberg
Ch. Minka (pedigree unknown)
Ch. Harry v. Nahetal
Ch. Daisy v. Wohlen
Ch. Max
Ch. Oak Ridge Frigga v. Magdeburg
Ch. Rona v. Brunnenhof

All of these champions, with the exception of Minka (whose breeding is unknown), were of good German breeding of that day.

Glossary

TRANSLATIONS FROM GERMAN PEDIGREES

Rude	male	*WT-Wurf Tag*	date whelped
Hundin	female	*Z-Zuchter*	breeder
Wurf	litter	*B-Besitzer*	owner
Welpe	young puppy	*A-Amme*	foster mother
Eltern	parents	*V-Vater*	sire (father)
Gross Eltern	grandparents	*M-Mutter*	dam (mother)
Ur-Gross Eltern	great-grandparents	*SZ*	stud book
Gedeckt	date of mating	*Angekoert*	recommended for breeding

GERMAN SHOW RATINGS

VA	Select Class	*M-Mangelhaft*	Faulty
V-Vörzuglich	Excellent	*O-Zero*	Failed, N.G.
SG-Sehr Gut	Very Good	*Auslese Klass*	Selection Class (*See VA*)
G-Gut	Good	*SR-Sieger*	German Grand Victor
A-Ausreishend	Sufficient	*SGRN-Siegerin*	German Grand Victrix

GERMAN WORKING DOG RATINGS

PH-Polizei Hund	police dog
HGH-Herden Gebrauchshund	herding dog
BlH-Blinden Hund	blind guide dog
SH-Such Hund	tracking dog
FH-Fahrten Hund	trailing dog

DH-Dienst Hund	service dog
SH-Sanitats Hund	Red Cross dog
GrH-Grenzen Hund	border patrol dog
MH-Militar Hund	army dog
LawH-Lawinen Hund	avalanche dog
SchH-Schutz Hund	protection dog
KrH-Kriegshund	war dog
ZPr-Zucht prufung	has passed Breed Survey and is recommended for breeding
Leistungssieger and *Leistungssiegerin* . .	all around working dog champions of the year in their sex
Preishuten Sieger and *Siegerin*	sheepherding champions of the year in their respective sexes

GERMAN SHOW CLASSES AND CLUBS

JKl-Jugend Klasse	youth class, 12 to 18 months
JHKl-Junghund Klasse	youth dog class, 18 to 24 months
GHKl-Gebrauchshund Klasse	dogs with ·SchH 1, 2, or 3 training degrees. Over 2 years of age.
AKl-Alters Klasse	dogs over 2 years of age with no training degrees
SV-Verein für Deutsche Schäferhunde . .	German Shepherd Dog Club (National)
OG-Ortsgruppe	regional clubs
HGH Sonderklasse	dogs who have a sheepherding degree and work as herders. Over 2 years of age.
Zuchtgruppen	breeding groups (kennel)
Nachkommengruppen	sire and progeny groups

GERMAN TRAINING COMMANDS

Bei Fuss	Heel!	*Bleib*	Stay!
Sitz	Sit!	*Gib laut*	Speak!
Platz	Down!	*Pass auf*	On the alert!
Heir	Come!	*Fass*	Attack!
Such	Go find! (Search!, Seek!)	*Pfui*	Shame! (No!)
Bringen	Bring! (Fetch!)	*Hopp*	Hop! (Jump!)
		Steh	Keep standing!
Nein	No!	*Voraus*	In front! (Move ahead!)
Geh Weiter	Go on!		
Aus	Out!, Let go!	*Halten*	Halt!

Suggested Reading

Dog Breeding by Ernest H. Hart provides basic information for fanciers with all degrees of experience. From physiology of the bitch and stud dog to fertility, whelping, genetics, and heredity, all you will need to know to build your own strain of German Shepherd Dogs is here. Every area of canine breeding is covered in this useful handbook.

Dog Owner's Encyclopedia of Veterinary Medicine by Allan H. Hart, B.V.Sc. provides sections on nutrition, pediatrics for puppies, parasites, respiratory disease, muscular and skeletal disorders, first aid and nursing, and much more. This fascinating medical guide is not meant to be a substitute for one's veterinarian; it merely informs readers of canine diseases, their causes and symptoms, and the recommended treatments. Knowing what to look for could save a dog's life.

Encyclopedia of Dog Breeds by Ernest H. Hart is a comprehensive volume that lists the history and standards of most of the important breeds today, together with valuable sections on the evolution of the dog, methods of dog breeding, feeding, general care, showing, training, and diseases and first aid.

The Book of the German Shepherd Dog by Anna Katherine Nicholas is a tribute to our beloved Shepherd breed and written by a prominent judge and writer in the Dog Fancy. This yearbook, filled with some of the most important and impressive top show dogs today, contains many kennel stories, the history and development of the breed in Germany, German Shepherd Dogs around the world, and everything you need to know about selecting and caring for your Shepherd.

Successful Dog Show Exhibiting by Anna Katherine Nicholas offers practical tips on how to get started in the exciting dog show world. Selecting a pure-bred show dog, choosing a professional handler, traveling with your dog, completing the entry form, show etiquette, and junior showmanship are all covered in depth by an author whose name is synonymous with the Dog Fancy . . . the perfect guide for show enthusiasts.

Your German Shepherd Puppy by Ernest H. Hart provides answers to such questions as how to remove dewclaws, how to cull a litter, how to feed orphan pups, how to housebreak your Shepherd puppy, how and when to register your pup with the A.K.C., when to begin an inoculation program, and how to administer medicine. Whether you are a newcomer to the Fancy or a veteran Shepherd breeder, all of the vital information you will need to raise healthy puppies is here and has been treated with careful attention to detail.

Marko v. Mimosenweg by Petz v. Zollgrenzschutz-Haus, SchH III. Marko was out of the "M" litter Mimosenweg and is owned by Gary and Diane Green of Ultima German Shepherds, Northport, New York. Photo courtesy of Elli Matlin of Highland Hills Kennels.

Above is Erynbrooks Quincy, a black and tan male bred by Nancy Phelps and Susan Casey and owned by Glenice (Kathy) Davis of Noble-Haus Shepherds, Wichita, Kansas. *Below* is Quincy's fine pedigree.

++++++++++ **CERTIFIED PEDIGREE** ++++++++++

Name of Dog __ERYNBROOKS QUINCY__   Sex __MALE__   Reg. No. __WE988440__

Breed _____GERMAN SHEPHERD DOG_____   Color __BLACK & TAN__

Date Whelped __SEPTEMBER 6, 1981__   Breeder __NANCY PHELPS & SUSAN CASEY__

|7| CH DOPPELT TAYS HAWKEYE
WC978054 4-76 BLK TN

|3| CH LOCHWOOD SUNDANCE V STUTGART
WD792154 6-78 BLK TN

|8| CH LOCHWOOD'S ZAJA
WC758493 6-77 BLK RD TN

Sire-1 CH STUTTGART'S SUNDANCE KID
WE676475 7-81 BLK TN

|9| CH DOPPELT TAYS HAWKEYE
WC978054 4-76 BLK TN

|4| CH CAPRICE KITTY HAWK
WE168262 7-80 BLK TN

|10| GALEWYND'S T N T OF GAN EDAN
WC571457 2-77 SBL

|11| CH LAKESIDE'S HARRIGAN
WB963211 4-72 BLK TN

|5| CH COVY'S HONDO OF TUCKER HILL
WC608800 10-74 BLK TN

|12| CH KOVAYA'S JILL CD
WB113215 7-73 BLK TN

Dam-2 ERYNBROOKS FLIRT OF FARMIL
WE878492 2-82 BLK RD

|13| COBERT'S WHISPER JET
WC464860 9-74 BLK TN

|6| FARMILS BETH OF DOLMAR
WE028019 9-80 BLK TN

|14| DOLMAR'S ILISE OF FAR-MIL
WD267067 3-78 BLK TN

The Seal of The American Kennel Club affixed hereto certifies that
this pedigree has been compiled from official Stud Book records

Date Issued __07/15/83__

315

Index

Copulation, 259, 261
Coughing, 283. *See also* Kennel cough.
Cowhocks, 173, 229
Crick, Francis, 90
Cross-fertilization, 82
Crossing over, 87, 106, 150
Cryotherapy, 296
Cryptorchidism, 150
Cynodesmus, 9
Cystitis, 282

Dandruff, 247, 287
Darwin, Charles Robert, 81, 83
Defecation, 188, 242, 251, 286, 294
Dehydration, 240, 282, 290
Demodectic mange, 276
Deoxyribonucleic acid, 89
Depression, 268, 282
Dermatitis, summer, 276
Deutscher Verband der Gebrauchshund-sportvereine, *See* DVG.
De Vries, Hugo, 83
Dewclaws, 161, 173, 243, 264
Diabetes mellitus, 287, 294
Diarrhea, 268, 269, 271 272, 274, 283, 284, 286, 290
Diet, 236
— for puppies, 239, 241-245
— for pregnant bitches, 239
— for mature dog, 245
— for aging dog, 294
Discharges, nasal and ocular, 268, 274

Disinfectant, 251
Distemper, 268, 270, 274, 283, 285
Distemper, feline, 269
DNA, 80, 89-90, 296
Doberman Pinscher, 256
Dog house, 253-255
Domestication of dogs, 11-13
Dominant traits, 81, 83, 88, 89, 91, 95, 99, 259, 278
Double handling, 185-186
Drooling, 286
DVG, 205, 206
Dysplasia, *See* Hip dysplasia.

Ear canker, 250, 281
Ear care, 279-280
Ear mites, 250, 280, 281
Eczema, 276
Electric goads, 192
Encephalitis, 286
Endurance test, 233
Enema, 290, 292
Enteritis, 283
Entropion, 281
Epilepsy, 52, 286
Estrus, 261, 263
"Erich" coat, 20
Evolution, 80, 81, 87
Excrements, 255
Exercise, 247, 259, 264, 274, 294
"Experiments in Plant Hybridization," 82
Eye color inheritance, 83-84
Eyes, opening of puppies', 243, 266

Fats, 236, 237, 238, 239, 241, 243, 245
Fatty acids, 236, 237, 248, 277, 294

Faults, breeding out, 42, 47, 78, 88, 94
FCI, *See* Federation Cynologique Interna-tionale.
Fecal examinations, 262, 271, 272, 283
Federation Cynologique Internationale, 142, 182, 183
Fence dogs, 256
Fertility, 232
Fertilization, 85, 264
Fever, 269, 282, 283
Fighting instinct, 215, 233
First aid, 290-292
Flea collars, 275
Flea repellents, 248, 250, 275, 280
Fleas, 250, 251, 252, 271, 272, 274-275, 276, 287
Flies, 249
Floating rib, 229, 279
Flu, *See* Parainfluenza.
Fluid therapy, 282
Flying insects, 249
Food rewards, 188, 191
Force feeding, 247
Fortunate Fields experi-ment, 22, 26
Fractures, bone, 239
Frozen semen, 107-110, 262, 296
Fungal infections, 276, 280, 286
Funk, Dr. Werner, 53
Furniture, jumping on, 191-192
Futurity shows, 131-134, 146, 147

Gaiting, 162-164, 169-170, 202, 225, 232, 233, 278
Gametes, 85